STARDUST
THE VISUAL COMPANION

GOE, AND CATCHE A FALLING STARRE,
GET WITH CHILD A MANDRAKE ROOTE,
TELL ME, WHERE ALL PAST YEARES ARE,
OR WHO CLEFT THE DIVELS FOOT,
TEACH ME TO HEARE MERMAIDES SINGING,
OR TO KEEP OFF ENVIES STINGING,
AND FINDE
WHAT WINDE
SERVES TO ADVANCE AN HONEST MINDE.

— FROM 'A SONG'
JOHN DONNE (1572-1631)

STARDUST

THE VISUAL COMPANION

Paperback ISBN-10: 1 84576 422 6 • Paperback ISBN-13: 9781845764227
Hardback ISBN-10: 1 84576 681 4 • Hardback ISBN-13: 9781845766818

Published by Titan Books
A division of Titan Publishing Group Ltd
144 Southwark St
London SE1 0UP

First edition July 2007
2 4 6 8 10 9 7 5 3 1

Stephen Jones is the winner of 3 World Fantasy Awards, 3 International Horror Guild Awards and 4 Horror Writers Association Bram Stoker Awards, as well as being a Hugo Award nominee and a 17-times recipient of the British Fantasy Award. One of Britain's most acclaimed anthologists of horror and dark fantasy, he has more than 85 books to his credit, including *Creepshows: The Illustrated Stephen King Movie Guide*, *The Essential Monster Movie Guide*, *Clive Barker's A-Z of Horror*, *The Hellraiser Chronicles*, *The Nightbreed Chronicles* and the poetry volume *Now We Are Sick: An Anthology of Nasty Verse*, co-edited with Neil Gaiman. You can visit his website at www.herebedragons.co.uk/jones

ACKNOWLEDGEMENTS
The author would like to thank the following for their support in the research and writing of this book:
Matthew Vaughn, Neil Gaiman, Charles Vess, Mark Scruton, Gavin Bocquet, Sammy Sheldon, Nik Williams, Fae Hammond, Jane Goldman, Risa Kessler, Paul Ruditis, Christina Hahni and Mandy Slater. Special thanks to Tarquin Pack for all his help, and my editorial team at Titan Books: Joanna Boylett, Adam Newell, Nick Jones, David Barraclough, Katy Wild, and designer Martin Stiff.

Major reference sources: Adam-Buxton.co.uk, DMWmedia.com, EW.com, Greenmanpress.com, *Hanging Out with the Dream King: Conversations with Neil Gaiman and His Collaborators* by Joseph McCabe (Fantagraphics Books), Movies.About.com, MTV.com and *Stardust: Being a Romance Within the Realms of Faerie* by Neil Gaiman and Charles Vess (DC Comics/Vertigo).

Titan Books would like to thank the following for, variously, their help, support, contributions and patience:
Tarquin Pack, Matthew Vaughn, Jane Goldman, Neil Gaiman, Charles Vess, Sammy Sheldon, Nick Williams, Fae Hammond, Risa Kessler and Paul Ruditis, Christina Hahni at Paramount and Adam Buxton.

Visit our website:
WWW.TITANBOOKS.COM

———•I•———

Did you enjoy this book? We love to hear from our readers. Please e-mail us at: readerfeedback@titanemail.com or write to Reader Feedback at the above address.

To subscribe to our regular newsletter for up-to-the-minute news, great offers and competitions, email: booksezine@titanemail.com

———•I•———

STARDUST

THE VISUAL COMPANION

WRITTEN BY
STEPHEN JONES

WITH AN INTRODUCTION BY
NEIL GAIMAN

INCLUDING THE SCREENPLAY BY
JANE GOLDMAN &
MATTHEW VAUGHN

BEING AN ACCOUNT
OF THE MAKING OF
A MAGICAL MOVIE

CONTENTS

INTRODUCTION

he other day I started wondering what it actually cost me to write *Stardust*, and I started to tot up the numbers in my head: I bought a nice blue Watermans fountain pen — the first fountain pen I had owned since I was at school — and a large blank notebook with a green cover, then, when that was filled, another blank notebook, this one with a black cover; I bought ink for the pen, too, and ink isn't cheap; and tea — I drank many cups of tea while writing *Stardust*, after all. Probably, all told, and mostly because of the fountain pen, it cost me about a hundred pounds to write, especially if you count the tea. Given that he had to pay for nice paper and pencils and water-colours, it probably cost Charles Vess two or three times that. Which is the sort of

thing you only think of when someone tells you just how many millions a film is going to cost, and you realise that scenes and images and ideas and places that took you moments to imagine and write down are going to have to be built and made and will be transformed from being some kind of Platonic Ideal into a filmed reality, and that the film of your book will occupy that place in people's minds for ever and ever — or until perhaps one day, decades on, someone decides to remake the film.

While it's true that most writers are philosophical about what Hollywood can do to us (The anecdote, with insert-the-writer-of-your-choice-here, has the writer being told that Hollywood ruined his or her book. "Nonsense," says Hammett or King or Chandler or whoever, gesturing to the books on the shelf behind his head. "Look, at them, they aren't ruined, they're just fine."), it's equally as true that we don't want bad films made of our books. It's no fun, and people never quite understand why we didn't just fix it, why we allowed changes to be made (because changes will always be made).

There are two ways to deal with that, as an author. You can either distance yourself as hard and as solidly as you can from the process — in Raymond Chandler's metaphor, you drive up to the California border, shovel the money into the back of the car and drive home, not looking back. The other option is to get involved: either write the script and direct the film yourself, or simply find people you like and trust them to get on with it, and help them wherever you can.

With *Stardust*, I took the latter course. I'd said no to many directors and producers who had wanted to make films of *Stardust*. Matthew Vaughn, on the other hand, is someone I trusted, a man who had a vision of the kind of film he wanted to make, and the tenacity to make it happen. I was able to suggest Jane Goldman as a writer (I'd long admired her as a journalist and novelist) to work with Matthew on the script he had in mind. And then, for the most part, I got to step back, in the knowledge that, while my suggestions were welcomed, they were easily trumped by considerations of budget or time (the two battles that every film finds itself up against), but still content that I had played my part in the film-making process.

My sweetest *Stardust* memory — and there are many — was wandering the Pinewood Studios backlot with Charles Vess. We strolled around the outside of the witch's inn, Charles wistfully wondering whether he could, somehow, take the building home with him to Virginia. And then, on some wasteland behind the inn, we found the wall — in storage until they needed it again. A perfectly real drystone wall, able to bear the closest inspection, discoloured by time and stained by lichens, and it wasn't until we touched it that we realised that it had been made by craftsmen from wood and plaster and paint. Movie magic.

Because of the *Stardust* film I have walked on the deck of a flying ship hunting lightning, and I watched from a few feet away as Michelle Pfeiffer lifted her knife and prepared to cut out the heart of a star. You don't get to do either of these things every day, and I'm thrilled I did, and count myself extremely lucky.

Films aren't books. In my head the movie *Stardust* takes place in a slightly divergent universe to the book — it's perhaps the Earth-2 *Stardust* (to use a now archaic cultural reference) — and while the Tristan of the film is not the Tristran of the book, they are reflections of each other: they share many experiences and adventures, and each of the Thornes sets out to bring Victoria Forester what he believes she wants, and grows from a boy into a man on the journey. I'm proud of both the book and of the film — one, as if it were my child, the other, that child's faster, more colourful, and much more expensive twin.

I've known Stephen Jones for over a quarter of a century and was delighted that Titan Books chose him to write this book; David James's photographs are works of art in themselves; I'm grateful to both of them. Jane and Matthew's script is funny and smart. Most of all I'd like to thank the actors and the crew, the technicians and designers and wall-builders and wranglers who took a dream written in two large notebooks and turned it into something that people could eat popcorn during.

It was magic all the way.

I can't wait to see the finished film. In the meantime, I'm delighted just to be able to have a copy of this book.

NEIL GAIMAN
December 16, 2006

Opposite: Charles Vess, Neil Gaiman and his daughter Maddy, behind the scenes at Pinewood Studios.
Above: Editor Jon Harris, director Matthew Vaughn, scriptwriter Jane Goldman, Neil Gaiman, Maddy Gaiman and Charles Vess, behind the scenes.

Prologue

IN WHICH THE ORIGIN OF
STARDUST IS REVEALED

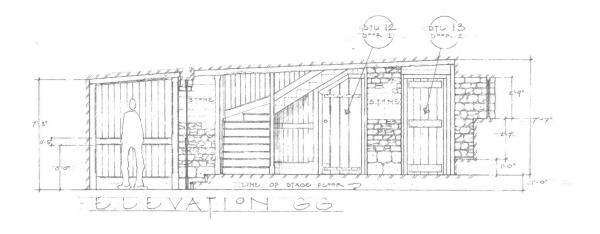

THERE WAS ONCE A YOUNG MAN WHO WISHED TO GAIN HIS HEART'S DESIRE.

– NEIL GAIMAN, STARDUST

hus began *Stardust: Being a Romance Within the Realms of Faerie*, a four-part illustrated novel published in 'prestige' format by DC Comics in 1997.

Written by British-born journalist turned comics writer and author Neil Gaiman, and illustrated by American artist Charles Vess, the collaborative work broke new ground within the comics industry.

"I wanted to tell a story about a young man who ran off to get his heart's desire and found out that it wasn't his heart's desire," says Gaiman. "What his heart's desire was, was something completely different, but he only learned that in the finding of it."

Unusually, the story was told without the use of word balloons and narrative boxes. Instead, Gaiman's evocative prose was presented as a short novel, with Vess' delicate watercolour paintings and line drawings integrated into the text in the manner of an illuminated manuscript.

Stardust tells the story of Tristran Thorn, a young man of uncertain origin yearning for adventure, who lives in the Victorian village of Wall in the sleepy English countryside. The secluded hamlet derives its name from the enigmatic stone edifice that stands just outside the village.

There is only one gap in the wall, through which can be seen a large green meadow. From time to time, odd shapes and figures can be glimpsed amongst the trees beyond a stream. This opening is guarded night and day by the villagers, and only very rarely is somebody allowed through the gateway. And that person invariably knows what they are looking for. There is a look in their eyes that once seen can never be mistaken.

Once every nine years, on May Day, the guard is relaxed when a magical fair comes to the meadow and the villagers and visitors from all over mix with those who live beyond the wall.

When Tristran loses his heart to the town beauty, the cold and aloof Victoria Forester, he rashly vows to fetch his beloved a star that falls from the sky on a crisp October night. When Victoria promises to give Tristran anything he desires if he keeps his vow, he sets out on a lover's quest through the gap in the ancient wall and into a world beyond his wildest imaginings to find the fallen star...

Gaiman and Vess first met at the annual San Diego Comic Convention, where they talked about their mutual interest in author James Branch Cabell. They subsequently worked together on an issue of DC's *The*

Books of Magic ('The Land of Summer's Twilight'), whose teenage wizard protagonist Tim Hunter is often cited as a pre-cursor to J.K. Rowling's Harry Potter. Prior to collaborating on *Sandman* #62 ('The Kindly Ones') and the final issue in the series, *Sandman* #75 ('The Tempest'), their *Sandman* #19 story, 'A Midsummer Night's Dream', uniquely won the World Fantasy Award for short fiction in 1991.

"We actually astonished ourselves and everybody else by winning the award," Gaiman recalls. That night, the writer celebrated at a party, held at a friend's home in the Arizona desert. There he watched a falling star. "In England, they're just a streak of light across the sky, but I discovered that if you're in the desert and you watch, it's like this little diamond coming down."

As Gaiman observed the tiny pinpoint of light in its fateful plunge to earth, he began to wonder, "What if you went to get that falling star? And what if it wasn't a star? It was a girl. And what if she had a broken leg and a foul temper and had no desire to be dragged halfway across the world and presented to anybody's would-be fiancée?

"Suddenly, there was a story," he remembers.

Gaiman returned to the hotel, where he found Vess, who was celebrating their win at a different party. "Okay, let me tell you this story," Gaiman said to him. "I think I've come up with something."

After listening to his friend relate everything that was

in his head about the fallen star, the artist smiled. "I can't wait to draw it," Vess said.

"That really was where it all began," recalls Gaiman.

———————————

Born in Porchester, England, in 1960, Neil Gaiman was fifteen years old when he was told by a school advisor that it would be impossible to become a comic book writer. As a youngster he read voraciously, including the works of J.R.R. Tolkien, C.S. Lewis, Hope Mirrlees, Ernest Bramah, James Branch Cabell and Lord Dunsany, and his love of traditional fairy tales and epic quests was established at an early age.

"They showed me that fairy stories were for adults too," Gaiman recalls. "I was also lucky enough to be growing up when Lin Carter was bringing two hundred years of great fantasy back into print with his Adult Fantasy series for Ballantine Books.

"More than anything, it was the idea that all these books were written when there wasn't such a thing as a 'fantasy' shelf in a bookstore. You were just a novelist, and you happened to write a fairy story, or whatever. I thought it would be really interesting to write something from that perspective – to pretend to myself that I was almost writing it from the perspective of the 1920s."

Because of pressing deadlines on other projects,

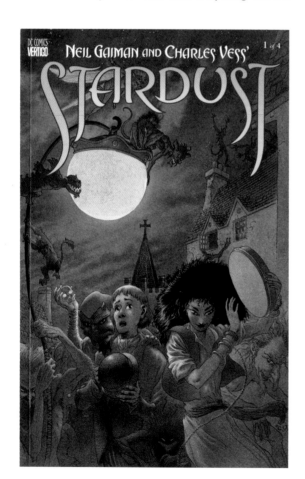

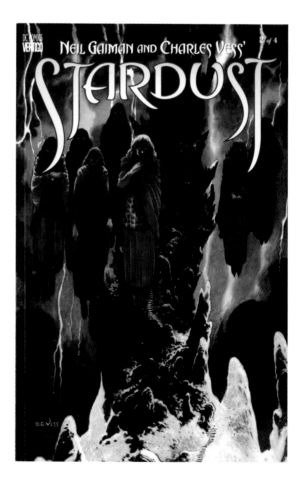

Gaiman did not actually start work on *Stardust* until 1994. "I decided to give it a comfortable authorial voice," he continues, "and tried to use a language that, although not antiquated in the sense that I was doing something that was cod-Victorian, was still very much 'of the period'."

The story was written in longhand with a fountain pen in two large volumes of blank pages; the first bound in green leather, the second bound in black. "I could not quite have told you why, but I thought it was a really good idea," muses the author, who had not written with a fountain pen since he was a schoolboy. "It made me think differently. Not just because I was pretending to be a writer from the 1920s, but also because I could write multiple drafts with a pen, whereas it is always a first draft that just improves on a computer."

Among several ideas and concepts that never made it into the final manuscript of *Stardust* were outlines for a scene in which Tristran grew wings and another sequence involving cloud-herds, which the writer eventually decided that he did not want to include.

"It was always meant to be a story for adults. There were things I knew I was going to do before I ever put pen to paper, including the sex scene in the fairy market and that the star would use an expletive when she landed on the ground. I loved that. It seemed right.

"I wanted to do a book that *wasn't* a children's book, and I'm slightly pleased and baffled that it won an award as a young adult book, as a result of which it has now come out in young adult editions around the world with completely the same text."

"Once we had sold the project, Neil sent me a photocopy of the hand-written manuscript of the first several chapters that proved completely impossible for me to actually read," Charles Vess recalls.

After Vess had telephoned Gaiman to complain that he could only make out a few words, the author narrated the book onto tape for the artist to listen to. "So I had the first half of the book read to me that way. After that, Neil would call me every few months and read me the first draft of whatever he had just finished over the phone. Subsequently, his wife Mary or assistant Lorraine would transcribe his errant scribbles into a legible manuscript and I would work from that."

That first chapter of *Stardust* was written in London, in a rented house belonging to Gaiman's friend, American-born singer-songwriter Tori Amos, who was away attending the Grammy Awards. "All Tori asked in exchange was that I make her a talking red-headed tree," reveals the author, who was also working on his novel *Neverwhere* at the same time.

"Because Neil's work is steeped in mythology, it pulled me in immediately," remembers Amos. "He makes magic carpet rides tied together with words that take us to worlds we would never go to – Neil's worlds."

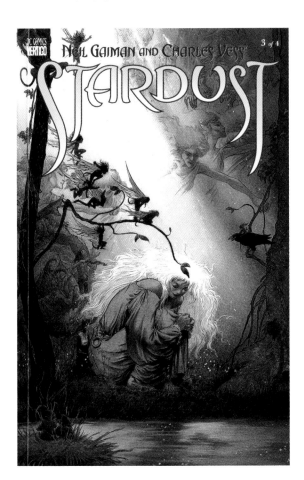

Left: The original four-issue run of Neil Gaiman and Charles Vess' illustrated novel, published by DC Comics in 1997.

"Upon being shown one of my paintings by Neil, Tori Amos said that she wanted to be a talking tree in the tale," Vess recalls. "So she was. She mentions it in the lyrics of one of her songs from that period ['Horses', on Amos' 1996 album *Boys for Pele*].

"The image was based on a dream I had had of Neil and I walking through that same forest with him telling me the initial story," continues Vess. "In the dream I kept feeling that someone was listening in. I finally looked up to see the great god Pan with a broad smile on his face. At the time I was studying the Swedish artist, John Bauer, and so I aped his trees on either side."

Born in Lynchburg, Virginia, in 1951, Charles Vess drew his first comic at the age of ten, and graduated with a Bachelor of Fine Arts degree from Virginia Commonwealth University in 1974. After briefly working as an animator, he became a freelance illustrator two years later. After contributing artwork to such magazines as *Heavy Metal* and *National Lampoon*, he began specialising in fantasy and fairy tale art, starting with his own book, *The Horns of Elfland*, in 1977.

Since then, his award-winning work has graced the pages of numerous comic books, such as *The Raven Banner: A Tale of Asgard*, *The Book of Night*, *Marvel Fanfare: The Warriors Three Saga*, *Spider-Man: Spirits of the Earth* and *Swamp Thing*. In 1991 he illustrated the official comics adaptation of Steven Spielberg's fantasy film, *Hook*. More recently, he has also illustrated such books as *Medicine Road* by Charles de Lint, *A Storm of Swords* by George R.R. Martin and *The Ladies of Grace Adieu and Other Stories* by Susanna Clarke.

Starting in 1989, the artist's work has been featured in a number of gallery exhibitions and museum shows across America.

"The book illustration allows me to spend more time on a single image," reveals Vess, "which is not something you can really do when you're doing a comic."

After sketching the work out lightly in pencil first, the artist then traces an outline with a pen before building up the image into a full colour painting with multiple washes of transparent inks. It is delicate and time-consuming work.

"I spent about two years illustrating *Stardust*," reveals Vess, "and a lot of that was at an intense deadline speed. So sometimes I really didn't get to think about the pictures as much as I wanted to."

The artist's approach to the book was a simple one: "I often just filled the image space with as many characters and made-up narratives as I could. Many of these characters never actually appeared in the book. I always wanted to know the story of a wee man astride the raven around whose neck is dangling a gold key, but that was not to be…"

Neil Gaiman has described Vess as "the nearest thing we have to one of the great Victorian fairy painters," and admitted that without the inspiration of his artwork, *Stardust* would never have existed. "Every time I finished a chapter I phoned him up and read it to him, and he listened patiently and he chuckled in all the right places."

Vess is quick to return the compliment: "Working with Neil made me realise that the better the writer you work with, the better your drawing is going to be."

At one point during the creative process, Gaiman suggested that the artist produce a tape of various songs and ballads that featured imagery that he would like to paint. "We had done this before for the third issue of the original *Books of Magic* mini-series," explains Vess. "The tape had lots of Steeleye Span, Pentangle, Fairport Convention, etcetera, on it, but I don't remember which particular songs they were."

As the story evolved, it became even more of a collaborative effort between writer and artist. "I just loved the idea of doing something as heavily illustrated as it could possibly be," recalls Gaiman, "and Charlie loved the idea of not doing it as a comic as he would not have to keep drawing the next panel. Of course," he adds with a smile, "towards the end of the process of having to complete more than 170 different paintings, he also started to grumble about having to do the next painting!

"A lot of the story was actually pushed into existence

by me going, 'Wouldn't it be fun to see Charles drawing so-and-so?'" Sometimes the artist would come up with something that was so good that Gaiman would want to return to it later in the book.

"We did the art as a sort of presentation to publishers first," he explains.

"*Stardust* was always a very collaborative process," agrees Vess. "To accompany Neil's original page-and-a-half prospectus that was to be used to sell the project, I painted three fairly major pieces and two not-quite-so-major."

These presentation pieces included Yvaine, the fallen star, crouching by the water and surrounded by the faerie folk; Tristran leading Yvaine through the forest with Pan above them in the trees; a double-page spread of the fairy market; and an illustration that appeared on the back of the first serialised issue of a farmer beside the wall watching a giant stride away into the distance. A fifth painting, showing the three witchy Lilim and a confrontation between Tristran, Yvaine and a tree-man was never used.

Early in the creative process, Gaiman had come up with a list of what might be found in the fairy market. "There was no story at that point," remembers Vess. "Then I thought of various things and did this big double-page drawing featuring lots of imagery and characters. Like I said, neither the book nor any of the characters had been written about yet, so I had free reign. I decided

to put Neil (in dark glasses and trench coat – he is cut off in the trade paperback edition due to proportion constraints) over on the far left-hand side at the bookstall. Also at the bookstall is the Victorian fairy painter Richard Dadd, who is reading the book that eventually drives him mad and into Bedlam [Bethlem Royal Hospital, the world's oldest psychiatric hospital] where he painted his greatest masterpieces. And Merlin and Nimue discussing a book of magical recipes.

"A bit further back is Beethoven listening to a tune from a fairy fiddler. At the top are the backs of two of my favourite Japanese *anime* characters, KiKi and Totoro, about to enter the tent of a goblin palm-reader. Coming back down into the middle, there are the characters out of Jeff Smith's comic book series *Bone* getting a cow shoed. Continuing across, you will find Prince Valiant choosing some new armour. And below that is myself wearing a Tintin sweatshirt flanked by a fox and a Musketeer. Below that and under the curtain is a woman walking a dragon out of the long-running British newspaper strip *Rupert the Bear*. And finally, the young boy and girl standing before the goblin market seller are my niece and nephew, then very young and now all grown up and married.

"Appropriately enough, the appearance of the goblin market sellers are all inspired by Laurence Housman's illustration for [Christina] Rossetti's 'Goblin Market' poem."

Right: The evil Lamia (Michelle Pfeiffer) watches over the sleeping Yvaine in the magical inn.
Below: Charles Vess' original version of the Lilim.

In the end, Vess produced around 175 paintings – many full-page and double-page spreads – for *Stardust*. "We had always envisioned the world of *Stardust* as being a very real and breathing one. A place in which the characters would continue to live and have adventures even when they weren't written about on the page," he explains. "So I found it an immense delight to place various characters into the backgrounds of many scenes wherein they weren't described. I thought it made the whole work breathe that much better. And Neil noticed, but never said anything about it. I'm sure that he would have if their placement had been detrimental to the tale we were telling.

"Since the story was serialised, and the work was done as it was being written for each issue, I never really knew exactly where it was going to end up," the artist admits.

Stardust had initially been conceived by its creators as a "story book with pictures" to be released in a single, illustrated volume aimed at all ages.

"The one thing that drives me crazy about *Stardust* is that everyone says it's a comic book," says Vess. "There are no panels – it's a story that's illustrated."

For the 1993 World Fantasy Convention in Minneapolis, Minnesota, Gaiman and Vess produced an illustrated prospectus to show to editors from all of the major publishing houses attending the event. "Over the next week or so," Gaiman recalls, "they contacted my agent to explain that the idea of a book with colour illustrations on every page was something that they just couldn't do. Meanwhile, DC Comics – who we had not even planned to pitch to – was saying, 'A new Charles

THE VISUAL COMPANION

Vess and Neil Gaiman project? We'll do that. We aren't scared by pictures.'"

Stardust: Being a Romance Within the Realms of Faerie, appeared as a four-part mini-series in 1997 and has never been out of print since. The following year it was collected into a single hardcover volume by DC Comics' Vertigo imprint, quarter-bound in *faux* leather, with cover text and several stars inlaid in foil. A subsequent softcover edition featured a different cover design, and both editions came complete with reproductions of the original comic covers and various concept sketches by Vess.

"It was classy and a lot of people saw it," says Vess.

"For me," says Gaiman, "*Stardust* really was a lovely example of an idea I had in my head. I started it, I followed it to the end, and I was very proud that I had made the thing I set out to do.

"I remember this incredibly puzzled phone call from a journalist in Canada who had read *Stardust* and was trying to understand what the book was for. Eventually I said to this guy, 'Look, it's an ice cream. You read it, and it makes you feel better. It has no social purpose at all, but it tastes really nice, and afterwards you're happy and you have a little sugar high.' And that's what *Stardust* is – it's happiness, and a little sugar high."

Publisher's Weekly praised the author for employing 'exquisitely rich language, natural wisdom, good humour and a dash of darkness to conjure up a fairy tale in the grand tradition', while the *San Francisco Chronicle* said that 'Vess' generously detailed paintings perfectly capture the beauty, oddness and terror of Faerie'.

In 1999, *Stardust* won an Alex Award from the American Library Association and also the Mythopoeic Fantasy Award for Adult Literature, presented by the Mythopoeic Society. The illustrated hardcover edition is long out of print and now commands high prices on the collectibles market.

That same year, Gaiman's text was published on both sides of the Atlantic as a separate hardcover, without any illustrations. "DC wrote us a terrific contract," says Gaiman, "which allowed me to do that."

However, a plan to issue the American paperback edition with three different covers, which would form a triptych when placed side-by-side, was never implemented.

An exhibition of Vess' artwork from the book was held at the Cartoon Art Museum in San Francisco, California, during the first half of 1998. The following year, the artist's Green Man Press imprint produced the portfolio *A Fall of Stardust* that included, among other items, a chapbook by Neil Gaiman entitled *Wall, A Prologue*, and another booklet containing Susanna Clarke's short story 'The Duke of Wellington Misplaces His Horse', which is set in the *Stardust* universe.

There has been much talk of a follow-up to *Stardust* over the years, but the initial idea for it dates back to an earlier time in the author's career. "When I was twenty-eight," recalls Gaiman, "I plotted my first novel, which was called *Wall*. It was about a successful romance novelist in her forties who returned to her native England after ten years in America and went to live in the town of Wall. It was a contemporary novel, but you met many of the descendants of the characters in *Stardust*, and it was basically about her relationship with Mr Bromios in the inn.

"A few years ago, I thought it was about time I wrote this book. Then I suddenly realised that the readers would think that this author character was *me*. So I again put it on hold for a while, but I would love to write it someday as there's some really fun stuff in it."

To tie in with the release of the movie version from Paramount Pictures, a new hardcover edition of the original illustrated novel was published in May 2007 by DC Comics/Vertigo. Along with all of the content of the original book, this edition has a new cover painting, end paper designs that feature a new version of the fairy market, plus a sixteen-page section of bonus material that includes five newly-drawn images that Vess was unable to include in the previous edition due to text and deadline constraints.

"For the new cover I really wanted a more nineteenth-century poster effect for the piece than strict naturalism," Vess reveals, "hence the more densely outlined contours of Yvaine and her hair.

"There were really only minor surprises waiting for me in the translation from pencil to paint. The biggest of which was a large slippage of the dark-blue background sky colour over the top of Yvaine's hair due to my slopping the paint around much too casually. I thought that a bit of opaque hair colour would quickly fix that right up. Two or three hours later, major portions of her hair had been repainted. This type of thing can be maddening when on a tight deadline, but I like the effect gained."

A sixth image in the new edition is from a proposed sequel that is far in the future for both writer and artist. "There's a story that I nearly did for a collection of novellas based around my various books," explains

Below: Matthew Vaughn discusses an idea with Neil Gaiman, behind the scenes.

Gaiman. "The *Stardust* novella would have been called *Hellflyer*, about how Tristran had to go to Hell in a hot-air balloon to bring back a wizard who has tattooed his soul onto the back of the new king. Actually, Charlie did the illustration for it to encourage me to write the story."

All six of Charles Vess' new paintings are also available as the final plates in the deluxe portfolio of *Stardust* prints that the artist has been producing for a number of years.

A decade after it was first published, *Stardust* remains an enduring tale of romance, magic and glamour from one of the most innovative and accomplished writer and artist teams currently working in the illustrated book medium.

As early as 1999 there was talk of a *Stardust* movie.

That year Neil Gaiman spoke to a large audience of fans at the San Diego Comic Convention about his various upcoming projects. These included a proposed film version of *Stardust*.

"I was having a meeting in Los Angeles with Bob Weinstein at Miramax," explains the author. "I had just scripted the English-language version of *Princess Mononoke* [1997] for them, and Bob asked me why I was in town. I told him that I was on a signing tour for *Stardust*, and he asked me, 'What's *Stardust*?' I told him, and he immediately said, 'I'm buying it.'"

Gaiman wrote an outline and, over the next couple of years, various other studios became involved and several top Hollywood actresses were considered for the role of the fallen star, before the option finally lapsed. "I was feeling fairly disenchanted with Hollywood at the time," Gaiman comments.

"In the summer of 2002, my agent suggested I have lunch with Matthew Vaughn in Los Angeles. We really got on and, on the way home, he read my story 'Snow Glass Apples' and wanted to make a short film of it."

Born in 1971, Vaughn grew up in London and, after

Right: Charles Vess' original designs for Tristran in his Victorian and 'fairy' garb.

Opposite: Tristan (Charlie Cox) encounters the old Guard (David Kelly) the second time he tries to cross from England to Stormhold at the gap in the wall.

dropping out of university, worked with music video presenter Simon Fields, who has collaborated with some of the top music recording artists in the world.

Vaughn made his début as a film producer with the 1996 crime drama *The Innocent Sleep*, directed by Scott Michell and based on the true story of Italian banker Roberto Calvi, who was found hanged under London's Blackfriars Bridge in 1982.

Two years later he teamed with writer/director Guy Ritchie to produce the hugely influential and award-winning British crime comedy *Lock, Stock and Two Smoking Barrels*. Made on a budget of just £900,000, the film eventually became the third highest grossing British movie of all time.

After producing a spin-off TV series of *Lock, Stock* in 2000, the pair reteamed for another offbeat crime story, *Snatch* (2000), and *Swept Away* (2002). Between those two credits, Vaughn also produced the soccer movie *Mean Machine* (2001), a remake of the 1974 film *The Longest Yard* relocated to a British prison.

As a result of the deal over 'Snow Glass Apples', in 2003 Vaughn produced Neil Gaiman's directing début, the twenty-seven minute *A Short Film About John Bolton*. "You rapidly discover that if you want it to be the way it was in your head," explains Gaiman, "and

you want to put that on the screen, then you direct it because that's the way to get it to be the way that you wanted."

Gaiman's script concerned a documentary team attempting to discover where the eponymous horror artist (played in the film by John O'Mahony) found his ideas. The answer was both surprising and scary.

"Neil wanted to make a short," explains Matthew Vaughn. "We got on and trusted each other, so I said I would put the money into it."

"Matthew was always there when I needed him," says Gaiman. "They put it out on DVD in America and it sold a lot of copies."

Vaughn made his own début behind the camera the following year with the critically-acclaimed Brit gangster film *Layer Cake*, starring the latest James Bond, Daniel Craig, as a cocaine dealer forced to do one more job before he retires.

By the summer of 2005, Vaughn had decided that his next project was going to be *Stardust*, which he had initially been shown by his agent.

"I thought it was one of the most original, wonderful stories," he enthuses. "I'm very interested in stories in cinema, and I think most modern movies forget to tell a story."

Right: Vess' 'The Fairy Market', developed from the drawing for the original *Stardust* presentation to publishers in 1993.

Act 1

IN WHICH VARIOUS CHARACTERS
EMBARK ON A QUEST

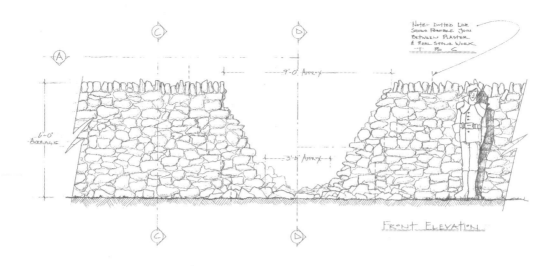

FRONT ELEVATION

I SEEK A FALLEN STAR.
– LAMIA

"It's a love story adventure," is how Matthew Vaughn describes *Stardust*. "It's a story about true love and about following your heart. And if you do, you can achieve happiness."

"*Stardust* is about the collision of two different worlds," explains Neil Gaiman. "The idea that you have Victorian England on the one hand – stuffy, straight-laced, pre-scientific, but a world in which science is just beginning to happen. And on the other hand you have Faerie and you have the Kingdom of Stormhold, and you have lions and unicorns and talking trees, and all sorts of strange, wonderful, magical, dangerous things. It's all about going into the kingdom of the imagination.

"But I think for me, when I was writing *Stardust*, I liked the idea of somebody figuring out what took them from being a boy to becoming a man."

In April 2006, Matthew Vaughn phoned Gaiman.

"Whenever I came to England," Gaiman reveals, "we would try to see each other, because we are friends. And Matthew would say, 'I want to do *Stardust*.' And I would say, 'When you are ready, let's talk.'"

"I like graphic novels," says Vaughn. "That's how I got to know Neil Gaiman. Neil is a really good friend of mine, a lovely bloke. I like being entertained, I like good stories, and I think comics have that. People who write comics take them very seriously."

"He phoned me up from England," continues Gaiman. "I was staying at the holiday home of British television presenter Jonathan Ross and his wife Jane Goldman in Florida, doing the final proofreading on my novel *Anansi Boys*. He said to me, '*Stardust* is the next thing I want to do.' Then he started talking about the problems he was having finding a scriptwriter.

"He started mentioning writers he was seeing and I thought, 'Hang on, all of the writers he's talking to here are boys' writers and Matthew is a boys' director. If the balance here isn't right, then it is going to be *Lock, Stock and Two Smoking Fairies*.

"I didn't want to write it because I had just started work on the script for the *Beowulf* [2007] movie, and I don't really like adapting my own material because I'm too precious about it in the wrong way.

"*Stardust* was not built to be a film," admits Gaiman. "I wrote it as a novel, and a lot of the delights of *Stardust* as a novel are not cinematic delights. An obvious example happens during the last third of the book. Part of the joy for the reader comes from watching a bunch of characters – all of whom the reader knows more about than

they do themselves – missing each other.

"You watch Primus and Septimus and all the Lords of Stormhold trying to kill each other off to get to the star, and none of them wins. And it all ends rather messily, and that is an absolute delight for the reader. It's great fun. It would completely not work as a movie, because a film is not a book.

"A lot of what works at the end of the book is how these people feel about what has happened. In a film you have to try and dramatise that. You have to turn that into an event, and turn it into action.

"That left me thinking that somebody else should do the script. There's so much damage that you need to do to turn a book into a film, and I didn't want to be the one doing the damage. I'm very happy with my novel.

"Jane Goldman had written a murder mystery novel called *Dreamworld* that I really enjoyed, and she really wanted to do a screenplay. I had loved Jane's writing for around eighteen years, and so I asked her if she had ever read *Stardust*. It was one of the few things of mine she hadn't, so I rang her in London and told her to read Jonathan's copy over the weekend and we would talk again on the Monday. And when she said, 'Can I ask what this is about?' I said, 'No.'

"When we next talked, she said that she had really, really loved it but still wanted to know why I had phoned. I asked if she was still really interested in writing

Previous spread, left: A concept illustration for an early unrealised scene, taken from the novel, in which a lion and a unicorn fight for a crown.

Previous spread, right: Sienna Miller and Matthew Vaughn, behind the scenes on location.

Above: Tristan dreams under a tree in the forest, before experiencing a rude awakening.

Right: Yvaine rides off on the unicorn after escaping her bonds in the forest.

screenplays, and when she said she was I told her that I would put her in touch with Matthew Vaughn, but there was no guarantee that she would get the job.

"Jane Goldman began her writing career in journalism, and is the author of nine books, including the best-selling two-volume non-fiction series, *The X-Files Book of the Unexplained*. She also produced and presented the Livingtv series *Jane Goldman Investigates* (2003-2004), before making the move behind the camera to write and produce other shows for British television. Gaiman's suggestion piqued her interest, and she called Vaughn right away and arranged to meet for coffee.

"I loved the fact that she was doing it because she loved the book," Gaiman recalls. He had suspected that she and Vaughn would be a well-matched creative pairing, and his instinct was spot on.

"It was just one of those lovely, serendipitous things," recalls Goldman, "where we seemed to think along very similar lines. Matthew and I got on well, and I was extremely excited and grateful when he said that he'd

like me to write the script.

"I respect Matthew enormously as a director and as an utterly brilliant producer. He's a complex and interesting person, and I don't think he would have worked with me if he didn't think I was capable of doing it.

"Writing is something that I am very passionate about," continues Goldman, "and it is also something that I work very hard at. My experience has always been that if you put enough love and effort into something you will achieve something you can be proud of."

Using Vaughn's script as a starting point, Goldman and Vaughn discussed the project over a number of meetings. "He had clear ideas about how to tell the story," recalls Goldman, "and for certain scenes from the book that he definitely wanted to include. He also had a really clear idea of the structure, which was very useful, and we worked on that together."

"To my amazement," Matthew Vaughn reveals, "it took us about five weeks to write the script, and then two weeks after that we got the money to make it. So it's

Above: Jane Goldman, Charlie Cox and Matthew Vaughn discuss a script point on the witches' lair set at Pinewood Studios.

one of those rare occasions where I think it was a film
that was definitely meant to be made."

Stardust is co-financed by Paramount Pictures, in
association with Matthew Vaughn's British-based
MARV Films. It is a Matthew Vaughn/Lorenzo di
Bonaventura Production, with Paramount handling
worldwide distribution.

"I figured that if you made *Stardust* into a film," says
Neil Gaiman, "it would be about two people who had no
idea that they were in love, and had every reason to dis-
like each other, heading off through a world in which
every hand was against them, and discovering along the
way that actually they liked the other one more than
anybody else in the world. And I think that had the
simplicity of what kind of film it was. And everything
else, the magical stuff – the flying ships, the trees, the
unicorns, the sword-fights, dangerous witches – everything else made that happen."

Soon after negotiations began, Vaughn offered
Gaiman a producer credit on the film. "He was right up

front about it very early on," explains the author. "He
came up to me later and said, 'You know, you actually
earned your producer credit by getting Jane Goldman as
the screenwriter.'

"But you know, I've definitely worked for it. I had a
lot of input into the script. In November 2005, when we
got to the second draft, I stayed for a weekend at
Matthew's home with him and Jane and we read the
whole thing through."

"Neil very sweetly left us to get on with the script
initially," recalls Goldman, "until we thought it was
ready for him to take a look at. We then all spent a really fun and interesting weekend at Matthew's house in
the country.

"It was surreal. At one point Matthew said, 'I wish I
had the camera on,' especially when Neil and I were
doing the pirate accents. But it was really useful to hear
the script out loud, and it was really nice to have Neil
there, contributing his comments."

"I think Neil Gaiman obviously wrote a great book,"

says Lorenzo di Bonaventura, whose other credits as a film producer include *Constantine* (2005), *Doom* (2005) and *Transformers* (2007), "and Matthew and Jane put together a script that Neil loved and approved of. It was at that point that I got involved. They brought the script to Paramount, and they needed a producer.

"I'm a big Neil Gaiman fan myself, having developed a few properties of his when I was President of Worldwide Theatrical Production at Warner Bros. I came onto the project in January 2006, and it's been a really fun ride. We put together a great group of movie stars, and Matthew and Jane did a phenomenal job on the script.

"Like any adaptation, we've certainly tried to be faithful to the source material, and in this case we used Neil – the author himself – as a barometer. Neil really embraced both the adaptation in script form, and the movie in its execution. So I think that's the best thing for the book, and the best thing for our movie.

"In terms of adapting books – and I've been involved

in a lot of adaptations – I think people have many different ways of looking at it. You simply have to be true to the spirit of the book more than you have to be literal. If you're true to the spirit of the book, the audience will actually think that a scene was in the book when it wasn't."

"They'd send me scripts," recalls Gaiman, "and I'd say every now and again, 'You don't want to do this.' Or they'd say, 'Oh, we're thinking of doing this.' And I'd say, 'Don't. It's not a good idea. The fans would kill you if you did, because they'd think that you didn't care.' And they'd go, 'But our reason for doing this is this, this and this.' And I'd say, 'Okay, absolutely fine.'"

"I wanted stay as faithful to the book as possible," says Matthew Vaughn, "while also bearing in mind that I had to make a good film. There are a lot of things in the book that aren't cinematic enough, so we had to ensure that the audience had a good ride."

"I think *Stardust* suggested itself as a film very readily," Jane Goldman points out, "and that is a testament

Above: Matthew Vaughn and director of photography Ben Davis shooting a scene on location.

to what a great book it is.

"You can make an incredibly faithful adaptation, but that doesn't mean it's going to be a perfect movie. There are things that are different, but the spirit of the book is very much there."

"Obviously," continues Vaughn, "to make it into a movie, we had to change it a bit, and add a new third act."

"Of course, it's never like you imagined it," agrees Neil Gaiman, "but for me that's one of the cool things about film. One of the great things about the book is that anybody owns it and everybody owns it. When you only have the text, it's yours to imagine. The people who have read the novel of *Stardust* have half-a-million Tristran Thorns wandering around in their heads, and half-a-million Yvaines, and half-a-million witches, and half-a-million Ditchwater Sals. They all look different."

"They've taken what we did and developed it into a slightly different world," Charles Vess observes, "but it's just as full and rich and wonderful."

"When I read the first draft of Jane and Matthew's script," Gaiman remembers, "I felt good that there were places where they had done – differently – things that I had known that I had to do in my original outline for Miramax back in 1999. They are very different, but there are occasional moments where I could see that we hit the same beats in the storytelling."

"I loved the atmosphere of *Stardust*," continues Jane Goldman, "and I loved the idea of the challenge of getting that into a movie, because it is a particularly nuanced fairy tale. It is a beautiful, many-layered book. I could see that it might be easy to miss the mood and tone of that, so I enjoyed the challenge of trying to translate it for the screen. I also really responded to the characters."

"If you give the audience what they expect, they'll be bored," believes Matthew Vaughn. "There are no rules. You do what you want, while respecting the boundaries. You do things they haven't seen before and make it accessible, funny and clever."

Once a second draft had been completed, that basically became the shooting script, with only a few minor revisions as the production went along.

Pre-production work on *Stardust* began in late September 2005. By the end of that year, all the major departments were hard at work creating a fantasy world set partially in Victorian England and for the most part in the Realms of Faerie, now retitled Stormhold in the script – a name coined from the original book. "That was something that Neil seemed to be comfortable with," confirms Jane Goldman.

"It was an ambitious film when we started," recalls production designer Gavin Bocquet, "which is often the case. There is usually never quite enough money, quite enough time and quite enough resources to do what everybody is hoping to do, but in theory you all pull together and you make that happen."

"It's really a balance of both cost-effectiveness and creativity," explains producer Lorenzo di Bonaventura, "and that's sort of the argument that goes back and forth. Matthew comes from an independent perspective, so he brings a certain skill set that is different to large-scale movies. We made some creative choices about how to visually handle the movie, which allowed us to bring the budget down as well. And Jane Goldman also comes from a very independent spirit. So there was sort of this fusion of big filmmaking and independent filmmaking in a unique setting."

"Whether it's a small film," continues Bocquet, "or a film like *Stardust*, the challenge for us is to put every penny of the art department budget up there on the screen and make it look like we had a great deal more to spend as well. That's all about pre-planning. Planning from Matthew, planning from me. Co-producer Michael Dreyer always stressed when we started that preparation is the crucial thing on a film like this.

"This kind of film, which is set in a fantastical world that involves visual effects, and stunts, and action, just requires a lot more preparation. You can never underestimate on a film how important that prep time is for the art department."

Bocquet should certainly know. In a career dating back to *Star Wars Episode VI: Return of the Jedi* (1983), he has worked on a number of high-profile productions, including *Supergirl* (1984), *Return to Oz* (1985), *Young Sherlock Holmes* (1985), *Dangerous Liaisons* (1988), *Kafka* (1991), *xXx* (2002) and its sequel *xXx: State of the Union* (2005), plus the TV series *The Young Indiana Jones Chronicles* (1992-93), for which he won an Emmy Award, and all three episodes in George Lucas' final *Star Wars* trilogy.

"When I came on board *Stardust*," Bocquet recalls, "Matthew had done about a week's work with a concept designer. There were sketches for five or six different key elements – Stormhold Palace, witches' lair, Primus' coach – but very loose designs. It was interesting to see those first ideas, just to get some general principals from

Above and right:
Pre-production sketches by the art department for Stormhold Palace.

Matthew about trying not to make *Stardust* just a fairy tale, but more of an edgy, urban fantasy within that fairy tale world.

"There's not a lot there that ended up connecting with what we did, but that's just a sequence of events. Many of our early designs ended up being nothing like the final result. The whole process is so organic. Some things you hit upon immediately as a design, others take six months of discussion and ideas to come out. We were trying to put things in front of Matthew to help him along with telling the story visually.

"When you are talking about a fantastical parallel world in Victorian times, you just don't come up with that concept instantly in the first week. It was a question of discussing it, getting reference books, showing ideas, getting images, doing designs and finding locations."

Costume designer Sammy Sheldon joined the production two weeks before Christmas and was faced with creating more than 200 major costume designs. "I thought the script was really magical," she says. "From a costume point of view it was kind of a dream script to design, but it was also something of a challenge, because it was both a fantasy and a period drama. Everything had to be made from scratch to create a believable world. Luckily, there were certain ideas that Matthew gave me to start researching."

Sheldon did not read the original illustrated book or consult Charles Vess' drawings before she began working on the costume designs. "In some ways, I think that it is easier not to be influenced by somebody else's version of the story. I wanted to get a pure view from Matthew, and Gavin Bocquet, and what I felt, so that what we achieved was as original as I could make it."

In fact, Sammy Sheldon is no stranger to working on adaptations from other media, and her recent film credits include *The Hitchhiker's Guide to the Galaxy* (2005) and *V for Vendetta* (2006).

"At the outset it was quite intimidating," she continues, "given that I always try to dispense with boundaries when I'm designing, and here was a script where almost anything goes. I struggled for a long time with how, exactly, we were going to create this fantasy world that seems believable without it looking corny in some way, or looking like just another fantasy movie."

There were a different set of challenges awaiting production designer Gavin Bocquet and his team. "The way the art department works is very much like an architectural studio," he explains. "I use 3-D architectural card

Below left: Costume designer Sammy Sheldon on location.
Below: Sammy Sheldon's original pre-production sketch for Ditch-Water Sal's costume.

models, as well as sketches, of everything we do. It's a 3-D world we live in, so we became a bit of a hub for every department, because if there was any discussion – stunts, action, visual effects – they would all head to the art department with Matthew because we had physical models of these designs.

"The good thing about card models is that they are very tactile. You can pick them up, you can move them around, you can pull walls out. With the 3-D models we created on the computer, you can actually get in there with a virtual camera and get a good idea of scale."

With sets and costume designs well under way, the producers' thoughts turned to casting. Unusually for a major studio film, scriptwriter Jane Goldman found herself included in the decision-making process.

"I felt very privileged that Matthew allowed me to be involved," she admits. "I watched auditions and made suggestions about casting, but in the end it was very much up to the director to make those decisions."

"Matthew brought to *Stardust* a single-minded vision that actually made something happen," says Neil Gaiman. "The effort involved in turning a film from a dream into a reality is absolutely unbelievable, and what Matthew has had is an absolute focus on the story he wanted to tell.

"He went out and got the money, he got his actors, and roughly six months after they started work on it they were shooting at Pinewood, which is astonishing."

Filming started on April 25, 2006, in Iceland, with two days devoted to a lakeside sequence and aerial shots of the wild, rocky coastline. The production then moved to the world-famous Pinewood Studios, Buckinghamshire, situated approximately twenty miles to the west of London.

Built on the site of former seventeenth-century manor houses, Pinewood was created in 1935 and has since played host to some of the biggest film franchises in the world, including the James Bond series.

Over the course of the production, *Stardust* utilised six of the large soundstages at the studios, along with the backlot, moving between each area as used sets were broken down and new environments were constructed.

Screenwriter Jane Goldman was on set almost every day. "There was always something for me to do," she remembers. "It was a big production, and there were a lot of actors, so when someone had a question they came to me if Matthew was busy."

"I didn't get on set as much as I wanted to," admits

Neil Gaiman. "I went on a location scout to the Isle of Skye, in Scotland, and I was around for the final ten days of pre-production before they started shooting, including rehearsals. I also came back twice more during the production. It was useful for me to be there.

"During the pre-production period, I had access to the casting website, so even though I was still in America I could see all the auditions as soon as they went up online. In fact, at one point, I found myself in Los Angeles operating the camera at a casting session while we auditioned potential Yvaines.

"The day filming started, I flew back to America and then went off to Australia and around the world on a book tour. Actually, I was quite nervous about what was going on in Scotland and Iceland and Pinewood Studios. When I finally returned to Pinewood, they showed me half an hour of footage. I wound up with a big grin on my face. It's funny and the scary bits are scary. It's my thing and they made it into a film."

"We had the advantage of going to some spectacular locations in Scotland, and in Iceland, and all through England," reveals producer Lorenzo di Bonaventura. "We did as much of our special effects as we could in-camera, and we have digital imagery as well. But our magic is really about the magic of the movie, and the locations, the people and the costuming were also all very important."

Left: Development blueprint of the witches' lair fireplace.
Below: The ornate witches' lair set at Pinewood Studios.

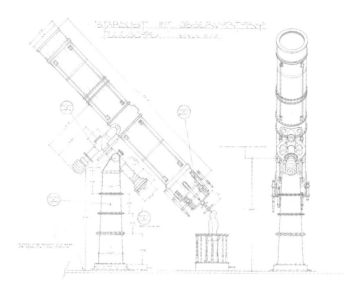

IT BEGINS WITH A LITTLE VILLAGE CALLED WALL.

– NARRATOR

The story of *Stardust* starts in Victorian England, the heart of the British Empire. It is the age of invention, and across the world that heart is bursting with a new-found love for the wonders of science.

At the Royal Academy of Science in London, a distinguished scientist replies to a letter received from a young country boy named Dunstan Thorne. In the opinion of the scientist and his esteemed colleagues, the stories told in the small English village of Wall – about an enchanted kingdom that exists alongside the village, filled with witches, fairies, unicorns and other magical creatures – can be safely dismissed as local folklore…

Stowe School in Bedford, England, was used as a location for two nights to shoot the Victorian observatory that opens the film, along with scenes of Stormhold Palace stables (later cut from the movie) and the climactic coronation, which involved more than 200 extras.

"There was a very grand entrance room," explains production designer Gavin Bocquet, "which we used for the opening sequence in the movie. It was difficult to find a circular or elliptical-shaped room that had no windows and was big enough for the thirty-foot telescope.

"The telescope was a big prop that we had to make. We knew we wanted this kind of 'Jules Verne' design – that mahogany and brass look. So we obtained

some old reference books, and did some concept sketches and built some miniatures. Got the scale right, got the size right. It was quite an expensive build, but it had a bit of a 'wow' factor when everybody walked into that room and saw it in place, surrounded by Peter Young's great Victorian set dressing."

As soon as Dunstan (Ben Barnes) receives his reply from the Royal Academy of Science, he rushes down to a strange dry stone wall on the outskirts of the village, and attempts to get the aged Guard (David Kelly) to allow him to pass through a tumbled gap in the edifice.

Neil Gaiman's initial inspiration for the village of Wall and its location came during a touring holiday in 1988. "My wife and I had left the children behind, and we had gone for a week driving through Ireland," recalls the author. "Somewhere in Cork I drove past a field, and there was a section of a wall, and there was a hole it. And you could just sort of see this wonderful forest beyond it and I thought, 'Wouldn't it be cool if just a hole in a wall away was Faerie land. It's everything you've ever dreamed of.' And that was the start."

"The film starts – as does the book – with Dunstan Thorne," explains screenwriter Jane Goldman. "Dunstan is a young man who lives in Victorian England, in a little village called Wall. We realise very quickly that he's very determined to get through the gap in a slightly mysterious dry stone wall that's guarded by a somewhat peculiar

**Previous spread,
left:** The scientist's letter to Dunstan.

**Previous spread,
right:** The scientist (Alasdair Macintosh) looks through the telescope in The Royal Academy of Science in London.

Right: The thirty-foot telescope prop situated in the entrance room of Stowe School in Bedford, England.

Far right: An art department mock-up of how the Victorian observatory would look in the final film.

Below: A blueprint of the telescope's pivot point.

Opposite: Art department scale miniature of the 'Jules Verne' design telescope.

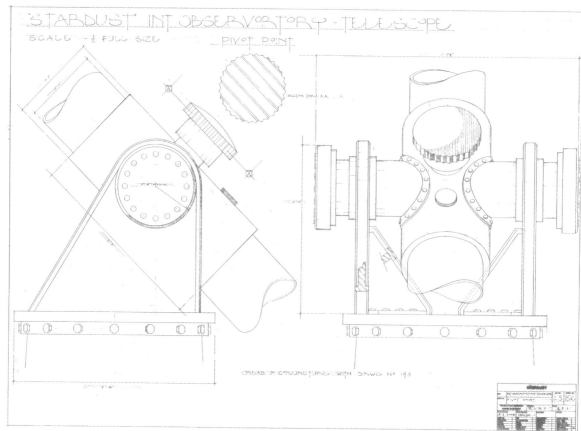

old man.

"Dunstan tricks his way through the gap in order to prove that there is nothing mysterious or magical on the other side. But he very quickly realises that his theory is wrong when he discovers a bizarre world beyond the wall."

After stumbling through a forest of tall trees, Dunstan emerges into an otherworldly market town and, for the first time, he realises that he has crossed over into an enchanted realm.

"He finds himself in an odd kind of market," continues Goldman, "where there are all sorts of things the like of which he has never seen before. Dunstan meets a rather saucy and mysterious young lady, and nine months later a baby is delivered to his doorstep in a basket. And that baby is Tristan Thorne, our hero."

Whereas the fairy market in the book was an impermanent market occurring every nine years, the film has it as a permanent fixture of life in Faerie. "It was felt that establishing the transient nature of the market in a way that would do the concept justice, would take too long," says Goldman. "It wouldn't have fitted in the way that Matthew wanted to pace the story. But otherwise, the market of the film is unchanged. It's Dunstan's first glimpse of the realm beyond the wall, and ours too, and it's where it becomes clear that Stormhold, as we call it, is a completely different, and captivatingly magical, world."

It was decided early on by the filmmakers not to make the people of Stormhold look too ethereal, as hair and make-up designer Fae Hammond explains: "We were very aware that this was Victorian England, and Matthew and I wanted to make sure that when we went through the wall, it was like a cross between Glastonbury Festival and the trendy Camden Town area of London.

Inset and above: The young Dunstan Thorne (Ben Barnes) makes his way through Stormhold Market.

Right: Dunstan meets the seductive Slave Girl (Kate Magowan) amongst the wonders of Stormhold Market.

"Matthew wants the audience to be able to relate to these characters, so it is almost as if they are people you've seen in the street. If you look carefully, you'll see them all around us. We wanted to keep it real, and so I tried to use elements of real people."

"It's sort of a world with two halves," explains the director. "You see Victorian England, which we actually shot in a very quaint, fantasy way. Then you have Stormhold, which is the fantasy element, and we gave that a modern, edgy, stylistic approach. I think a lot of people when they make fantasy films think, 'Well it's fantasy, so we'll just make it full of clichés,' which is what we wanted to avoid."

Eighteen years later, and Tristan has grown up to be an awkward young man who works behind the counter of the local grocery store in the village of Wall. He is infatuated with the conceited and flirtatious Victoria Forester, who much prefers the romantic attentions of the wealthy and dashing Humphrey.

For the pivotal role of Tristan Thorne – the spelling of the character's name was changed from 'Tristran' in the original book to prevent any confusion over pronunciation – Matthew Vaughn cast the relatively unknown young British actor Charlie Cox after auditioning him several times.

Born in London in 1982, Cox had previously appeared in *The Merchant of Venice* (2004), *Casanova* (2005) and the BBC remake of *A for Andromeda* (2006).

"Tristan is a character who has to go from a nerd to a swashbuckling hero," producer Lorenzo di Bonaventura explains. "He has to travel a long way as a character."

"This is Charlie Cox's first starring role," reveals Neil Gaiman. "He just came in and nailed it on the audition. Once we had seen him, there really wasn't any doubt in our minds. He was so obviously right for the role. There were lots of young men who could come in and play gormless and awkward, and there were others who could be wonderfully cool heroes. But there was nobody else who could go from one part to the other as convincingly. You really believe in the progression of his character throughout Tristan's adventures."

"Most actors will audition once or twice, get the part, and then start the character work," reveals Charlie Cox, "whereas I kind of found it during the audition process, which is really interesting."

"I think Charlie has such amazing screen presence," says Jane Goldman. "There's something so unbelievably genuine and truthful about his performance. He brought an incredible naturalism to what is basically a fantasy film."

"When we first meet Tristan," hair and make-up designer Fae Hammond explains, "we see him living in a small Victorian house in a small Victorian village. We had to make him look very ordinary, so I kept his skin tone very pale. Charlie Cox is a handsome guy, so we couldn't do anything too over-the-top to

Opposite: British actor Charlie Cox stars as Tristan Thorne, a young man searching for his Heart's Desire in a world of magic and mystery.
Left: Sammy Sheldon's costume design for the "awkward" Tristan.

make him ugly, but we gave him a geeky haircut and a pale complexion with no definition around the eyes, so he just looked a bit gormless."

Hammond, who won an Emmy Award for her work on *Elizabeth I* (2005) and had previously worked with Matthew Vaughn on such films as *Snatch*, *Swept Away* and *Layer Cake*, came onto the production late, and was helped immensely by Sammy Sheldon's distinctive costume designs. "Sammy was amazing," confirms Hammond. "So long as the hair and make-up matches the costume, it is key to the look of a character."

"Tristan's a young Victorian man who hasn't got a lot of money," says Sheldon. "His costume is slightly off-kilter; the trousers are a bit too tight, the coat could have been his dad's. It had a funny little Peter Pan collar that looked a little bit geeky and not quite right, and I think it really works for him. Then we had a bowler hat made for him that was right for the period but squashed a bit, so again it wasn't quite right. Basically, it's just a very, very simple Victorian working-class design."

"He lives in a very small village in the middle of nowhere," Charlie Cox reveals about the character he portrays. "He just lives with his father. He doesn't have a mother, or at least he's not aware of his mother's whereabouts. And his father doesn't have any other children, so it's an unusual situation and he's feeling a bit different, like an outcast really."

"I think I always saw Tristan as someone who, despite not knowing his history and his family background, and actually believing that his mother had died in childbirth, has always had a sense that he didn't quite fit in," says Jane Goldman. "And in many ways I think that's probably a sense that a lot of people at eighteen have. A sense that the town that they come from may not be where they're destined to end up, especially when they're not accepted by the popular crowd. I liked that element of the story.

"Actually, I think that's what makes *Stardust* a very, very interesting fantasy movie – because it's not just about the spectacle, it's about real people."

"The main thing on Tristan's mind at that stage in his life is absolute infatuation with Victoria Forester," explains Goldman, "who is the prettiest girl in the village and is completely disinterested in him. She really feels that she's quite a lot better than him, and that she can do better."

"Tristan is in love with the village beauty, Victoria," says Charlie Cox, "and his goal is to win her heart. There isn't a boy in the village who wouldn't want to be with Victoria. All the other boys just accept that that person will be Humphrey, except Tristan, who believes that it's him."

The vain and conceited object of Tristan's affections is played by New York-born British actress Sienna Miller.

"Victoria Forester is this quite glamorous girl in a small village," explains Miller. "At the beginning of the film there are two people who are after my character. One is Tristan, and the other guy is called Humphrey. So, she's in this dilemma because she's being pursued by these two suitors, although it's quite obvious for her which one is the more attractive.

"It's also clear to the audience from the beginning that she thinks one of them is pretty pathetic and weak and the other is very strapping and handsome."

For the actress, whose credits include Matthew Vaughn's *Layer Cake*, *Alfie* (2004) and *Factory Girl* (2006), the role of the flighty Victoria was basically an extended cameo. "It's just a very light-hearted, very fun kind of film," she says. "It's sort of an adventure, and I guess Victoria is a catalyst for the story.

"I actually did Matthew's first film, so I'd worked with him before, which was great. I felt very at home. I

Opposite, above: Tristan is smitten with the vain and conceited Victoria Forester (Sienna Miller).
Opposite, below: Tristan and Victoria share a romantic evening picnic.
Below: Tristan receives a beating from Humphrey (Henry Cavill), Victoria's dashing suitor.

think he's naturally a very good director, and he's very good at being in control. I think he knows exactly what he wants."

Miller had also previously worked with Charlie Cox, when they played brother and sister in Lasse Hallström's historical drama *Casanova*. "We go way back, so it was obviously great to work with him again," enthuses the actress. "And Henry Cavill is playing Humphrey, and he's fantastic. Very dashing, and tall, and kind of perfect for the part. They were both great to work with, and it was just a lot of fun."

"I talked with director of photography Ben Davis about the style of the lighting and where should we go with strong colours," costume designer Sammy Sheldon recalls. "While Matthew wanted Stormhold to have a really rich pallet, the Victorian flip-side was quite toned-down and muted, but also very real. Therefore everybody wasn't just dressed in black or bustles.

"Victoria is the froth within the village of Wall. She's a playful character, so the colours that I gave her were always pretty and she stands out. Tristan's costume is a quirky little jacket that doesn't look quite right, with his funny little bowler hat and hobnail boots. He tries, but he doesn't quite get it right. Then Humphrey is the dashing suitor who sweeps Victoria off her feet.

**Previous spread,
above left:** Tristan tries
to convince the aged
Guard to let him pass
through the gap in the
wall.
**Previous spread,
below left:** Tristan
attempts to cross the wall.
**Previous spread,
right:** Early concept
drawing of the wall.

"Humphrey is really quite posh, and we thought it would be quite funny to have him in a sort of driving outfit rather than just a suit for one of those scenes, just to give another aspect to him, that he's got everything.

"All the Victorian characters are generally quite real. I didn't want to get into the frilly sort of pretty Victorian. You don't notice it, it's just a background to what's going on."

In an attempt to win Victoria's affections, the besotted Tristan spends all his savings laying out a romantic nighttime picnic for the two of them in a field near the mysterious wall.

"So Tristan and Victoria go for a picnic," explains Sienna Miller, "and she sees a shooting star. Tristan promises that he will go and cross the wall that is sort of the divide between their world and this more mystical land, to retrieve the fallen star for her. And she says that if he gets it, then she'll marry him."

"The picnic doesn't go very well," Charlie Cox reveals, "and in his kind of drunk, delusional state he promises that he will fetch the shooting star for her without really considering what that entails at all. But he makes the promise and fully intends to stand by his word."

"She rather thinks it's quite the most absurd thing she's ever heard," continues Jane Goldman. "But at the same time, she wants to hedge her bets because she likes the idea of having something that nobody else has in

the world. So Tristan blindly goes off to fulfil his side of this rather odd deal, which is actually his ticket to manhood and adventure."

The streets and houses of the sleepy village of Wall, "a countryside town boarding on a magical land", were mostly based in Castle Combe, in Wiltshire. Situated not far from Stonehenge, and used as the location for the original *Doctor Dolittle* (1967) movie and the 1980s television series *Robin of Sherwood*, the village houses are all constructed from typical Cotswold stone with thick walls and roofs made of split natural stone tiles. Dating back several hundred years, these unique properties are listed as ancient monuments.

"We looked all over to find the perfect English village," recalls production designer Gavin Bocquet. "You'd think there would be hundreds, but there were not many that worked for us and hadn't been seen in other films recently."

The production finally settled on using both Castle Combe and the Cotswold village of Bibury – the latter once famously described by nineteenth century Arts and Crafts designer William Morris as "the most beautiful village in England" – to represent Wall.

Following three weeks' intensive preparation, filming there began in early May 2006 and lasted for a week. Director Matthew Vaughn wanted the location to look picturesque but not manicured. The small street leading down from the Market Cross to the By Brook provided a postcard-perfect background for the film crew, who gave each of the forty or so ancient buildings a make-over; applying a lick of paint, changing double-glazed windows, replacing front doors, substituting modern plants for more traditional varieties, and adding French-style

Clockwise from left: Tristan makes his way through the streets of his sleepy home village. The exterior of the grocer's shop, Monday & Sons, where Tristan works. Production sketch of the interior of Monday & Sons. Scale model of Wall's central square.

Above: Tristan finally learns about his unconventional heritage from his father, Dunstan (Nathaniel Parker).

Opposite: Various Babylon candle pre-production designs and the final version (far right).

shutters to the television aerial-free cottages. Straw and turf were laid over the main road to create a dirt track and a completely new village green was created.

When the director needed a specific shot that linked Victoria's house to the local store where Tristan works, the perfect building was eventually found after a difficult search for exactly the right location that combined both elements. The art department then went to work, transforming a charming holiday cottage into the grocer's shop, Monday & Sons. "Sometimes you come across a location, and you know it is perfect for the script," says Gavin Bocquet. "Castle Combe was a beautiful town in a really nice valley."

During filming, security guards and police kept curious onlookers and the paparazzi at a safe distance. 200 extras were selected from amongst the village population, and Castle Combe Parish Council chairman Adrian Bishop told a local newspaper: "I believe there are quite a number of extras taken from the village and they were all bussed up to London to audition. It's very exciting for Castle Combe, and the village has really been transformed."

When shooting was completed, the streets and

houses were returned to their natural appearance. Pressure washers were used to remove the biodegradable pulp paper mixture applied to darken down the buildings' usual colourful exteriors.

Emboldened by Victoria's promise to marry him if he brings her back the fallen star, Tristan unknowingly follows in his father's footsteps as he approaches the gap in the wall and is challenged by the same Guard.

"It was one thing I was thinking a lot about when I was reading the script," says Charlie Cox. "What do the villagers, the people of Wall, think is on the other side? If no one has crossed it, or at least anyone who has doesn't talk about it, then what do they think they're going to find? It's interesting. Do they think that there's nothing really there? Do they believe it's just a fairy tale? Or do they really believe that there is something magical and dangerous on the other side of the wall? They're not allowed to go through, and it's been guarded for as long as anyone can remember, so there's no reason to question why it's guarded.

"Tristan attempts to just walk through because the Guard is ninety-seven, and a young boy of eighteen would not worry about getting past an old man. But when he gets there, he's in for a bit of a shock."

"In the book, the way that I had it is basically that all the men in the village guard the wall," Neil Gaiman recalls. "They take it in turns, and there are always two people on wall duty, normally an older person and a young person. In the film, for reasons of economy in the sense of just compressing the storytelling, they have a Guard on the wall who is more than ninety years old. In the next scene he's eighteen years older than that. So I guess he's probably about 108.

"But it's lovely, and in *Stardust* the film we learn that you shouldn't mess with little old Irish men, because they're even more lethal than some of those little old Chinese men in the movies."

When Tristan attempts to pull the same stunt that his father did, and bolt through the gap in the wall when the Guard's attention is distracted, he ends up on the receiving end of some high-flying kicks and a good thrashing.

"As for David Kelly," says hair and make-up designer Fae Hammond, "who plays the old Guard at the wall, we made him Victorian, but slightly odd Victorian. There's just something a little disconcerting about him. He has obviously been there for a long, long time, but there is also something otherworldly about him which makes

you think that he could sneak through the gap in the wall and he wouldn't seem out of place."

"When he fails to cross the wall because of the Guard, Tristan goes back home," explains Charlie Cox. "In an earlier version of the script we had a sequence in which he attempted to climb the wall away from the Guard using different methods, and he fails every time.

"It's a major setback, and he doesn't really have any new ideas of how to cross the wall. And when he does eventually cross the wall, it's through the help of his mother."

When Tristan returns home to nurse his bruises, his father (Nathaniel Parker, as the older Dunstan Thorne) takes him up to the attic and finally reveals to him the truth about his unconventional heritage. Within the basket that he was delivered in, Tristan discovers a partly-used Babylon candle and a note from his mother (Kate Magowan). For them to finally be reunited, she tells him the safest way to travel is by candlelight.

"He makes the decision to light the candle," continues Cox, "having no idea what will happen at all. And when he does light it, he disappears and travels by candlelight beyond the wall. I don't think Tristan has even enough time to really consider what will become of him."

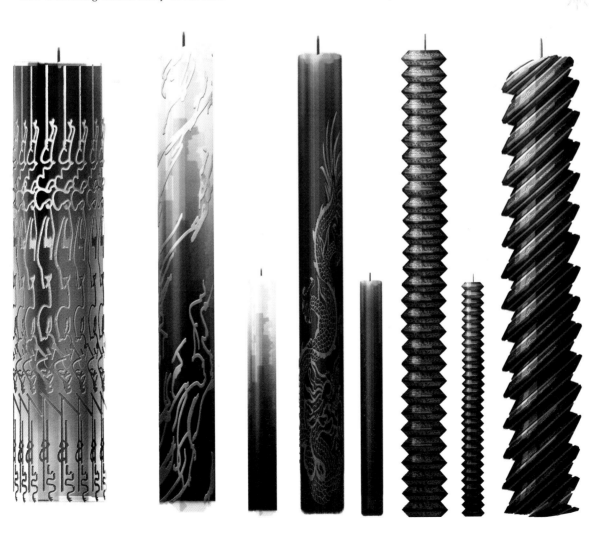

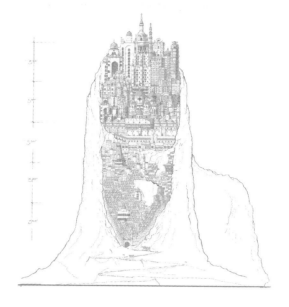

ONLY HE OF ROYAL BLOOD CAN RESTORE THE SAPPHIRE. AND BE THE NEW KING OF STORMHOLD.

– KING

"You have a kingdom called Stormhold," says Neil Gaiman, "which I always liked to imagine was carved out of the top of a mountain. A whole city carved out of a mountain, and right at the top the old King of Stormhold is dying."

In the King's bedroom, his surviving sons Primus (Jason Flemyng), Secundus (Rupert Everett), Tertius (Mark Heap) and the ruthless Septimus (Mark Strong) are gathered around their dying father.

"I couldn't believe our luck that we got Peter O'Toole as the King of Stormhold," exclaims Jane Goldman. "At the point in the film where that scene happens, he brings just the right amount of sly humour to the proceedings."

Also observing the old King's final moments are three other figures. These are the shades of his dead sons, Quartus (Julian Rhind-Tutt), Quintas (Adam Buxton) and Sextus (David Walliams).

"The tradition of Stormhold is that usually by the time it comes to decide succession most of the princes have all killed each other," continues Goldman.

"Unfortunately," Gaiman observes, "as he finds himself dying, the King notices that his sons have not yet succeeded in assassinating each other. Four of them are alive, while the other three are dead but still hanging around as ghosts and commenting on the action.

"When I did the original outline for *Stardust* for publishers to see in 1993, I listed a number of things that

Right: Concept design for the Kingdom of Stormhold.

Opposite: The dying King of Stormhold (Peter O'Toole) surrounded by his avaricious sons.

Tristran and Yvaine were going to encounter in Faerie. One of which was that they would come up against the seven Lords of Stormhold, some of whom are dead. It was just one line that came straight out of my head. And then Charlie Vess took it and drew seven Lords of Stormhold.

"It amused me while I was writing the book to have dead people standing around commenting on the action and, occasionally, when another one of them would get killed and shuffle into the line, they would say, 'Cor, you should have seen that one coming.'"

When the King tells Secundus to look out of the window, Septimus grasps the opportunity to send his brother plummeting to his death. Moments later, a flat-faced Secundus appears alongside his phantom brethren.

"Rupert Everett is magnificent," Gaiman enthuses. "His little scene as Secundus, where he comes on as Prince Charming and gets pushed out of the window, is magic."

Clockwise from opposite below: The nut tree and various art department designs and scale models of Stormhold Palace, a city carved out of a mountain.

Below: Blueprint of the King's bedroom tower.

Right: Art department design for the dying King's bed.

Opposite: Peter O'Toole as the dying King of Stormhold.

Opposite, inset: The King's ruby pendant.

"The scariest ghost for me was Rupert Everett," reveals comedian Adam Buxton, who played the spectral Quintus, "who, like Dave Walliams and Julian Rhind-Tutt, was having to do his scenes under five hours of prosthetics to achieve the look of a man who had just died a grisly death."

"The princes were always one of my favourite things in the book," admits Jane Goldman, "So I particularly enjoyed writing dialogue for them. Neil has a very dry sense of humour, and I wanted to stay true to that spirit. Matthew and I liked the idea of them functioning as

a Greek chorus. There was just something slightly dark and funny and quirky about them, and that was the appeal to me."

"It's Ealing comedy," says Gaiman. "Even when I was writing it, it felt like *Kind Hearts and Coronets* [1949] – you can imagine Alec Guinness playing all the ghosts."

"It's a very haunting and magical book," Goldman continues, "but you can read it on a humorous level as well, and I just wanted to bring that element a bit more to the fore. And hopefully that is what we have done.

"The ghostly princes are cameo roles, but I think they

make a big impact in terms of the tone of the whole piece. We've got some amazing British actors and comedians playing them, and what they all have in common is great timing."

"I now can't imagine anyone else playing Septimus and Primus other than Mark Strong and Jason Flemyng. Jason brings such a sweetness to Primus that is very, very appealing."

"Primus has redeeming features," agrees Gaiman. "He is the only one of them that you kind of like. He's a little bit pompous, but he wouldn't have been a bad king."

"For the scene in the King's bedroom, where the old King dies," production designer Gavin Bocquet recalls, "we spent six months looking for a grand, opulent location, maybe something with a religious connotation. With the location managers I saw more than sixty different locations from Scotland to Wales to London, but we couldn't really get a handle on it. Everything we saw looked architecturally too 'English', by nature of the fact

that that was where we were filming.

"We finally ended up shooting that scene at Elveden Estate, in Suffolk, which had a style of decoration that was very exotic, in an ornamental way. It just fitted perfectly into the world that we had imagined Stormhold to be.

"The reason that we couldn't really pin down that location earlier was because back at the beginning we probably didn't completely understand what that world was. That's part of that organic process. The most difficult thing for a designer is when you sit there on that first day and you have a piece of blank paper in front of you. No matter how many times you do it, that first morning is still the blank piece of paper, and you know that it will take six or eight months of gradually working and scheduling your design time to achieve all the results you want."

With his waning strength, the King removes a pendant and chain from around his neck. At its heart is a large ruby. As the pendant floats in the air, all the colour drains from the precious stone. Only someone of royal blood can restore the jewel, and the person who does so will become the new King of Stormhold.

Incredibly, all the intricate jewellery and finely crafted metalwork seen in the film was specially created by the costume department. "The jewellery is very specific to the film," explains costume designer Sammy Sheldon. "Early in the pre-production process, the art department had come up with a coat of arms for the King of Stormhold, depicting a boar and an eagle. So I took that,

and basically distorted it into the King's ruby pendant, which everybody is chasing after, with the two animals holding the stone. Through that process, I was able to link the pendant to this whole heraldic tradition of Stormhold. I drew up the design and sent that to my jeweller and he sculpted it.

"With the King's crown, I took the boar and the eagle motif and used them on the sides, so they looked as if they were chasing each other around the circumference. We just took the basic design and adapted it for whatever was needed."

As the King's head falls back onto the pillow and his eyes close in death, the pendant hurtles out of the window and high up into the night sky... where it knocks a twinkling star out of the heavens. As the fiery mass plummets toward the Earth, it passes over the wall and into Stormhold.

It is the same fallen star that Tristan and Victoria observed from their picnic.

"The surviving princes are after this magical jewel, the power of Stormhold," confirms Neil Gaiman, "which was

thrown up into the sky by the dying King and which actually knocked the star out of the sky. So they are after this jewel, and they are also out to murder each other."

"Once we got into Stormhold," explains Sammy Sheldon, "I completely went any way possible to make the costumes not look Victorian. I tried to use designs from all kinds of periods, but also ignore the idea that it had to look like a period movie.

"As much as possible, I tried to make the princes look really sexy. The starting point Matthew gave me was using the style of Sergio Leone Italian Westerns – like they were really cool cowboys.

"It really didn't matter to me if they were wearing modern boots or low-cut trousers. We mixed it up a bit. So, when you look at the clothes, they look a little bit eighteenth century, but they've also got a modern twist to them as well. I always feel that it is easier to go with

the way people wear their clothes, rather than try to dictate their character with a costume. I often change designs of collars and cuffs and waistlines to accentuate how the clothes are worn. I think that the characters should look like they are *wearing* clothes, not costumes, and that's why I like actors to sit around in their costumes. I hate it when clothes look neat and tidy. Wrinkles happen, and I'd rather that was part of what the look is.

"It's the difference between the costume wearing the actor or the actor wearing the costume. That's really important to me – to make them comfortable, but to also make them look cool.

"Matthew was very keen on in some way incorporating the princes' numbers into their costumes," continues Sheldon, "so that they each have an individual

Below: Mark Strong as the ruthless Septimus.

identity. Not just by their names, but that they have actually embellished themselves by weaving roman numerals into the fabric. It was hugely expensive, but I came up with some designs that incorporated each of the numbers into a different pattern.

"From there, I looked at how we could use this idea in conjunction with the duster coats and that whole cowboy look. We started with Septimus, because we shot him first in Iceland. His coat was made out of wax fabric. Then I started designing each belt so that they also incorporated the appropriate numbers in a pattern. The belt buckles feature the heraldic coat of arms with the number in, and each one is slightly different. Septimus also has his own pair of spurs with his number '7' on. We even did the buttons and the rings. So everywhere on their costumes you'll see numbers.

"Then I had to give each of the princes a character, using different colours and textures. Septimus is the evil one, killing all his brothers, so his costume is very different from Primus, who is the nominally 'good' son. So we've given them all an identity."

For the scenes in which they appear as ghosts, Sheldon's department had to completely remake the costumes for the princes, giving them a muted colour to go with their ethereal appearance. "Actually, I found a shot of Clint Eastwood as the Man With No Name for reference but, when I printed the picture, it looked sort of washed-out. When I showed it to Matthew he thought it would be really cool if that is what they looked like when they were ghosts. That's where the idea came from.

"So what we did was replicate the costumes for every single prince, but this time in shades of grey. I even used pictures from the stills photographer to work out the various tones of greys, so you get an identical look to the costume, but without any colour in it. Also, anything that was gold was changed to silver, so that you can still see the glint of all the metal.

"I think it really works," adds Sheldon. "It's quite an exciting thing to do a whole wardrobe of costumes all in grey, because the princes really do look dead, without anyone having to do it digitally."

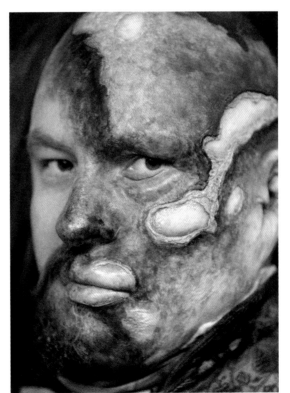

Above left: Julian Rhind-Tutt being made-up as the chilly shade of Quartus.

Above right: You axed for it: Adam Buxton as the dead Quintas.

Far Left: Sammy Sheldon's costume design for Quartus.

Left: David Walliams as the scorched phantom Sextus.

WHEN I RETURN WITH OUR PRIZE, ALL OF US SHALL BE YOUNG AGAIN. NEVER FEAR, MY SISTERS. I WILL NOT FAIL.

– LAMIA

As the star hurtles through the night sky, it is observed by three wizened old witches, Lamia (Michelle Pfeiffer), Mormo (Joanna Scanlan) and Empusa (Sarah Alexander). For four hundred years they have waited to claim the heart of a fallen star so that they can regain their youth and replenish their magical powers.

"In the book the three witches are nameless," Neil Gaiman points out. "I didn't name any of them, other than they are known collectively as 'the Lilim', the daughters of Lilith. In the film we really did need to name them, so Jane called the witch queen Lamia, and her sisters Mormo and Empusa, which are two classical names of dangerous goddesses.

"They are thousands and thousands of years old when we meet them, and in the film they are living in a corner of what was once their palace.

"In order to regain a little bit of her youth, Lamia eats the last piece of star heart that they have. She goes back to being stunningly beautiful, but with every small amount of magic that she expends as the story goes on, she ages just a little more. And so, by the end, she's even older than she was at the start."

Hollywood star Michelle Pfeiffer had played a member of a witchy trio before,

opposite Jack Nicholson's smooth devil in *The Witches of Eastwick* (1987). However, she had never before had to endure the complicated and time-consuming make-up process that she did on *Stardust*.

"It's not every day you get the opportunity to make one of the world's most beautiful women into a centuries-old hag," recalls prosthetics make-up designer Nik Williams. "It was a hell of a challenge."

Williams and his team from Animated Extras are based out of Shepperton Studios, just outside London. Since the mid-1990s the company has created a wide variety of animatronic and prosthetic effects for such films as *Mary Shelley's Frankenstein* (1994), *Mary Reilley* (1996), *Resident Evil* (2002), *Shaun of the Dead* (2004), *AVP: Alien vs. Predator* (2004) and *Dog Soldiers: Fresh Meat* (2007).

Williams himself has a career dating back twenty years to *Little Shop of Horrors* (1986) and is recognised as one of the leading animatronic designers in the world. However, his work on *Stardust* mostly involved prosthetic make-ups.

"It was important that it was obviously still Michelle Pfeiffer behind the make-up," he says, "otherwise there

Previous spread, left: Sarah Alexander as Empusa.

Previous spread, right: A rejuvenated Lamia travels in her cart, pulled by Billy and the transformed Bernard.

was no point in her doing it."

Williams also points out that putting prosthetic make-up on women is possibly the hardest type of make-up to achieve successfully. "Usually prosthetics are used to create something horrific in films, but it is different when you have to use them over a long period. To actually use prosthetic make-up on somebody every day, for six weeks – which is what Michelle had to endure – we had to be very sure that the pieces could be removed without damaging her skin. That was probably our major concern when designing the make-up."

Still, he has nothing but praise for the Hollywood star: "I don't think Michelle had ever had to wear prosthetic make-up like that before, but she was fantastic. I was amazed. She would sit completely still for nearly three hours while four of us applied the various pieces. She was a very easy person to work with."

Starting out with a series of concept drawings created by Jeremy Woodhead, Williams travelled to San Francisco to make a life-cast of the actress, which he then used to refine his designs for the Lamia make-up over the next four or five weeks. He then returned to California to film the finished test make-up.

"By this time, the whole thing had evolved from simply being a make-up to being an ageing process. Now the character starts old, becomes young, and then gradually ages again as she uses her magic. We therefore had to create all the in-between stages as well, although we didn't have time to test them all beforehand.

"We therefore had to test certain make-up effects almost as we did them, or perhaps the day before. We would show Matthew something and ask him if it worked for a particular intermediary stage we would be shooting in a few days' time. So we came up with ideas as we were going along."

Williams' task was also not helped by the script being shot totally out of sequence, which is usual in filmmaking. "That was one of the biggest challenges," he reveals. "The problem is that you can't change a make-up mid-day. It took three hours to put on and another hour to take off, and by the time we had done that they would have lost so much shooting time that it wouldn't have been worth it.

"So it was very much a case of Matthew shooting everything he could with Michelle in one set of prosthetics before we changed over to another set."

Because of the use of various stunt doubles for the three witches, Williams' core team of six prosthetic make-up artists would often swell to around fifteen for some scenes.

"My job was to connect the other two sisters to Michelle Pfeiffer's character," explains hair and make-up designer Fae Hammond. "We loved the idea that as they had lost their hair over the centuries, that they would go around the floor collecting pieces of animal fur, bits of dusty old fabric, and gradually build up these big, ridiculous wigs."

For Hammond and her team, getting the

Opposite: After eating the last piece of a star heart, Lamia regains her youthful appearance.
Left: Sammy Sheldon's costume design for the "innkeeper" Lamia.

Above: Empusa and Mormo (Joanna Scanlan) consult the entrails.

Right: The cast made by the make-up department for Joanna Scanlan's role as Mormo.

witches ready for the camera was probably their biggest challenge on the film. "On average it took around three hours, because it is not just their faces you had to make-up. There were also necks, and chests, and the hands to be aged up. We didn't really age the teeth, nor the eyes, sort of deliberately, so that we didn't get the classic 'old witch' look. We didn't want old hags, we wanted something fresh and different.

"My job was to connect up the various different units, so I would come in at the end of one shoot and the beginning of another. As I would leave the studio at around five in the morning, I would see the next group coming in."

"I think they made completely the right call with the three witches," says Neil Gaiman. "They could have had two old women and Michelle Pfeiffer, but instead they had three actresses of around the same age under some very disturbing old-age make-up.

"It was really disturbing meeting them," he recalls. "I'm talking to Joanna Scanlan, who plays Mormo, and in the back of my mind I'm thinking that this is that nice woman I met, who is probably younger than I am, but has all these crows-feet covering her face and pendulous earlobes. She told me that it was like she caught sight of her grandmother in the mirror sometimes."

"Although this wasn't a big crowd film," explains Fae Hammond, "it was quite a big cast film. We ended up doubling most of them so, for example, when we were doing the sequences of Lamia in the witches' lair, we had several Michelles walking around, all in full prosthetic make-up. There were only three of them, but because we had to treble or sometimes quadruple them, there seemed to be witches everywhere.

"That happened a lot during the last few weeks of filming. We were shooting with a number of units, so there were three Claire Danes and four Charlie Coxes. Doubles were everywhere. That takes a lot of time, as usually it is more difficult to make a double look like the real thing. You have to work hard to make it believable.

"During the final month I had an extra team coming in just to do the witches' doubles."

"There was so much additional stuff to do, just on the three main witches," agrees Nik Williams. "*Stardust* is one of the first big films where we used silicon make-up pieces instead of the traditional foam rubber appliances. The nice thing about using silicon is that it has a translucent quality that films beautifully. The downside is that it takes longer to prepare the moulds and turn the pieces out, and with silicon it is much harder to hide the edges of the make-ups."

"Michelle Pfeiffer is absolutely astonishing as Lamia," enthuses Neil Gaiman. "She's very scary, yet also gorgeous and sexy. As I watched her work I thought, 'Okay, this is what it means to be a star, and she gives a star performance.'"

"She really was amazing," agrees Jane Goldman.

Below: Sammy Sheldon's designs for Mormo and Empusa's costumes.

Right and opposite: Art department concept sketches for Lamia's goat-drawn cart.

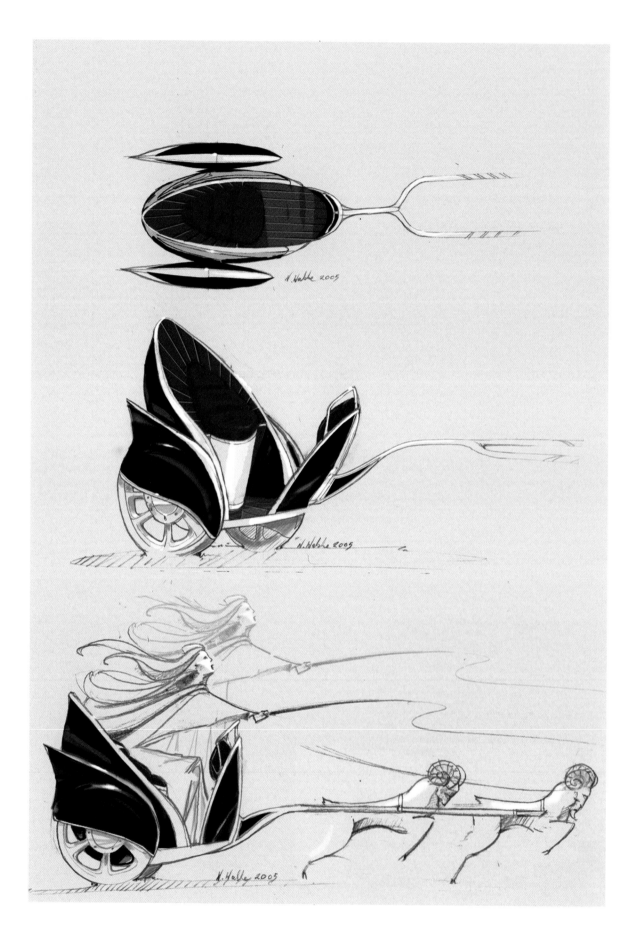

"She's so scary, but also brings an interesting layer of poignancy to the role. I was really excited that she responded so positively to the script. She liked the idea that the witches were in pursuit of youth and beauty. She brought so much to the part of Lamia, and it's a great testament to her skill that she's absolutely terrifying."

As well as Fae Hammond's full-time hair and make-up team, Michelle Pfeiffer also worked with her own personal make-up artist, Ronnie Specter. "Michelle had a tremendous amount of input into the look of her character," reveals Hammond. "She had full-on glamour make-up and this wild, long, fabulous hair, but wearing a sort of period costume. So it gave you this interesting feeling – what is this? It's not period, it's not modern. You just got this edginess of someone wearing lots of make-up, yet wearing a period frock. It was a very interesting look."

After Lamia has been rejuvenated, she tears off her tattered robes and changes into a beautiful dress before setting out on foot to find the fallen star.

"Some of the casting was quite late," reveals costume designer Sammy Sheldon, "but it always is on a film. I went to San Francisco a couple of times for fittings with Michelle. She was very thoughtful and logical about what she would suggest so far as the costume was concerned.

"Because of the amount of action Lamia has, and the distance she travels in the film, we had to create something that was believable that the witches would have given her to wear.

"I initially designed a dress for her that was based on a Salvador Dali painting of a skeleton. After we did initial fittings with that, we quickly realised that what with the prosthetics and the action, and trying to work with body doubles and stunt doubles, it just wouldn't work. So we discarded it. It was a very slinky thing, but it wasn't a dynamic enough shape. In fact, Michelle liked the green and gold dress she ended up in more. It was supposed to be the transformation dress I had designed for the beginning of the movie, but I designed another dress to use in that scene.

"With the three witches, I again kept that slightly ethnic feel to them," Sheldon continues. "I based them on the Renaissance period. I thought that the best way was to start off with a colour. So I found a painting that had three Greek women pouring water, and they were dressed in green, red and purple. Those are very jewel-

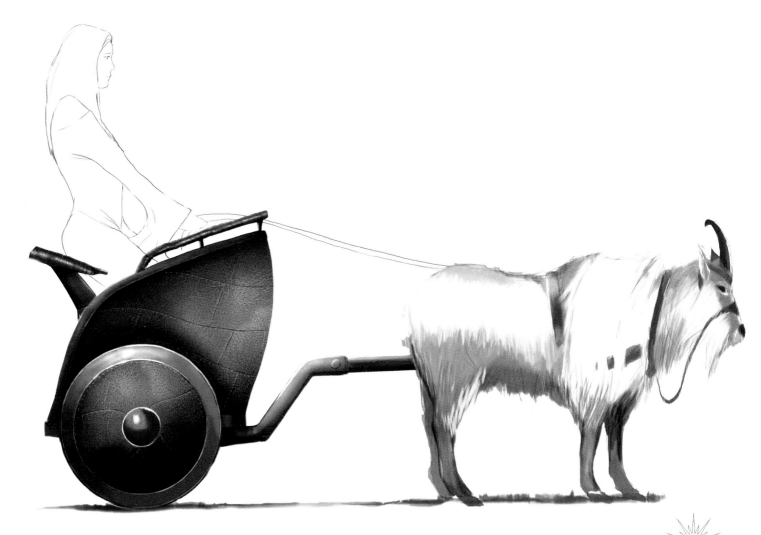

like colours.

"In fact the witches are meant to be like three jewels in a black box. Their world is all black and silver and very faded grandeur. So to make them stand out in that environment I started off by thinking of them as jewels. Then I added a blackness over the top of them to get a real muted colour and keep that heavy, dark, slightly sinister feel.

"Lamia's character is based on a half-snake or reptile woman in Greek mythology. I used some of that in the choices of fabrics for her, so she's in green, and gold, and black. And then, with Mormo and Empusa, I again chose some things from the Renaissance period and then added something slightly Victorian-esque there. So it's all a bit eclectic again. I gave each of them a different texture too: Lamia is sort of snake-like, Mormo's very lacy and Empusa's more velvety and soft.

"One of the things I said to Matthew was I thought it would be great if we had a large witch instead of three thin witches, and use that in a more interesting way.

You get three completely different body shapes, and I tried to design the dresses around the idea of women actually sagging, and becoming shorter and wider, so they're sinking into their dresses because they've been wearing them for so long. I wanted them to look like they had dropped into their costumes because they are all so old. And because they're kind of heavy, big shapes, they make a huge impact in the big black palace that they live in.

"These are three women who have lived in this place for thousands of years trying to eat these hearts to keep themselves young, and they're very vain. And maybe over the years they've added things, which is why there's sort of the funny little belts, and strange bits of fringing that they've added to make themselves look grander, basically.

"I hadn't realised that they were going to put straw down on the floor in the witches' lair, and the costumes just kept gathering all this stuff up. I thought that it was great that the bottoms of their dresses were gathering

bits of the set as they moved around. We ripped the dresses to shreds anyway, but it really looked like where they live. The set and the costumes worked wonderfully together."

Setting out on her quest to find the fallen star, the now-beautiful Lamia encounters farm boy Bernard (Jake Curran), who has been ordered by his mother to sell their goat at market. When Lamia transforms the dim-witted teenager into a second goat to pull her cart, she notices with dismay that using magic has already aged her hands.

Continuing her journey, Lamia stops to share a meal with another witch, Ditch-Water Sal (Melanie Hill). Sal's Slave Girl, who she keeps transformed as an exotic bird tethered to her caravan by a magic chain, is the same beauty who Dunstan Thorne had his fling with many years before.

"Ditch-Water Sal has badly applied make-up on in odd places," reveals hair and make-up designer Fae Hammond. "She has orange eyebrows, her hair's a mess and very badly dyed, and her costume is slightly period yet with ethnic qualities. It was a wonderful mix."

Lamia's first encounter with Ditch-Water Sal was shot at the end of April around the Uig and Staffin areas on the Isle of Skye, off the west coast of Scotland. The largest and best-known of the Inner Hebrides, Skye is known for its wild, natural beauty, Gaelic history and abundant wildlife.

The main road between the Flodigarry Country House Hotel and the township of Digg was closed off by the production and covered with soil, while new trees were planted along the verges.

Unfortunately, bad weather hampered the production, with Michelle Pfeiffer reportedly forced back into her trailer by the torrential rain on her first day of shooting. As a consequence, a few sequences had to be re-shot some months later. *Stardust* creators Neil Gaiman and Charles Vess travelled to Skye to watch the later filming and, as Gaiman recalls, "Charles was somewhere out beyond happy. When Charles is extremely happy he gets sort of quiet and twinkly, and he twinkled a lot."

"I expected certain transformations dictated by both the personality of the director and the requirements of the screenplay," explains Vess. "And I was quite nervous about those changes up until I visited the sets. The re-imagining of the world of *Stardust* was lovely. I believe I've described it as an alternative world just slightly over to the left of mine. Each medium has its own inherent

needs and requirements. What looks good or is satisfying for the written word may not suggest itself to best advantage when transformed into film. So all in all I'm very happy with what they've done."

When Lamia discovers that Ditch-Water Sal has sprinkled her food with limbus grass, which magically compels her to reveal the object of her quest, she erases the old woman's memory of their encounter. However, Sal's captive bird has witnessed the whole incident.

Meanwhile, as Lamia resumes her journey in her goat-drawn cart, Septimus poisons his brother Tertius but fails to kill Primus. The two remaining princes then set out on their own quest for the pendant that will make one or the other of them the new King of Stormhold…

Opposite: Melanie Hill as colourful witch Ditch-Water Sal.
Above: Concept painting for the sequence where Ditch-Water Sal shares her meal with Lamia.
Left: Ditch-Water Sal uses her magic chain to restrict the Slave Girl's movements.

Act II

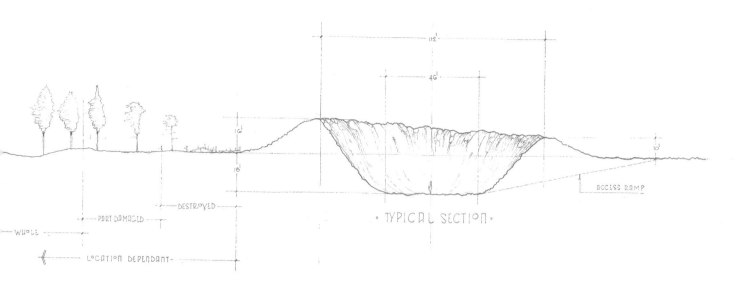

I'M A STAR.
I EAT DARKNESS.
I DRINK LIGHT.
– YVAINE

"he first thing Tristan encounters when he finds himself across the wall is very much proof that he's not in Kansas anymore," explains Jane Goldman. "The star has fallen not in any form you'd expect a star to land in, as a meteor or what have you, but actually in the form of an incredibly beautiful and incredibly cross young lady. Such is the strange power of the universe beyond the wall.

"So he realises almost immediately that the task which already seemed difficult is actually going to be a lot harder. Because he has to contend with persuading the star to come with him – to come back and be a birthday present to win Victoria's heart."

"We probably auditioned every actress between the ages of seventeen and thirty in Hollywood, Britain and Australia," Neil Gaiman recalls. "It was fascinating to watch some of them. But Claire Danes, like Charlie Cox, aced the audition. She came in right at the end of the casting period, when we were down to a few actresses to choose from, and we knew we had found our Yvaine.

She is a star, and she is *the* star."

"Yvaine is a fallen star," adds producer Lorenzo di Bonaventura. "We haven't seen one of those before, so everybody had a different point of view about what that meant. The role was tricky because when you first meet her there is a caustic – one could even say bitchy – quality to how the character is. I think Claire Danes is tremendous in the role."

"The moment Claire Danes' name came up," reveals Jane Goldman, "I got very, very excited because she is such an amazing actress. She has a real wisdom and vulnerability about her that fitted the part. When I saw Claire's audition I was absolutely enchanted, and it just worked for me immediately. And I know Matthew felt the same way."

Born in 1979 in New York City, Claire Danes' mother is an artist and her father a photographer. She remembers herself as "a very confident child", and knew that she wanted to be an actress from the age of five, after watching Madonna perform on television. She attended New York's Professional Performing Arts High School, whose other alumni include singer Britney Spears.

Danes' first big break came in 1994, when she was cast as fifteen year-old Angela Chase on the ABC-TV teen drama series *My So-Called Life*. The following year the young actress won a Golden Globe Award for her performance and her career really took off. "I never thought of myself as a child actor," she says. "I knew I was a kid, but they weren't related."

Since then she has appeared in such films as *How to Make an American Quilt* (1995), *Romeo + Juliet* (1996), *U Turn* (1997), *The Mod Squad* (1999), *Terminator 3: Rise of the Machines* (2003), *Stage Beauty* (2004) and *The Flock* (2007).

"I'm familiar with Neil Gaiman's writing," reveals the actress, "and had been before I became involved with *Stardust*. I actually wrote a forward for a graphic novel

Previous spread,
left: A concept sketch of
Yvaine in the crater.
Previous spread,
right: Yvaine is rescued
by a unicorn in the forest.

that he wrote called *Death: The Time of Your Life* (1997). I also did a voice for the Japanese animation movie *Princess Mononoke* (1997) that Neil scripted the English version of. So our paths have crossed a number of times, and I think he's brilliant. His stories are so obviously full of imagination and wit. He's very special."

Danes was also already familiar with the illustrated novel of *Stardust* when she was asked to read the script. "I found it really charming," she recalls. "That struck me most. I hadn't read anything quite like it before. It's unique, like a lot of Neil's stories. I thought my character was so dreamy. I mean she's a riot. It's just totally bizarre to have to portray a star, but it was definitely a worthy challenge.

"I wasn't so concerned with playing her as a celestial being. She's written as a very normal, accessible person, and so I kind of concentrated on her state of being in any given circumstance, and her desire to get home."

Having been knocked out of the sky by the King's pendant and fallen to Earth in human form, it is perhaps no surprise that Yvaine is slightly irritable when she first encounters Tristan in the crater. Especially when he initially mistakes her for his long-lost mother.

"After taking the decision to light the candle," says Charlie Cox, "Tristan thinks he's going to meet his mother, because that was how the candle was supposed

Opposite: The fallen star takes on human form.
Opposite inset: Concept painting of the crater formed by the fallen star.
Left: Sammy Sheldon's "liquid" costume design for Yvaine.

Above: Filming the crater at Pinewood Studios.
Right: Tristan discovers the fallen star in the middle of the crater.

to work. Instead, he ends up bumping into Yvaine in the middle of a crater."

"She's not terribly impressed with him because he's not terribly impressive," adds Claire Danes. "He's got a pretty bad haircut, and makes quite a few inane comments. But he's totally committed to getting this star back to the silly girl that he's infatuated with. So he's tenacious and capable. Surprisingly capable for a guy with such a bad haircut!"

"It takes a while for him to establish that she is the star," continues Cox, "and that he hasn't met his mother. He figures out how that happened and, at the beginning of the relationship, Tristan and Yvaine don't like each other. They have both upset each other very quickly and said hurtful things. They don't really have any interest in getting on, but they both need each other. Tristan needs Yvaine because she is the gift that he must give to Victoria, and Yvaine has broken her leg and has no escape from the crater. So they make the decision to help each other, to stick with each other, but they bicker and they argue."

"She is not an entirely agreeable, forgiving character," agrees Danes. "In fact, she's pretty angry. She's been hurled out of the sky, her home, and has crashed very

Above: Tristan leads Yvaine through the forest.
Left: The unicorn.

Above: Yvaine is rescued by the unicorn.

painfully onto the surface of our world. Then, almost immediately she is kidnapped by some silly boy who she has no patience for. When we are first introduced to her, she is not very sympathetic, you know. But she softens, and she matures as the story progresses."

"I liked the idea of exploring Yvaine as a character," explains screenwriter Jane Goldman, "especially her fury at the injustice of her predicament."

"You care about Yvaine while she is being irritating," Neil Gaiman points out. "It was always important to me that the star was bad-tempered, after all she doesn't want to be there, she has broken her leg, and all sorts of people want to drag her off across the country. She doesn't like this, nor should she. Claire handles that progression beautifully. She starts out properly grumpy, and she grows and she changes, but she is still that lovely, sympathetic person.

"Both Tristan and Yvaine do a little bit of growing up together, even though he is only eighteen or so and she is many millions of years old."

Tristan ties a piece of the magic chain around Yvaine's wrist so that she can't escape him. Then, after he promises her that she can have what is left of the Babylon candle, which will enable her to return to her rightful place

in the sky, Yvaine reluctantly agrees to accompany Tristan back to Wall as a present for Victoria's birthday.

So they start out on their long journey across Stormhold. But as their travels continue, a reluctant respect gradually begins to turn into something deeper...

"I mean, it doesn't come as an enormous surprise that the adversaries become quite fond of each other ultimately," comments Danes. "That's how it works in the movies."

"With Claire Danes," says hair and make-up designer Fae Hammond, "special effects put this wonderful glow around her. But we felt that she should simply look gorgeous – lovely long blonde hair, not much make-up, just very natural."

"The fallen star costume was quite difficult to design," Sammy Sheldon admits, "because it really could have gone different ways. It could have been all sparkly, but instead we went in the other direction. I played around with using crystal fabric and making it shiny. Then we talked with visual effects supervisor Peter Chiang about it. 'Could we get away with this blue, or that green?' Also, any material that's got a very hazy edge to it is important, because that makes it quite difficult if you're using green screen. But I wasn't comfortable with the concept, because Yvaine's glow comes from inside her. The moment you

make something that somebody wears have an effect like that, which has to do with an inner soul, it simply becomes a fashion item. I wanted to get away from that.

"If this star had fallen to Earth and become a human being, it wouldn't be wearing something earthly, but at the same time what *isn't* earthly? Anything that you put on her, if it's anything fashionable, immediately becomes an item of clothing.

"I wanted the fabric I chose to have an almost metallic quality to it, so that she looked like she was part of the molten crater that she's landed in. I thought it would be great if what she was wearing was almost like a liquid, hence the fabric we chose is just a silk satin, but it's quite heavy, and I wanted it to kind of move like a liquid. So we used a very simple, natural fabric, and had it cut in a way that it just fell to the ground.

"I went back to the most simplistic form I could think of," continues Sheldon, "without any fastenings on it at all. So there's no way you can ever identify it with any time period. It's just a very simple shroud, with all the decoration taken away to keep it 'pure'. However, the dress does have a slightly Renaissance feel to it, just to keep that period flavour.

"As for the colour, I was also really keen that we didn't use cream or white. So it's metal grey because, when she lands, she almost looks like she's merging with the molten rock and it has that whole elemental feel to it, like something of the earth.

"With Claire we had quite a few fittings because that

Top: Tristan is surprised by Billy nibbling the hem of his jacket.

Above: Concept design of Primus' coach.

dress, particularly, had to fit like a glove without any fastenings. Which meant that it had to go on over her head and still look like it fitted her perfectly."

One of the most memorable scenes in the book occurs when Tristran and the star first encounter the unicorn during their journey through the forest. They come across a clearing where the noble creature and a huge lion are locked in a deadly battle over an ornate golden crown studded with jewels.

"Matthew and I both liked the sequence with the lion and the unicorn," reveals Jane Goldman, "and it was in the first draft of the script. But in the end it was just one of those budgetary decisions that you sometimes

have to make."

Although also scripted, a sequence from the book involving a talking tree and a dream in which Tristan converses with Yvaine's mother, the moon, also failed to make it into the final print. However, Yvaine does encounter a unicorn and rides off on the creature after escaping her bonds.

"Tristan chains Yvaine to him so she can't get away," explains Charlie Cox. "After tying her to a tree in the forest, he goes to get some food and a crutch to help Yvaine walk, but when he comes back she's not there."

While the ghostly princes play I Spy in the back, Primus' coach almost runs over Tristan in the forest. They agree that it would be to both their advantages if they teamed up.

"He meets Primus, one of the princes," continues Cox, "who explains his mission and that of his evil brother, Septimus."

The scene where Septimus forces a hapless Soothsayer (George Innes) to use his runes to reveal the location of the King's pendant – which is now hanging around Yvaine's neck – was one of the early sequences Matthew Vaughn shot on a black sand beach near Höfn in Iceland at the end of March 2006, before full production commenced. Background plates of the rugged lava fields of Hafnarfjörður (reputed by the locals to be inhabited by elves and dwarfs) were filmed at the same time to add verisimilitude to sequences to be shot later.

"Mark Strong is pant-wettingly scary as Septimus in that scene," says Jane Goldman. "The way Mark carries himself, I think he looks amazing. He created such a powerful character in terms of what he brought as an actor to the role."

"I loved Mark Strong as Septimus," agrees Neil Gaiman, "because his character is very different from the book, but really cool. In the original book, Septimus is thin, crow-like and extremely dangerous and nasty. In the film he is like a guided missile – he knows exactly what it is he wants, which is the throne of Stormhold, and he will kill anybody and everybody who gets in his way. He would probably make a very good king, if you didn't anger or upset him, in which case you would find yourself very dead."

According to reports, more of *Stardust* was scheduled to be filmed in Iceland. However, when it was discovered that it is illegal to import horses into the country – because the local herds are particularly vulnerable to disease as they have been isolated for so many centuries – it was decided to move the bulk of the shooting back to the British mainland.

"We could have shot for two or three weeks up there," confirms production designer Gavin Bocquet, "and made Stormhold be this extraordinary, otherworldly landscape. But we had a lot of horses and carriages, so when the logistics of that became difficult, the Isle of Skye was suggested."

Left: Sammy Sheldon's costume design for the Soothsayer.
Above: The Soothsayer's runes.

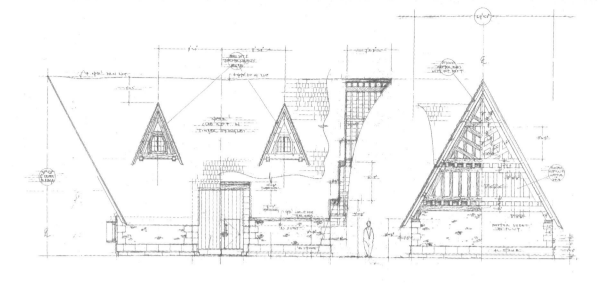

WE HAVE FOOD AND DRINK. A WARM BED. PLENTY OF HOT WATER FOR A BATH.

– LAMIA

"Tristan doesn't know that he's not the only one after the star," reveals scriptwriter Jane Goldman. "The heart of a star in this universe beyond the wall is an incredibly valuable commodity – possibly the most valuable commodity – to people who trade in magic. So unbeknownst to Tristan, there are three absolutely horrible witches who have also seen the star fall, and this is their big chance because they're getting incredibly decrepit. It's been four hundred years since a star last fell, and they are determined that this will be their salvation. So the eldest of the three sisters sets out to find the fallen star."

Lamia contacts her sisters, Mormo and Empusa, through a magic mirror, even though using her powers costs her more of her precious youth. After consulting

the entrails of one of their sacrificial animals, they inform their sibling that the star is coming to her.

"I'm pretty popular," says Claire Danes. "Everybody wants to kill me. The heart of a star is very valuable because it can provide everlasting life, or at least many, many thousands of years of youth."

Waiting at the crossroads, Lamia transforms her goat into Billy (Mark Williams), while the goat-formally-known-as-Bernard is changed into a young woman. The witch then conjures up an old inn and, with her newly-created family, awaits the arrival of Yvaine.

"I loved Bernard," Neil Gaiman reveals, "the young man with the goat, who then gets transformed into a goat, and then having been a goat ends up for a while as a zombie pot-maid. It's one of those gorgeous little moments when you have the actress, Olivia Grant, giving a magical performance as a boy-who-has-been-transformed-into-a-goat-into-a-girl gawking at Yvaine as she gets into her bath in exactly the way that a rather gormless young teenager would."

"There are some funny, strange little things going on," explains costume designer Sammy Sheldon, "particularly with characters like Bernard and Billy, because they're meant to be goats. Rather than just make a costume that looked like a goat, I tried to choose elements that sort of made their bodies look animalistic. I also gave them clogs so they had to sort of trot. Their buttons were all made of horn, and some of the colours in them relate to the colours of the fur."

"We didn't want to make Billy too hairy," adds hair and make-up designer Fae Hammond, "but I gave him a beard that was very goatee, if you'll excuse the pun. It was made from real goat hair, and his fingers had little bits of goat hair left on them still. He also had slightly furry ears. These were all just little odd elements that I

Previous spread,
left: Development artwork
for the sign on Lamia's inn
**Previous spread,
right:** Yvaine and the
unicorn arrive at Lamia's
inn.

wanted to bring to the character, but you'd have to look twice to probably even notice them."

With Yvaine now her unsuspecting guest, Lamia's well-laid plans are thrown into disarray when Tristan and Primus also arrive at the inn. One of the most shocking scenes in the film is when Primus has his throat slashed by Lamia while he is taking a bath.

"Michelle Pfeiffer cut poor Jason Flemyng's throat with a big black obsidian-glass knife," recalls Neil Gaiman. "It was Matthew's idea that Primus' blood would be blue. It was a way of getting around an automatic R rating in the US when you show red blood. So Matthew said, 'They're aristocrats, they would have blue blood…'"

Having been saved from certain poisoning by the intervention of the unicorn, Tristan bursts into the inn to warn Primus, but it is too late – he has already joined his dead brethren. Tristan is no sooner reunited with Yvaine than Lamia sets the dead-eyed Billy on them. However, the unicorn once more intervenes to protect the couple.

"One of my favourite characters in the film," continues Gaiman, "just in terms of things that give me a little warm feeling and

Opposite: Olivia Grant as the boy-who-has-been-transformed-into-a-goat-into-a-girl, Bernard.
Left: Sammy Sheldon's costume design for Billy.
Above: British comedian Mark Williams as the transformed goat, Billy.

Above: Primus recognises the pendant Yvaine is wearing.

Right: Actor Jason Flemyng displays his slashed-throat prosthetic.

because it wasn't in the original book, is Billy the goat. Everything he is and does is implicit in the book, but I didn't do any of those gags like chewing a tea towel. Mark Williams is so funny.

"And then you get that shot of him going head-to-head with a unicorn, and I always thought the idea of a guy who is really a billy-goat deciding that the way you deal with a unicorn is by head-butting it always had a certain dark humour."

As Lamia creates a wall of magical fire, Tristan tells Yvaine to think of home as they use the stub of the Babylon candle to escape.

"He finds her again," says Charlie Cox, "and ends up having to save her from the witch."

The scenes of Lamia's inn and the crossroads were shot on Chobham Common, one of the largest areas of natural heath land in Surrey. Once notorious for the highwaymen who preyed upon the coach travellers crossing its "wild wastes", the common is now an area of outstanding wildlife interest and was designated a National Nature Reserve in 1994.

"Because of the heather," explains production designer Gavin Bocquet, "the location matched the scenes we shot in Scotland. For Lamia's inn we built the interior set

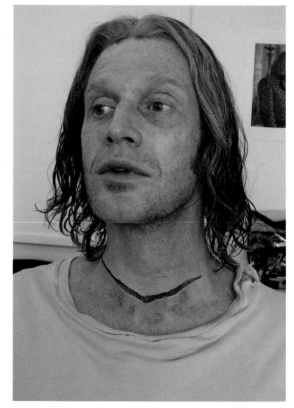

on a soundstage at Pinewood. An exterior was created on the backlot, and then this was combined by [visual effects supervisor] Peter Chiang with the location on Chobham Common where it magically appears."

"All the sets have been so beautifully designed," says Claire Danes. "Lamia's inn was a little eerie, of course, as there were all these horns poking everywhere, and evidence of dead animals, which is appropriate because it's the witch's inn. So it smacked of evil."

"It was interesting visiting the art department," recalls Neil Gaiman, "where they had reference books of castles, books of markets, and Charles Vess' *Stardust*. There wasn't any point when they went, 'We are not going to do what Charlie did.' Charlie's stuff would just be one of many other elements."

"The way Charles paints is very Victorian in a way," says Matthew Vaughn, "but I wanted the film to have more of a modern look. I think the problem is that people say, 'We're going to do a fairy tale, so therefore let's shoot it in a fairy tale way.' I wanted to shoot it in a far more modern, grittier manner."

"Lamia's inn is so incredibly Charles Vess," continues Gaiman. "The whole building is Charles Vess, with those weird sloping roofs, and it's like walking into a Charles Vess place. There are moments in the film that are pure Charles Vess – like the scene of Yvaine riding the unicorn."

"None of the designs look quite like my original drawings," agrees Vess, "but they are nevertheless very satisfying in their own right. Much as if they were from an alternative world of *Stardust* just slightly over to the left from my own."

Early in the schedule, Charles Vess was invited by the filmmakers to visit the set and watch the filming. "I got the call to be at the airport at 5:30pm to fly to London," he explains. "Neil had called the day before, so I was already packed and ready for the adventure.

"I stumbled off the plane at Gatwick and was met by a driver and taken, first to a hotel to freshen-up, then on to London to pick up Neil, and then to Pinewood Studios where the film was being shot. The cast and crew were scheduled for a night shoot, so it was still quiet when we arrived mid-afternoon. We toured the costume and art departments then casually wandered through several gorgeous full-size sets.

"The re-creation of the inn that the witch queen conjures up in order to trap the star was lovely. The set is what I would have drawn if I had had a week to draw it. But you know, I only had a night to do it. So it's really fun to watch your imagination be expanded upon by other people who are so good at it. It's really remarkable and pretty exciting.

"The next day I was overcome with the need to draw and retired to the art department and there, surrounded

Below: Septimus finds the body of his brother (and Billy) on the site where the magical inn once stood.

Clockwise from above: Art department concept sketches of Lamia conjuring up the inn at the crossroads. The Lamia's inn set. Scale model of Lamia's inn with Primus' coach in foreground (inset). Development sketch of Lamia's inn.

Above: The unicorn bursts into the inn.

Right: Concept sketch of the interior of Lamia's inn.

Opposite left: Yvaine takes a bath at the inn.

Opposite right: Lamia and her knife.

by miniature constructions of all the sets, I did just that. Several hours later I'd pencilled out a nice concept drawing for the new hardcover edition of *Stardust*. The only trouble was the drawing was too large for my portfolio, so we scanned it onto disc for future reference and Neil and I then presented it to Claire Danes. That earned me several big hugs!"

At around 11:00am on Sunday, July 30, members of the *Stardust* art department looked out of the windows of their offices in the Kubrick Building on the backlot at Pinewood and noticed black smoke rising from the world-famous 'Albert R. Broccoli' 007 Stage. They immediately raised the alarm and the Buckingham Fire Brigade dealt with the blaze. At least eight fire engines and sixty fire fighters were in attendance.

The 007 Stage was one of the largest soundstages in the world. It was originally constructed in 1976 to accommodate the 'super-tanker' set for James Bond film *The Spy Who Loved Me*, and was previously destroyed by fire in 1984 following the filming of Ridley Scott's *Legend*.

There was no filming taking place in the corrugated metal structure at the time, but *Casino Royale* (2006) had recently completed shooting and was in the process of removing its sets when the fire started. The roof covering the stage collapsed, and fire services had to use special equipment to deal with exploding gas cylinders. An adjacent exterior set of Lamia's inn from *Stardust*, on which shooting had fortunately been completed, had to be torn down by firemen tackling the blaze.

Although there were no casualties, the damage was so severe that it was subsequently decided that the 007 Stage would have to be demolished and rebuilt a second time.

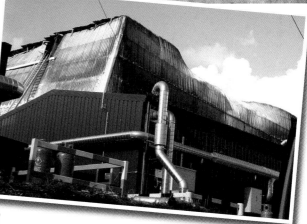

Left: The burned-out 007 Stage at Pinewood Studios.

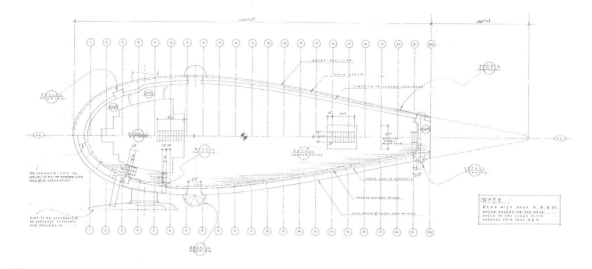

NO ONE TANGLES WITH CAPTAIN SHAKESPEARE AND LIVES! PREPARE TO MEET YOUR DEATH!

– CAPTAIN SHAKESPEARE

ristan and Yvaine find themselves standing on a grey cloud, while around them a storm rages. Each had thought of their own "home", and now they are trapped halfway between the two. But not for long. They are suddenly caught up in the metallic nets of a pirate crew and deposited on the deck of a flying vessel in front of the fearsome Captain Shakespeare.

"So Robert De Niro is the captain of a flying pirate ship," explains Neil Gaiman, "and they are lightning catchers. They fish for lightning with their copper nets up there in the clouds, and they put it into bottles and they sell it. They are dealers in lightning which people can use for incredibly wonderful, magical purposes."

"What we wanted was an actor who is indisputably a tough guy who has a surprise to him," producer Lorenzo di Bonaventura reveals. "And the tougher he comes across as a character, the more of a surprise it will be what his other life is.

"So we were considering a list of people, and Bob De Niro's name came up a lot from me because I've done a bunch of movies with him, and I really like working with him. He's one of the great actors. So Bob's name came up and we all went, 'Captain Shakespeare – let's go for it.' Stormhold is a place that has a lot of exotic characters, so why can't you have a pirate from New York? It ended up playing to the strength of the movie."

Considered one of the greatest actors of his generation, for the Oscar-winning star of such films as *Taxi Driver* (1976) and *Raging Bull* (1980), the role of the flamboyant pirate captain was definitely something of a departure.

"Matthew had a very clear vision of how to use Bob," continues di Bonaventura, "from the haircut to the clothing that he would wear. We used it as an opportunity to have Robert De Niro in our film, and I think he had a lot of fun."

When Matthew Vaughn urged Charlie Cox and Claire Danes to look terrified for the scene in which they are captured by De Niro's Captain Shakespeare, Cox reveals that it didn't take that much skill: "Bob's a pirate and he has us tied up," recalls the actor. "He's doing his Mafioso, intimidating stuff, and Matthew's going to us: 'This is scary, this is really scary.' But by that time we were scared of Bob for real, so there was no need to act!"

"Robert De Niro was fantastic," confirms Vaughn, "and people will see a side to him that's never been seen before in movies, which I'm excited about and proud of."

Previous spread, left: Costume concepts for the pirate crew.

Previous spread, right: Tristan and Yvaine are snared in the sky vessel's net.

Above: Captain Shakespeare shares his wardrobe with both Tristan and Yvaine.

Right: Sammy Sheldon's design for Captain Shakespeare's costume.

Far right: Captain Shakespeare hatches a plan.

Opposite: Oscar-winner Robert De Niro as the enigmatic Captain Shakespeare.

Opposite inset: The sky vessel's motley crew.

As it turns out, Captain Shakespeare is not all he seems, and the two young captives are soon enjoying the hospitality of the captain's cabin.

"In the novel we have a captain named Captain Johannes Alberic who is very nice," explains Neil Gaiman, "and the sequence on the flying ship is more or less a small holiday from the incredible adventures and vicissitudes surrounding Tristran and the star.

"Jane and Matthew's script expanded the part in the book of the captain of the sky vessel fishing for lightning, which made a great deal of sense because we needed to up the ante for the film at the point where in the book I had given us a little breathing room.

"I congratulated Jane on having come up with a part that was perfect for a guest star to come in for two weeks and do it and then go home. And she replied that she

wished she had known that when she wrote the script.

"What Matthew did was quite brilliant. First of all, he took that sequence and he quite rightly felt that at that point in the film you didn't need a little holiday, you really needed to ramp up the excitement a bit. So he ramped up the excitement.

"The other thing Matthew realised was that he really needed another major Hollywood actor. So he took the part of the captain of the flying ship and he just made it bigger, and made it meatier, and made it seriously chewier. Then he just sent the script to Robert De Niro, and De Niro read it and said 'Absolutely, count me in,' which I think is really wonderful."

"When somebody's name comes up for a comedy role, it's really great when the mere idea of it makes you laugh," says Jane Goldman. "It was an absolute dream that De Niro was up for it."

"I remember when we started filming with the pirates," Charlie Cox recalls. "I remember thinking there's a real different energy to this part of the movie, these scenes. It felt different, and I thought maybe it was because Robert De Niro was on set, or because we were surrounded by all this green screen.

"But actually, if you look at the script, it's the only time in the film where Tristan and Yvaine aren't actually endangered. So much outside of the ship involved running away, and being scared. You know that once they've got past the initial introduction to Captain Shakespeare that they're not in danger anymore. It's the only time during the film that they're safe – he keeps them safe. So it did feel totally different."

"Tristan and Yvaine needed some time in safety, during which they could have breathing space to allow their relationship to grow," says Goldman. "It also marks a turning point where Tristan begins the transition from boyhood to manhood."

Under the guidance of Captain Shakespeare, Tristan is transformed into a handsome, swashbuckling hero.

"Tristan certainly comes into his own," Charlie Cox explains. "There's such an obvious visual transformation. We had problems with my hair, because they wanted me to look young at the beginning and older at the end. The obvious way to do that is to have long puffy hair, and then cut it into a cool haircut. But then the problem with that was that people look much younger with shorter hair. We were sitting in the make-up chair trying to figure it out, and Matthew said, 'Well, why can't Captain Shakespeare make your hair grow because we're in a magical world? There are no rules. You can make that stuff up.'"

"I think it's an extraordinary transformation," says Jane Goldman, "which can be credited as much to Charlie's performance as it can to anything we did with make-up or costumes."

"Without question, Tristan's pirate costume was the most difficult challenge," Sammy Sheldon admits. "I just did not know what Captain Shakespeare would

give him. We played around with so many designs before we came up with something everybody liked.

"The idea was that he becomes dashing and very sexy, completely the opposite to the Tristan that the Victorian world knows. So the shape of his coat is sort of eighteenth century, but with a bit more Victorian in the detail. Then I put a brown collar on it – that's kind of dapper – and just sort of mixed it up a bit. I also added modern elements in there, so you can't really tell which period it comes from.

"Because it's also Captain Shakespeare's wardrobe, and he would have worn it himself once, there was also the idea that there's a little bit of decoration in there. All the buttons are hand-embroidered, so it's got those little details that Captain Shakespeare would have really appreciated.

"When the captain dresses Yvaine, I chose a blue fabric because I thought that if she was faced with a row of dresses, she would go with something that was sort of a night sky colour. It's quite an electric blue. For her, it's the first time that she's ever worn a normal dress."

"When you first meet Yvaine," adds Claire Danes, "she's in her star costume, which is a silvery kind of silk dress. Then she's kidnapped by pirates, and the captain eagerly makes her over and gives her this beautiful Victorian frock to wear.

"It was really fun to shoot actually," continues the actress. "It was great. I really felt like we were shooting a movie when there were pirates involved. It's such a classic motif. Occasionally I'd sort of pinch myself and think, 'I'm being dragged across the floor of a pirate ship by Robert De Niro.' But it was really good fun."

Above: The Captain teaches Yvaine how to dance while Tristan and the crew look on.

Along with giving his guests a fashionable make-over, Captain Shakespeare also teaches Yvaine to dance the waltz and Tristan how to sword-fight. "I'd seen *The Mission* [1986]," explains Charlie Cox, "so I knew that Robert De Niro had fenced before. It was just a really wonderful, bizarre experience to work with him and to be fencing with him.

"He trained independently of me because he was in New York prior to the start of shooting, and I trained in England. He came over a couple of days before we started filming and we were put together for the first time. It was a really good way to get to know each other, because we had to work out how we were going to do the sword-fighting scenes. It was a really good fight."

"Walking onto those stages at Pinewood Studios, I thought to myself, 'They don't make sets like this anymore,'" recalls Neil Gaiman.

"We filled the entire soundstage with a ship," says producer Lorenzo di Bonaventura with pride. "It is a

mighty, mighty sailing vessel, and those people who have read the book know that it flies through the air. It's really spectacular and very complicated, and that's one of the learning experiences that Matthew went through on this film. The entire stage was green-screened, and in the middle of it was this giant ship.

"You don't get to shoot visual effects very often on independent budgets, and you certainly don't get to do it on that kind of scale. So that's a learning experience for anybody, and that's a pretty demanding way to just jump into the pool. Then we had Robert De Niro for a

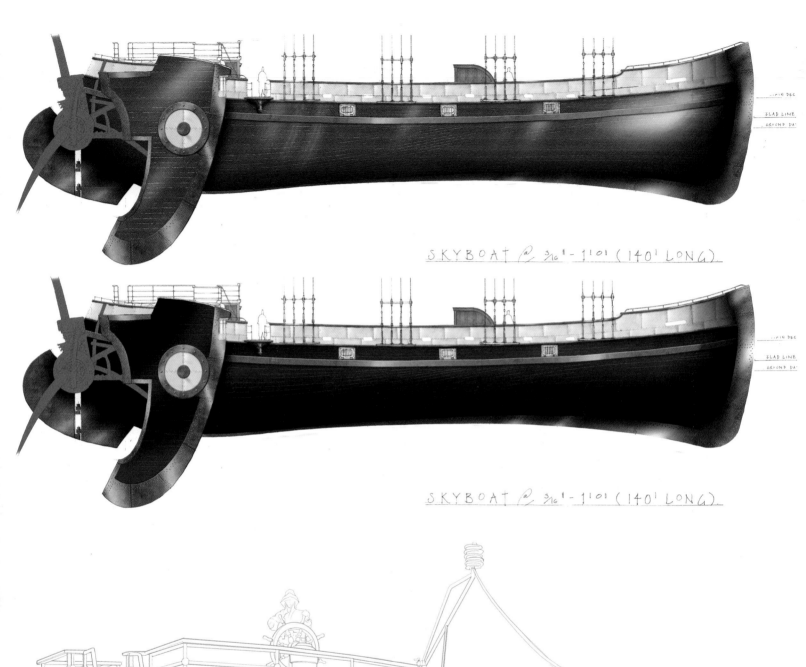

SKYBOAT @ 3/16" - 1'0" (140' LONG)

SKYBOAT @ 3/16" - 1'0" (140' LONG)

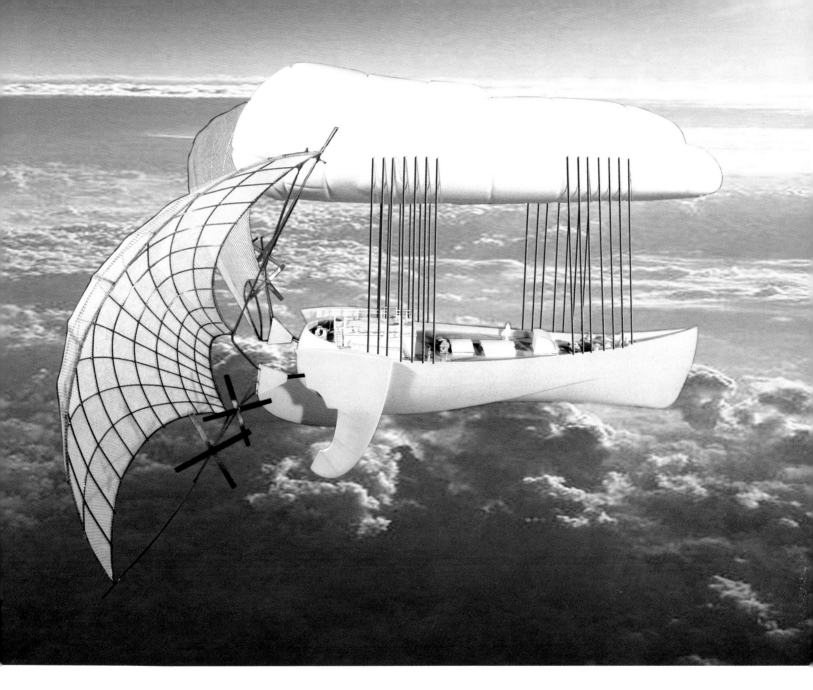

Opposite: Various concept designs for Captain Shakespeare's sky vessel.
Above and far left: Scale model of the sky vessel.
Left: Filming against the green screen at Pinewood Studios.

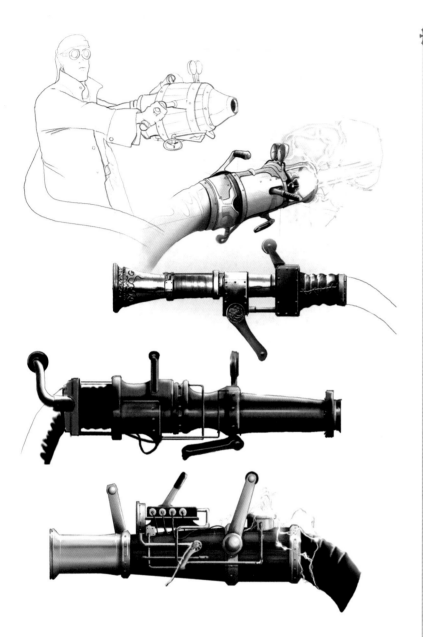

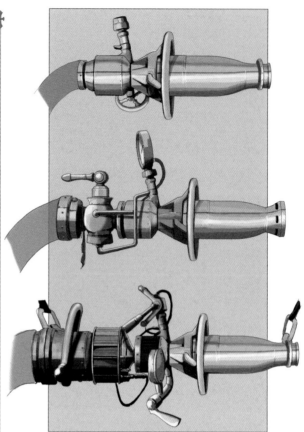

couple of weeks. So Matthew not only had to jump into the pool, he had to jump in with one of the greatest actors of our time, and had a limited time period to get it all done.

"That ship was lively," adds Bonaventura. "The pirates were jumping all over the place."

"What we did with the pirates," explains hair and make-up designer Fae Hammond, "is we wanted to get completely away from that 'classic' pirate look. We wanted to be the opposite. So we basically cut everybody's hair off. There was just one very old pirate, played by Terry Murphy, who we left with a kind of 'yo-ho-ho' beard.

"With everybody else we cropped their hair, disguised any scarring they may have and kept them really, really brown. That's because they are outside in the sunshine most of the time, but without being too dirty as there

would be no dirt in the clouds.

"It was really important that the pirates looked different," agrees costume designer Sammy Sheldon. "The basic concept was that they live on a flying ship and harvest lightning, so it is immediately obvious that they are not normal pirates! They are more like deep-sea fishermen."

"So I just went with the concept that if these people live on a ship that floats in the sky, they're going to be really weathered, they've probably been electrocuted hundreds of times, so their clothes will be slightly burned or distressed in some other way. Then we went with the idea of using rubber aprons, rubber boots and rubber gloves to protect them from being electrocuted. Also, the goggles were really important, because otherwise they would be blinded by the lightning-flashes, so they all had their own pair of goggles that had blacked-out lenses. Beyond that, we tried not to have any buttons or buckles that were made of metal, because they would conduct the electricity. So we used bone and other natural materials. It is definitely a weird look.

"Because they're a team, I didn't make Captain Shakespeare stand out too much from the others when we first see the pirates together. The only difference was his waistcoat is a bit more military in its basic tailoring, but he's got no metal anywhere on his costume that might attract any electricity."

"They built almost the entire ship on the Pinewood

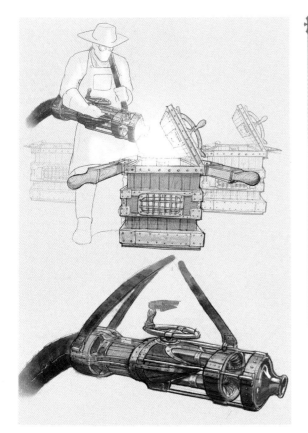

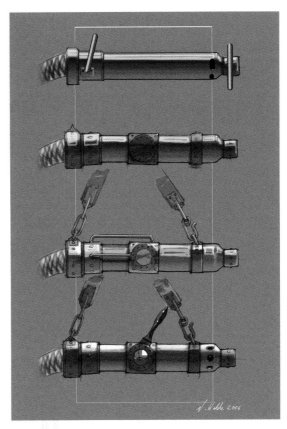

PULLEY CHAINS FADE UP INTO DISTANCE OF WHERE BALLON SITS.

LIGHTENING GUARD VERY BURNT.

LIGHTENING FLOWS DOWN NOZZLE

set!" says Neil Gaiman. "As Matthew pointed out, the budget for the ship cost more than *Layer Cake*. It was amazing. As I walked around it, I admit I felt a little guilty. It was just a pirate ship in the sky in the book because I thought that would be really fun for Charlie to draw. I'd get them stranded on a cloud, and have them picked up by this lightning-hunting pirate ship. It was the work of a paragraph to create a flying pirate ship. If I'd thought of something different at the moment where I needed to get them out of trouble, it could have been a submarine. It could have been anything. It was just a flying pirate ship because I thought it seemed like a fun thing to do.

"Now there I was, eight years and a huge amount of money later, walking into Studio H at Pinewood and standing on the deck of something I created. Thirty or forty craftsmen have been toiling for eight weeks at a significant cost to build a full-size flying pirate ship in the studio. I felt elated, I felt awed, but chiefly I just felt guilty.

"I never meant for anybody to actually have to do any work. It was just something fun that I made up. And now somebody was actually having to make it real."

"You don't design a set to fit in the stage," reveals production designer Gavin Bocquet, "you design the set and then see which stage it fits in. On *Stardust* we knew that we only had a certain number of stages available,

and the original concept was that the sky vessel would be about 110 feet long and would therefore have fit into our stage diagonally.

"We initially created four or five test versions of the sky vessel. The biggest was probably three or four feet long. We also had a digital version designed in the computer.

"After showing Matthew little models and drawing full-size mark-outs on the backlot, he felt that it just had to be 160 feet long. So the only option was to move to a bigger stage, except that everywhere was busy. So after talking with visual effects supervisor Peter Chiang, the decision was made not to build the front twenty feet of the ship as the two or three shots from that angle could be done with digital technology.

"The audience is never going to know that it's not real in the end."

⸻

When the pirates' sky vessel docks at a cliff-top port town, Captain Shakespeare, Tristan and Yvaine, along with several of the crew members, disembark and enter a dodgy den filled with many magical objects. There, the captain begins to haggle with Ferdy the Fence, played by British comedian Ricky Gervais, who created television show *The Office* for the BBC and portrayed odious boss

David Brent on the show.

"Ricky Gervais is hilarious," says producer Lorenzo di Bonaventura, "just fall-down funny."

"Captain Shakespeare gets to sell his lightning to an incredibly unsavoury gentleman named Ferdy the Fence," reveals Neil Gaiman. "It was great watching Ricky Gervais and Robert De Niro having a ball, pushing their games up because each one got a little bit sharper with every scene. Ricky would throw in another line, and De Niro would toss down an even cooler one just to match him, and suddenly it's really funny and sharp. Watching that was astonishing, and an education."

"My scene was with Robert De Niro," explains Gervais. "How could I turn that down? Just think of that, the world's greatest actor – and Robert De Niro – in the same scene!"

The day's filming is remembered with particular fondness by all of *Stardust*'s cast and crew, who were kept endlessly entertained. The two actors kept the ad-libs coming — some of which made it into the final cut. "They are doing this amazing little scene in which they are haggling," says Gaiman. "Although as Ferdy the Fence points out to Captain Shakespeare, it isn't

Above: Ferdinand (Ricky Gervais) and Captain Shakespeare haggle over the price of electricity.
Left: British comedian Ricky Gervais as the luckless Ferdy the Fence.

haggling because his numbers are going up and the Captain's are staying the same."

"I got to act with Robert De Niro and I loved it," Gervais recalls. "One day's work. And I spent the day ad-libbing, trying to put him off and make him laugh. When he eventually lost it and laughed, I wanted to run around the room celebrating.

"Then, when we finished, I did that thing of suddenly letting everything flood out and being a nerd. I had eight hours of bravado, being a normal person, and then before the last shot, I broke and went: 'I think you're the best actor in the world. You're brilliant. I've seen everything you've ever done…' And he looked at me and said, 'Thank you very much…'

"I'll always remember that day with Robert De Niro."

"Ricky has such a great comic mind," says Jane Goldman, "that Matthew and I were happy to let him improvise. When you have someone that funny, it would be ridiculous to make him stick to the script. We were all delighted, because it's all about anything that makes the finished movie better.

"It was such an honour and a delight to be on the same set as De Niro. He's charming, and funny, and just great. Everyone was so excited to have him there. It was a really interesting couple of weeks. I think everyone was initially slightly nervous, and I think what really broke the ice was the day we shot the scene with him and Ricky.

"No-one was quite sure whether he'd find it funny and then, when he did it, it was lovely. He has great

comic timing and was very receptive to Ricky's ad-libbing. Everyone was laughing. It was a great day, and Ricky is a lot of fun to work with."

"It was awesome, quite an experience," confirms Gervais. "I still pinch myself that I'm working with these people. It's ridiculous. It's madness."

When Lamia enters Ferdy the Fence's store, looking for the fallen star, she quickly tires of his babbling and puts a spell on him, so that he can only squawk in animal noises. When Septimus turns up a little later, still on the trail of the pendant now being worn by Yvaine, he interprets Ferdy's caterwauls as insolence and runs him through with his sword.

"One of the things that really appealed to me is that the danger to the characters in Stormhold is very genuine," Goldman explains. "There is certainly a darkness to the story. People get hurt, people get killed. It's not gratuitously violent at all, but it's a dark story in the sense that fairy tales are traditionally nasty. Bad things even happen to the nice characters.

"I think that's one of the things that make fairy tales so enduring, and so it made complete sense to retain that element in Stardust. I don't think there was ever a time when we questioned whether it was too dark, and because it's leavened with humour it's not nasty. It makes it darkly humorous, and that's a combination I'm very fond of."

Above: Ferdy receives a visit from Lamia, still hunting the fallen star.
Left: A soggy Septimus survives a fight with the crew of the sky vessel.

Act III

IN WHICH TRUE LOVE TRIUMPHS

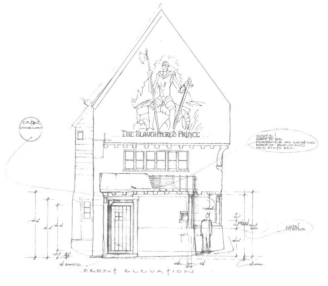

HE SAID THAT MY TRUE LOVE WAS IN FRONT OF MY EYES... AND HE WAS RIGHT.

– TRISTAN

Saying their goodbyes to Captain Shakespeare and his loyal crew, Tristan and Yvaine continue their journey across the Stormhold countryside. Meanwhile, the rapidly-ageing Lamia and hot-blooded Septimus are still in pursuit of the fallen star and the ruby pendant.

Coming across Ditch-Water Sal, who is unable to see Yvaine because of the spell cast on her earlier by Lamia, Tristan asks her to give him safe passage to the wall in her caravan.

The scenes of Tristan and Yvaine's encounter with Ditch-Water Sal were shot at Llyn y Fan Fach in mid-Wales. Situated on the north-western side of the Carmarthenshire Fans, the area is famous for its local legend of the mysterious Lady of the Lake.

"There was a very nice stone bridge sequence that we didn't get in Scotland," recalls production designer Gavin Bocquet. "Ditch-Water Sal's caravan comes across it and she meets Tristan and Yvaine."

"Bizarrely, I think that Ditch-Water Sal is probably my favourite costume," says Sammy Sheldon. "Her costumes came from me wanting her to be totally eclectic – all witches have accumulated stuff over the centuries, but they have not kept up to date. Sal's quite the poor relation in terms of grandeur, while the other three are faded princesses. So I wanted to create the impression that they are from this palatial world, while Sal lives in a caravan.

"She may not have any money, but she is rich in other ways. She is rich in her head. So I wanted to make her like an old carpet bag, something that looks really friendly and homely but actually has another side to it. Her coat is made out of pieces of an old African rug that I cut up and added material to, and I found this other fabric that was patterned Indian wool. She carries everything around, she's got lots of beads. Sal likes to put on a show."

Ditch-Water Sal agrees to Tristan's request, but only after he gives her the protective charm that he is wearing, and the wily old witch changes him into a mouse for the duration of the journey. Yvaine, still invisible to Sal, also hitches a ride in the caravan.

"By the time we get to the scene where she is talking to the mouse," says Jane Goldman, "I think it is impossible not to absolutely adore Claire Danes." The turning point in the couple's relationship comes when Tristan and Yvaine finally arrive at Stormhold Market Town, barely a mile from the wall. They decide to spend the night at a nearby inn before Tristan presents the star to Victoria on her birthday.

"I think they're forced to work collaboratively," Claire Danes explains, "and

Opposite: Concept art for the rugged Stormhold countryside Yvaine and Tristan must cross.
Below: The rapidly-ageing Lamia continues her pursuit of the star.
Left: Yvaine and Tristan continue their journey.

they have no choice but to solve these problems that they have together. I think that's binding. They both manage to save each other's lives, and that tends to lead to good, if not amorous feelings."

"They fall in love," confirms Charlie Cox, "but the interesting twist that I think this story has is that Tristan falls in love a lot earlier than he thinks he does. It takes Captain Shakespeare to first tell him that he's in love with Yvaine, and for him to then realise it.

"Even then it takes a while for that to sink in. I had this idea that once Captain Shakespeare tells him that Yvaine is the woman he loves, then there's a sense of denial that comes with that realisation. He doesn't think it's true, and he doesn't really want it to be true, until he can pretend no longer that it's not the truth. So they fall in love, and it's very sweet, I think."

Right: Scale model of Ditch-Water Sal's caravan.
Below: Filming the encounter between Ditch-Water Sal and Tristan on location in Wales.

For three weeks, the Medieval city of Norwich, Norfolk, became the location for Stormhold Market Town. Three hundred years ago, Norwich was considered the largest provincial city in England and today is still considered the 'Capital of East Anglia'. Amongst the cobbled streets and twisting alleyways stand two cathedrals and more

pre-Reformation churches than in any other city in Europe. It boasts 1,500 historic buildings within its walled city centre, including the Norman castle, one of the most ambitious secular buildings of its period in Europe.

"We had a lot of locations to deal with on this film," says production designer Gavin Bocquet. "We were trying to create a magical land and as we knew that we couldn't build the whole of that environment, we tried wherever possible to find locations that gave us some instant visual references that worked. Then we could adapt or add to them.

"We knew we wanted Stormhold Market Town to have this somewhat exotic architectural look to it. So we scouted all over Britain, and even went to France and Germany looking for locations. We looked at Medieval towns in both those places, and even considered building the street as a composite set on the backlot. Eventually, through the process of elimination, we came across a tiny little old Medieval street in Norwich with a lovely old building at the end that was perfect for the inn."

Elm Hill is one of the oldest streets in Norwich and it contains more Tudor houses than there are in the whole of London. Now a quaint, winding, cobbled street filled with antique shops and exclusive art galleries, it was destroyed by the great fire of 1507 and rebuilt during the sixteenth and seventeenth centuries. Most of the merchant houses lining the road date from that period, and the area is reputedly haunted by several ghosts, including that of a hellfire preacher who used to live in an old monastery at the top of the hill.

"We finally felt we had a handle on the look of Stormhold, our parallel world, around three or four months into the preparation period," explains Bocquet. "But it still developed even further along. We had ideas of how we were going to dress certain interior locations, such as the room in the Slaughtered Prince inn.

"It was one of the last things we shot, and by the time we got to that location, we realised that the way we had decorated and dressed some of the other Stormhold locations – in a slightly exotic and eclectic way, as if comprised of elements from everywhere else in the known world – it became obvious that we would have to dress the inn room in the same way."

The exterior of a local tea shop, The Briton's Arms, was painstakingly transformed into The Slaughtered Prince, complete with new doorway and a large painted mural of a triumphant young Peter O'Toole in knight's armour looming over his fallen enemy.

"First we had to design the image, and we showed Matthew a number of different sketches," says Bocquet, "and then a scenic artist spent three or four days up a crane painting the mural with water-based paint."

A mix of eclectic market stalls selling everything from bolts of material to wolf pelts were set up along the length of the street and a number of shop fronts

Top: Ditch-Water Sal is still unable to see Yvaine due to the spell cast on her by Lamia.
Above: Yvaine reveals her true feelings to the transformed Tristan.
Left: Tristan is turned into a mouse by Ditch-Water Sal's spell.

Opposite, above: Behind the scenes at Stormhold Market Town. **Opposite, below:** Concept painting of Stormhold Market Town. **Left:** Some of the colourful background characters that populate the market sequences. **Below:** Art department concept sketch of Stormhold Market Town.

Right: Concept sketches for the painted mural that adorns The Slaughtered Prince.

Far right: The exterior of a Norwich tea shop was transformed into The Slaughtered Prince inn.

were redressed and covered in a bio-degradable pulp-wash to age them. "One of the most expensive costs on location when we have to adapt buildings is the painting side of things," Bocquet explains. "If we have to change colours and then put the original colours back, it is usually the putting back that costs more. It's quite an expensive process. This black and grey paper wash we used works very well as a quick ageing technique when sprayed on a white building. It simply washes off afterwards."

Other scenes of Stormhold Market Town were shot in the large stable courtyard of a nearby stately home. To give the illusion that the two locations were connected, a huge green screen was erected across the High Street that was moved into position when needed on a mobile tractor, and the two localities were digitally combined for the finished film.

For the look of Stormhold, Gavin Bocquet says: "Imagine a parallel world to Victorian England that is sort of the same, but its influences are every other known world at that time. So you are kind of in the same world, but everything is mixed together with maybe an

element of magical fantasy.

"By the time you got all the strange inhabitants in their somewhat eclectic mix of clothes and with their exotic looks populating that street in Norwich, it worked very well."

For the costume department, Stormhold Market Town was the largest scene they had to deal with, necessitating an expanded crew of around thirty-five people to get all the cast and extras into their clothes. "It was the biggest crowd we had," says Sammy Sheldon, "around 250 people. We had lots of different characters in that, although I'm not sure how big it will look on the screen.

"A lot of the background characters look kind of Eastern or Asiatic. We sort of mixed it all up and made it a bit folksy, so that the Victorian stuff looks very neat. We hired the costumes for the background crowds, but we used a real mix of designs and put them together in a stylised way that kind of looked odd but which will hopefully blend in with the costumes we made especially. So you've got this quite colourful world where I've just put in loads of stuff from everywhere – it's quite eclectic."

"The crowd scenes looked fantastic," agrees hair and make-up designer Fae Hammond. "There were some fabulous designs. We used a lot of wonderful colours and shapes with the hair, and I thought the whole Stormhold 'look' was great.

"For the people of Stormhold, we did a lot of

Above: Realising the danger Yvaine is in, the Slave Girl steals Ditch-Water Sal's caravan.
Inset: The Slave Girl prevents Yvaine passing into England through the gap in the wall.

interesting things with their hands," she continues. "We thought they would dye their hands, so it would look like their finger-tips had been dipped in colours. They would also perhaps dye their hair, dye their costumes. That was interesting for me."

"The costume and make-up departments worked very closely together," confirms Sheldon. "We gave them bits and pieces of stuff from the costumes that they could incorporate into hair and beards. It was a really good collaboration. I also worked closely with Gavin Bocquet in the art department as well, trying to really keep in mind the colours and textures he was using for the interiors. I wanted the costumes to be as rich as the set dressing and the whole environment that they would appear in."

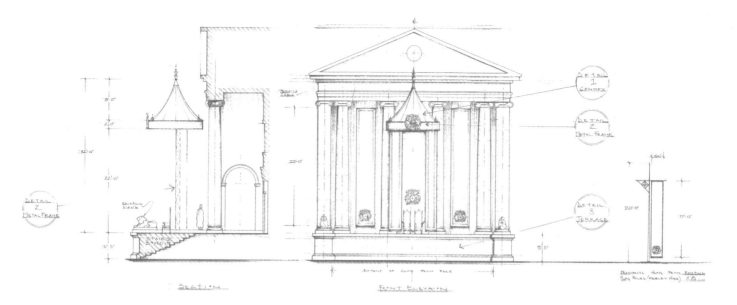

NO STAR CAN SHINE
WITH A BROKEN HEART.

– YVAINE

As events rush towards a conclusion, Tristan, slipping away from Yvaine, goes to tell Victoria that he has found the fallen star and his true love and no longer wishes to marry her. But a misunderstanding leaves Yvaine believing that he has abandoned her.

When a decrepit Lamia finally catches up to the fallen star, she takes her back to the witches' lair so that the three sisters can feed on her heart and once again regain their lost beauty and power.

"The witches' lair is really an extraordinary place," reveals producer Lorenzo di Bonaventura. "It's sort of half-Versailles, half-Edgar Allan Poe, with a few other things thrown in there. It is the building where the three witches brew their concoctions, where their victims are brought to, and the location where the film's finale also takes place."

Tristan and Septimus join forces to battle the three hags, who turn the last of their magic powers on the headstrong heroes. Lamia produces a clay doll that she uses to manipulate Septimus' enchanted limbs before dropping the effigy into a receptacle filled with water.

Jane Goldman admits that the scene of Septimus drowning in mid-air was, "just an image I had in my head. I was really delighted and proud at how that looks on the screen, and it's one of my favourite moments in the film."

As Septimus takes his place alongside his six ghostly brothers, his dead body is reanimated by Lamia and used to attack Tristan. "The dead Septimus sword-fight is just a very cool, fun sequence," says Goldman. "It appeals to that part of me that is basically a fourteen year-old boy."

"Matthew particularly wanted us to keep it as real as possible," recalls Charlie Cox, "he didn't want us to overdo any of the moments. But at the same time you discover that in order for the audience to believe what is happening – to believe that Yvaine is a star, that these are witches, and that we are in real danger – you have to up

Previous spread, left: Various concept designs for the witches' sacrificial knives.

Previous spread, right: The three evil witches prepare to cut out the heart of Yvaine's sister star in a flashback sequence.

Right: Lamia and Empusa show Yvaine their magic mirror.

Below: Yvaine finds herself about to be sacrificed.

Opposite above: Richard Ryan, Robert De Niro's fight double, and Charlie Cox rehearse a scene on the witches' lair set at Pinewood Studios.

Opposite below: Empusa is impaled during the final confrontation.

the stakes. You have to bring your performance up a little bit, because these are not everyday occurrences. If you were just to react to a witch's magical flying fire as if the toast had just been burnt, then it wouldn't really be sufficient. It was a real challenge actually, and really difficult.

"I really enjoyed it, but when I read it in the script, it was very hard to gauge what it was going to be, and how it was going to work. I literally come in at the very end and save the day at the last minute. All the stuff I did with Mark Strong was really enjoyable. It was a crazy scene. There was not much room for subtlety. If you're about to be killed by a witch, it's pure terror and then relief when it doesn't happen."

Perhaps the most impressive and spectacular set built for *Stardust* was the witches' lair. "From the very first week of concept drawings that were done prior to me joining the production, there was an idea that the witches' lair was a rather abstract, temple-like structure," recalls production designer Gavin Bocquet. "We also knew that we weren't going to find it on location and that it would be a big,

Right: Septimus prepares for a fight.
Below: The ornate staircase and fountain of the witches' lair set at Pinewood.

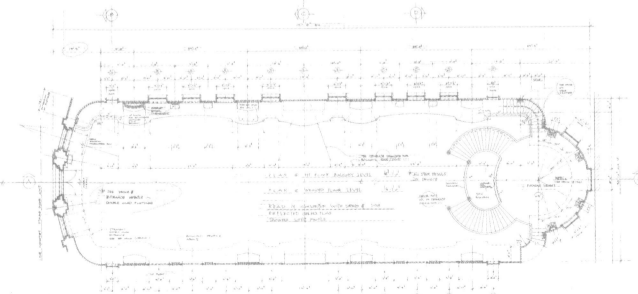

Above: Concept design for the witches' lair.

Left: Blueprint of the interior of the witches' lair.

Right: Witches' lair fountain detail, including angelic cherubs eviscerating a pig and an alligator.
Below: Concept design of a cherub mural for the witches' lair set.
Opposite, above: Concept design for the witches' sacrificial table.
Opposite, below left: One of the giant mirrors lining the walls of the lair.
Opposite, below right: Concept design for the witches' magical mirror.
Opposite, far right: One of the witches' sacrificial knives.

interior set that we would have to build. As soon as you started thinking about the wire-work, the action, the explosions and the water, it was just impossible to imagine anywhere that would be a suitable shooting location for what ended up being eight weeks on the soundstage."

Construction on the 160 foot-long set began in the middle of February 2006, well before principal photography commenced. Filming didn't start on the set until nearly four months later and it remained standing and in use for the duration of the shoot.

The colour design was basically black and silver. Walls were constructed in black wood, and black marble floors reflected the obsidian glass chandeliers. The intricate sculptures built into the walls, some depicting angelic cherubs eviscerating a pig, were trimmed in silver.

"It was a very ornate, cleverly sculpted set," explains Bocquet. "It had great marble finishes from construction

manager John Bohan and his team, great dressing from set decorator Peter Young, and great organisation from supervising art director Peter Russell."

Unusually, the set was built as one immense room, without the normal breakaway sections for ease of access. The roof was left open to allow for the numerous lights and complicated rigging, and the intricate vaulted ceiling would be added later using the latest in cutting-edge computer graphics.

"We had a thirty-four foot-high set that went up to the lighting rig," explains Bocquet, "which was as high as we could go. The next piece was the ceiling over the top. So not only was there no room for it, but there would have been nowhere for director of photography Ben Davis to light from. So we built what was classically a film set."

Above: Preliminary concept design for the witches' lair in the sink hole.

Right: Witches' lair sink hole development drawings.

Opposite above: Design sketch of the witches' lair sink hole.

Opposite below: Scale model of the witches' lair.

A number of the giant mirrors lining the walls could be removed, allowing the camera access from various angles. All these huge panes could also be slightly pivoted on gimbals to prevent the camera crew being reflected in them while filming. It proved to be a costly and complicated procedure as most of the ground floor of the witches' lair consisted of ten foot-high glass panels interspersed with columns.

The giant mirrors were later replaced with breakaway glass for a spectacular climactic sequence in which they explode into thousands of deadly shards. During the last few weeks of principal photography in August 2006, as the final battle scenes grew more dramatic and complicated than originally envisioned, alternating crews filmed on the set twenty-four hours a day, every day of the week.

"It felt pretty epic when we were doing it," recalls Charlie Cox. "I don't really have any frame of reference. I did a reasonably big movie [*Casanova*], but I'd never done this much studio work before."

Using various models and schematic drawings created by the art department, an earlier design of the witches' lair was based on the concept of a cave-like structure growing out of solid rock. This later became a building that more closely resembled an Aztec or Asiatic temple. But after being developed for two months, that monolithic structure was discarded for a design that was loosely inspired by the Palace of Versailles in France. It then took a further six weeks for production designer Gavin Bocquet to finalise

Left and opposite, above: Various preliminary concept designs for the witches' lair exterior.
Opposite, below: Concept painting for the final confrontation between Tristan and Lamia.

the shape and construction of the set, based on the idea
that it would consist of two very different areas.

"In the art department you schedule your design time
for each set and location very accurately," he recalls.
"We knew with the witches' lair that we had maybe
three months of general concept work. Every now and
again we would show ideas to Matthew, and we kept
working on this concept of a temple-like interior. They
all featured interesting things going on with them, but
we always thought that there was something missing."

It was eventually decided that the witches
would be living in a massive palace but, as
their powers faded, so did the grandeur
of their surroundings.

"Matthew gradually began to realise
that what he wanted was more of a
'living area' for the witches," continues
Bocquet, "and that was difficult for us to com-
bine into the temple-like environment. In the original
book, the three witches live in a very small house in the
middle of the forest, but Matthew just had this feeling
that having seen one of them create an entire inn out of
nothing, you knew that they could magic anything up.
They would have created their own living space, and the
idea became that it should be a grand palace."

"Sometimes they took an idea from the book and
made it cinematic," says Neil Gaiman, "which is why I
don't get precious about some of my work. The times I
get precious is when I think that somebody is doing
something that is simply wrong and it isn't what I would
have wanted it to be.

"In the book I had the witches living in a little hovel
with a huge mirror propped up against one wall which
reflected the palace that they also apparently live in, or

once lived in, and you are never quite certain whether they are in this world or another.

"What I love about the set design in the film is that they thought about that concept, then built a huge baroque hall and had the witches living in just one corner of it. The rest of it is empty and filled with dust. I thought that was great because it was absolutely spiritually and emotionally what I wanted, but it was a perfect way of achieving it for the camera."

"We had a brainstorming session over a week or so," explains Bocquet, "doing very quick sketches, with two or three people just jumping in and making some simple models. There were a couple of ideas that were of a chateau or mansion-type environment, with broken

roofs fallen in, and you could just see that that was where we should take it. Maybe the witches would just have created their own Versailles.

"The interesting take on it is, at that time in the story, their powers are waning, so they have decamped with various rag-tag bits of furniture into the entrance hall, which is all we built really, and they are living there with a small cooking stove, one bed and all their animals in cages."

Because the witches utilise entrails for their divinations, a number of live animals were used on set to represent a dwindling supply of sacrifices. Special cages were constructed by skilled metal-workers to house them in during the filming. For the more extreme scenes, stuffed stand-ins were used.

———— ✢ ————

For this final sequence set in the witches' lair, Matthew Vaughn wanted the battle to range up and down the length of the mirror-lined gallery between the two contrasting areas of the room, as the dead Princes of Stormhold commented on and interacted with the action while sitting on a fireplace mantel.

To achieve the complex effect of incorporating the ghostly chorus into the other live action footage filmed earlier, the main unit continued to shoot green screen special effects shots for two weeks in early September 2006 on stages B and C at Pinewood Studios.

Before the original sets had been destroyed or discarded, their contours and dimensions had been mapped in perfect 3-D detail by the latest laser technology and stored on computer software. The high-resolution 3-D modelling and visualisation process used, called LiDAR (Light Detection and Ranging), is more usually utilised by

airborne scanning companies for such applications as topography profiling, mining studies, architecture archiving, surveying and city modelling. Using rapid pulses of laser light striking a surface and measuring the time of pulse return, the system gave a high-resolution profile of every centimetre of the sets used. This then allowed the art department to recreate in exact detail certain portions of scenery from the crater, Lamia's inn, the Slaughtered Prince inn and the witches' lair mantelpiece, amongst other locations. These set pieces were then painted a fluorescent green, against which the actors would perform.

Orange tape was sometimes used as reference points to exactly mark the actors' positions in relation to the set design, and this separately-shot footage was subsequently combined optically with the earlier material to give the impression that the semi-transparent ghosts were in the same scenes with the other actors.

While filming took place on one soundstage, the other stage was being built and prepped with more green-painted sets so that the crew could move across when finished with the least amount of time wasted.

Using reference plates from the earlier shoots as a guide, Matthew Vaughn directed his cast and the multiple cameras from behind a bank of monitors. Although the director encouraged his phantoms to improvise in certain scenes, Jane Goldman remained on set to oversee changes of dialogue and action from the seven spectres.

Comedian Adam Buxton, of Channel 4 Television's

Above: The dead princes attempt to pool their power and influence the outcome of the battle.
Left: Adam Buxton and Julian Rhind-Tutt, working against the green screen.
Below: David Walliams and Rupert Everett.

Right: Some familiar faces in the crowd at the coronation.

Below: Concept design for the King of Stormhold's crown.

anarchic *Adam & Joe Show* (1997-2001), was cast as Quintus after Noel Fielding (from BBC television's *The Mighty Boosh* [2004-]) had to pull out at the last minute due to ill health. "It's been fantastic fun," says Buxton. "At first I was very nervous because I was aware of being an unknown and less celebrated quantity than the others.

"Myself, Jason Flemyng, Mark Heap and Mark Strong escaped without seriously crippling make-up, so we've probably had the best time, comfort-wise, but I've enjoyed being around all of the others immensely and I miss it now it's over."

"Doing the ghostly princes was great fun," says prosthetics make-up designer Nik Williams, "because they were slightly comic. But they were also challenging. It was a problem trying to make somebody look frozen without sticking icicles off their nose. Because their scenes were shot against a green screen with very flat lighting, it was very difficult to get anything to glisten like ice, so the challenge was to make something look frozen solid and

allow for the actor's movements at the same time."

The plan was for the ghostly princes to disappear heavenwards when finally released from their curse. But Matthew Vaughn and Jane Goldman remained undecided as to whether Septimus should disappear downwards. "We just weren't sure if we wanted to see him punished to that extreme!" explains Goldman. "But in the end the effects department did a very cool, subtle visual that is humorous rather than horrible, and works brilliantly well."

With the witches eventually destroyed, and Tristan surprisingly proclaimed the rightful heir to the throne of Stormhold, everyone gathers at the palace for a spectacular coronation.

These scenes, along with the opening sequence featuring the observatory telescope, were filmed over two nights at Stowe School, Buckinghamshire, where both

Above: The exterior location at Stowe School, Buckingham, for the coronation sequence.
Inset: Concept painting for the background to the coronation.
Left: Scale model of the coronation set.

director Matthew Vaughn and actor Henry Cavill (who plays Humphrey) were educated. Other notable alumni include Christopher Robin Milne (of *Winnie the Pooh* fame), actor David Niven and business entrepreneur Sir Richard Branson. The school had previously been used as a location for such films as *Indiana Jones and the Temple of Doom* (1989).

Founded in 1923 in the former home of the Dukes of Buckingham and Chandos, this country boarding school is set in 750 acres of landscaped gardens and parkland, described by the National Trust as 'Britain's largest work of art'. The gardens were created in the early eighteenth century by Sir Richard Temple, Viscount Cobham, and evolved with the help of various designers, including landscape painter William Kent and Lancelot 'Capability' Brown. The Georgian gardens boast temples, arches, bridges and caves built into the scenery.

"We had been looking for the basis of some architecture for Stormhold Palace," reveals production designer Gavin Bocquet. "We knew that we needed a large courtyard, and it was Matthew who mentioned Stowe because it has a very good colonnaded front."

For the 200 extras used in the coronation scene, Fae Hammond's hair and make-up team increased from five to around forty people. "The most challenging thing about this film was the stamina," she reveals. "We put in some long hours, did some big make-ups, but I thoroughly enjoyed doing it.

In the *Stardust* novel, Tristran and the star aren't crowned king and queen straight away, but decide to continue their wanderings across the world, leaving Tristran's mother, Lady Una, to rule Stormhold in their

Above: Yvaine and Tristan are crowned the new rulers of Stormhold.

Right: Sammy Sheldon's design for Yvaine's coronation costume.

Opposite: The unaged Yvaine and old King Tristan light the Babylon candle. This ending for the film, though shot, was replaced by a slightly different scene in the final version.

absence. Eventually, having ascended to the throne and ruled well for many years, Tristran dies, leaving an unaged Yvaine to rule the kingdom.

It was decided to add a new epilogue to the movie, set many years after the initial tale. A version was shot in which King Tristan, now an old man, is lying on his deathbed in Stormhold Palace, surrounded by his children and Yvaine, who has never aged. However, the final version shows Tristan and Yvaine in silhouette at a window as they light the Babylon candle, before the camera pans up to reveal two stars side-by-side in the sky.

"The ending of the book is bittersweet," reveals screenwriter Jane Goldman. "It actually made me feel very, very sad. It is a very beautiful ending and incredibly poignant. But in the conversations that Matthew and I had, we felt that for the tone of the story being told in the movie of *Stardust* it just wouldn't have fitted what had gone before. I think it's now very sweet, and the idea of an eternal existence together after a long and happy life together is a perfect ending for me."

Following two days of special effects shooting, covering Secundus' fall to his death from a window in Stormhold Palace, principal photography on *Stardust* was completed after seventy-seven days on September 19, 2006. The shooting schedule had been split between thirty-five days on location and another forty-two at Pinewood Studios.

Epilogue

IN WHICH ONE ADVENTURE
ENDS AND ANOTHER BEGINS

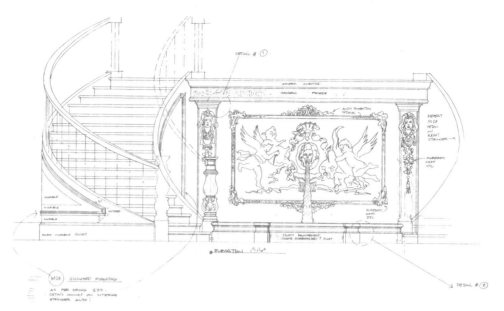

AND WE REALLY DID LIVE HAPPILY EVER AFTER...

– TRISTAN

"Wherever possible," explains Neil Gaiman, "Matthew did every special effect he could in the camera. CGI can only take you so far."

The director agrees: "I did as much in-camera as possible because I think that people are getting bored of CGI. So we went back to basics as much as possible with this movie. It's like the old James Bond movies. They're still entertaining because it's stuntmen doing real stunts, and they used real locations. So we've adopted that approach."

"In many ways I think we were really lucky," Jane Goldman adds, "because it was somewhat unusual that

we actually built quite a lot of huge and elaborate sets. So adding digital effects later was a lovely bonus."

Following the completion of principal photography, over the next few months visual effects supervisor Peter Chiang and his team used state-of-the-art computer technology to optically enhance a large number of sequences. Chiang's recent credits include *The Chronicles of Riddick* (2004) and *Kingdom of Heaven* (2005). These digitally-created shots included the star being knocked out of the heavens, Captain Shakespeare's flying sky vessel, the ornate roof of the witches' lair and the ghostly princes interacting with the other characters.

"The process is still basically the same as it was in the 1930s," explains production designer Gavin Bocquet. "It is still about the art department designing the environment, and then deciding how much do you build and how much you do as a glass painting or foreground miniature or model in the old days, or create using digital enhancement today. Back then they still painted ceilings in. They may have done it on a sheet of glass in front of the camera lens, but the methodology is basically the same. There's no point in building something if it is not economically sensible.

"The difference now is that digital technology is a lot more flexible than the old techniques. It can be thought of as a magic tool, but it is not a cheap magic tool. It really has to be thought about. As an art department we were always making those judgement calls early on, about which was the most sensible way to proceed. In our world, if we shot on a physical set for eight weeks, it wouldn't cost us any more than if we used it for a week. Our costs are finite once we've constructed the set. For the digital cost it's all about how many shots and the length of those sequences. For one shot of something quite extraordinary, we wouldn't build very much – because it would be much

more efficient for Peter Chiang and his team to paint that in. If it's something like the witches' lair, which we shot on for six weeks, then you want to have as many set-ups covered by real sets as you possibly can."

"From the first shots I saw, I thought to myself, 'This doesn't look like a fantasy film,'" says Neil Gaiman. "It looks like perhaps a slightly skewed historical film. It looks like a David Lean film. It reminds me a little of Richard Lester and *The Three Musketeers* films.

"The thing I hate about some fantasy films is you only have to watch them for five seconds on the screen and you go, 'Oh, yes, it's a fantasy movie.' It looks like everybody has been reading the same books, and there's a little bit of Arthur Rackham in there somewhere, and a little bit of Pauline Baynes, a little bit of Tolkien.

"I had a voice in the design of the film, but in the end it was up to Matthew. If I thought something was wrong, then I would tell him."

"The job of the art department is to basically

help tell the story visually," continues Bocquet. "That's our whole purpose. Neil Gaiman's book was the basis of a great script by Jane and Matthew, so my hope is that our design work has helped move that storytelling along. You don't want your work to stand out unless it needs to stand out in the story. I know that on a fantasy film it is very hard to say that, but it is always about the characters and the storytelling. All we do is help that process along.

"Working with Matthew was a very creative and enjoyable experience. He was always very involved in the art department and the work we were doing, and was very clear about what he liked and what he didn't like, which always makes the creative process so much easier. He had strong ideas about the 'look' of the film, but was also always very keen to see the designs and ideas that we came up with."

"I hope we helped bring *Stardust* to life," reveals costume designer Sammy Sheldon, "and I hope that when people watch the movie that they don't notice the costumes before they notice the actors. It is really important

Left: A Captain Shakespeare costume design, and Robert De Niro cutting a swashbuckling figure in the final version.

that you see the characters first and that anything I've done only enhances the performances. It's all about telling the story.

"I think it is definitely an adventure. I hope that's how it comes across. It is really enjoyable, and quite funny, but a bit dark and, you know, slightly off-the-wall."

"Visually it's a really rich movie," agrees producer Lorenzo di Bonaventura. "It's a hard movie to describe in simple terms, because the costumes done by Sammy Sheldon are really extraordinary, and very unusual. The world of Stormhold is a fantasy world, but we've used real locations and, with slight alterations, it has a very interesting sense of reality to it. Yet it also has the fantasy or magical aspects to it."

On July 21, 2006, prior to several hours of print and media interviews, scriptwriter Jane Goldman, producer Lorenzo di Bonaventura, Neil Gaiman and Charles Vess presented a reel of rough footage from *Stardust* to an expectant audience at the San Diego International Comic Convention. A non-profit, educational event designed to create a greater awareness of and appreciation for comics and related art forms, the *Stardust* alumni held a question and answer session in front of thousands of comics fans.

"On the day of our presentation," recalls Vess, "we were made-up and groomed in preparation for the media circus. It was a hoot. The stylist kept asking why I was laughing. A stretch limo was there to take us two blocks to the back of the convention centre so we wouldn't have to navigate through the crowds. Then there was a short wait in the Media Green Room, where I saw directors Alfonso Cuarón and Guillermo Del Toro and others. Then into Hall H where a crowd of 6,000-plus watched our presentation of *Stardust* footage. A slight look to the right or left while answering questions revealed your face projected up to ten feet on giant screens – weirdly amusing!"

"It was great," says producer di Bonaventura. "We were really showing our underwear, in a way. Some of the scenes we had just seen for the first time three days earlier. It really was a sense of, 'Am I showing all the warts and

blemishes before we've had a chance to work on it?'"

The presentation concluded with a video message from director Matthew Vaughn. "There was a lot of clapping and hooting," continues Vess, "so I think they liked what they saw."

"The challenge was always to have a film that is very different from anything else," says Neil Gaiman, who has described *Stardust* as being: "A little bit like *Shakespeare in Love* [1998] meets Richard Lester's *The Three Musketeers* [1973] meets *The Princess Bride* [1987], with a little *Pirates of the Caribbean* [2003] undertone." However, in the end, he admits that, "It's its own thing. I like that. I really do."

"It's gonna be several audiences that come to see the movie," agrees di Bonaventura. "There will be the family audience that comes, and then there will be the later teens and the Neil Gaiman fans, who either know Neil or like this kind of material."

"We also have the advantage that there's been several movies over the past ten or fifteen years that have really whetted the appetite of the audience for this type of film. I think it's going to be a lot of fun, and I think that we have a uniqueness that is rare in our movie business right now."

"I hope that *Stardust* will be the kind of film that people who get dragged to it thinking they don't like that sort of thing are really going to like," says Gaiman. "I also hope that it will do something good for the British film industry. It's the kind of film they don't make any more."

Charles Vess readily agrees: "After seeing some thirty-five minutes of raw footage from the film I was blown away. Michelle Pfeiffer makes for a very, very scary witch queen and Claire Danes is a lovely transformed fallen star. Charlie Cox evolves from loveable nerd to hero as naturally as if he were born for the role.

"If, in the editing process, Matthew Vaughn maintains

a delicate balance between the elements of adventure, humour and horror within the film, I think it will be a splendid entertainment indeed!"

"It should be very enjoyable," says Charlie Cox. "I think it's a really fun family adventure film, but you can't escape from the raw darkness of it at times. I'm interested to know how the audience will respond to it. It's very different to anything I've seen – even the book. Of course it's fantastical, but it's also got a bizarre edge to it.

"It was really difficult, and tiring, and hard, but I'm so grateful to have done it. It was a great crew. A lot of the crew members had done some of Matthew's previous movies with him, so there was a great sense of teamwork on the set."

"It's an epic fantasy," reveals Claire Danes. "I think it's going to have a really interesting tone because it's really funny, but not necessarily a comedy. And really action-filled, but not necessarily an action movie. Most importantly, it centres on real people who are having real relationships with each other, and that is the most engaging thing of all. It's not up to me as an actor to decide how it's going to ultimately turn out, but I think it'll be good fun."

"I think it'll end up being a really fun adventure," Sienna Miller agrees. "It's got some great, great people in it, and some great cameos. You've got Robert De Niro and Michelle Pfeiffer. Charlie Cox is brilliant, and so is Claire Danes. And then you have all these familiar faces – Peter O'Toole, Ricky Gervais, Jason Flemyng, David Walliams, Dexter Fletcher and tons of other fantastic people. So I think it'll be a really fun, very light-hearted movie. It'll be great."

"As a writer," reveals Jane Goldman, "it is really lovely to see your work given another dimension from what is brought to it by the actors and the director. All you can ever hope is that you have done your part in telling a good story and telling it well. So I want audiences to come away from this film feeling that they have been entertained."

"I'll guarantee that audiences will be entertained," says Matthew Vaughn. "They'll experience a wonderful story. I think a lot of times when they go to see a movie they probably think, 'Was that worth paying my six bucks for?' On this they will definitely get their money's worth."

"There are lots of moments in the film where it's like, 'Oh, I wrote that, I wrote that,'" says Neil Gaiman. "Occasionally there are lines that I recognise. 'That's my line, I wrote that in the book.' But what I love most is that it feels like the same sense of humour. The same mixture of light and dark. It's got the funny stuff, and it's got the sweet stuff, and it's got the romance, and it's got the horror, and it all seems to be very much that thing that came out of my head back in 1992. I also like the fact that the film has a few surprises for people who know the book."

And all those surprises are revealed in August 2007, when Paramount Pictures releases *Stardust*.

So, as is the tradition in any good fairy tale, all that is left to tell you about Tristan and Yvaine is...

They really did live happily ever after.

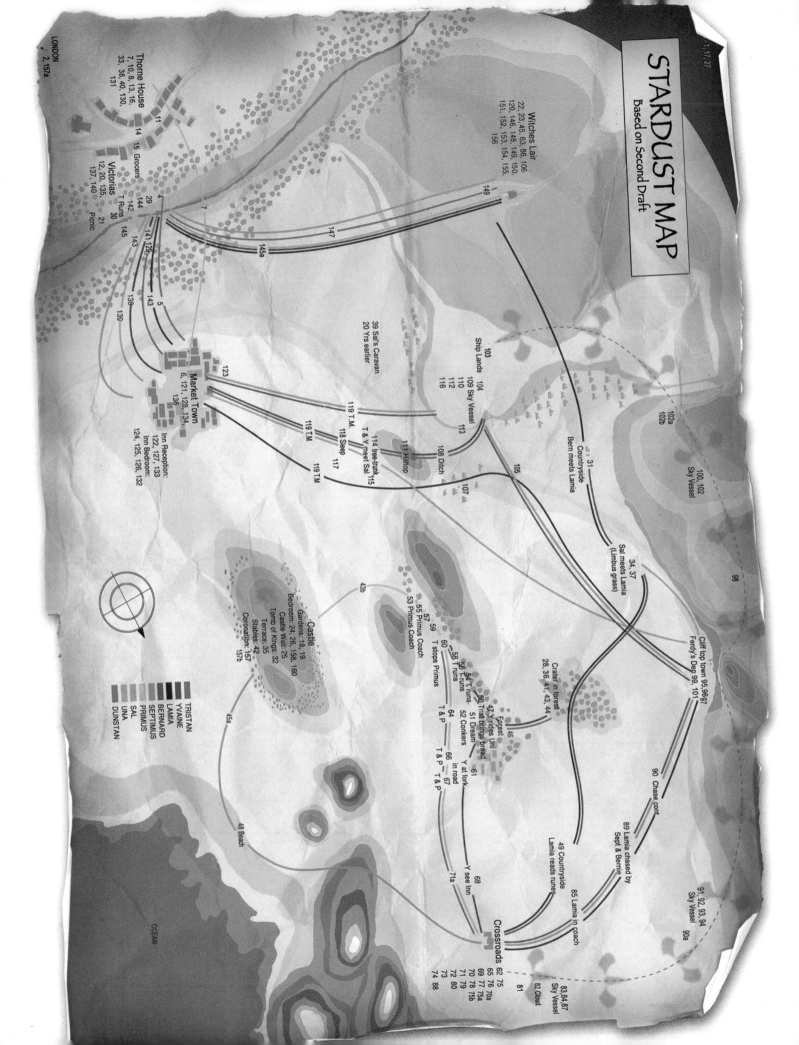

STARDUST

THE
SHOOTING
SCRIPT

EXT. SPACE – NIGHT.

Fade up from black to reveal a beautiful, twinkling STAR in the heavens.

> NARRATOR (V.O.)
> A philosopher once asked: are we human
> because we gaze at the stars or do we
> gaze at them because we are human?
> Pointless really. Do the stars gaze back?
> Now that's a question.

We pan over and find: THE MOON. Tracking back, further and further, we move through the barrel of a telescope.

We follow the beam of the moon's light through the lenses and splitters in the telescope, until finally we see the moon itself again, reflected on a human eye...

INT. ROYAL ACADEMY OF SCIENCE – NIGHT.

...Belonging to a DISTINGUISHED SCHOLAR in Victorian period dress. He gazes through a hulking brass telescope. We pull back to find him at the centre of a vast library, where other ACADEMICS are quietly busy with their own endeavours. A hive of dignified industry.

> NARRATOR (V.O.)
> But I'm getting ahead of myself... Our
> story really begins here, in England.

At a desk by a window, a YOUNG SCIENTIST types a LETTER. Outside, a view of BIG BEN, under construction. The CLOCK FACE is being slowly winched up the tower.

> NARRATOR (V.O.) (CONT'D)
> At the Royal Academy of Science in
> London, where a letter arrived con-
> taining a very strange enquiry. It had
> come from a country boy, and the sci-
> entist who read it thought that it might
> be a practical joke of some kind. But he
> duly wrote a reply, just in case...

The man removes the page from the typewriter and signs off with a flourish.

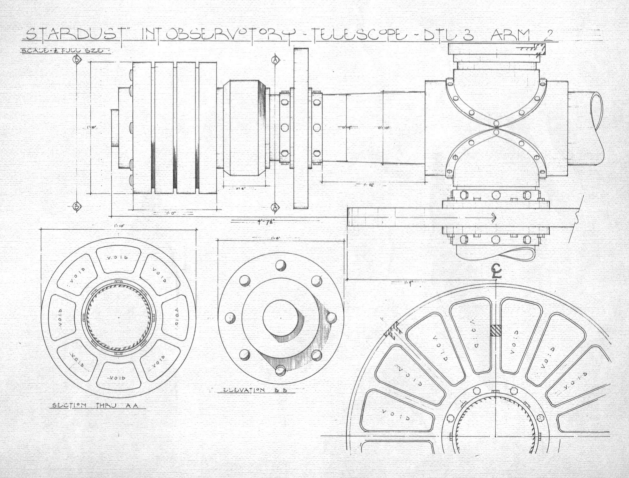

NARRATOR (V.O.) (CONT'D)
...And posted it to the boy, who lived in a village called...

The letter dissolves to...

EXT. WALL VILLAGE – NIGHT.

Lights burn brightly in cottage windows as we soar over a small country hamlet.

NARRATOR (V.O.)
...Wall.

We move over the treetops until we find a clearing bordered by a strange drystone wall of indeterminate length.

NARRATOR (V.O.) (CONT'D)
So named, the boy had said, for the wall that ran alongside it. A wall that, according to local legend, hid an extraordinary secret.

As we swoop down, a gap in the wall becomes apparent. It is here we that find DUNSTAN THORNE, 18, a boy who brings fresh meaning to the word 'awkward'. Resolutely blocking the gap is an elderly and furious GUARD, studying the letter we saw earlier.

GUARD
(reading from the letter, outraged)
"The hy... po... thetical... existence of such a gateway would run contrary to all known laws of science and, in the opinion of myself and my esteemed colleagues, may safely be dismissed merely as colourful rural folklore."
(horrified)
You spoke of the secret to persons outside of the village?

DUNSTAN
Not just persons: Scientists! And guess what? They agree with me! The entire story of the wall and what lies beyond it is fiction. Poppycock. Just as I've always said. And now, if you'll just let me through, I'll prove it to you.

GUARD
I'm charged with guarding the portal to another world and you're asking me to just let you through?!

DUNSTAN
Well... Yes. Because, let's be honest: it's a field. Look. Do you see another world over there? No. You see a field. Do you see anything non-human? No. And you know why? Because it's a field.

GUARD
Hundreds of years, this wall's been here. Hundreds of years, this gap's been under 24-hour guard. I wouldn't move if you brought me a letter from Queen Victoria herself.

DUNSTAN
(suddenly deflated)
Well that's... That sounds rather final. Better just go home, I suppose.

GUARD
(surprised and delighted)
Right, then. Night, Dunstan. Give my best to your father.

Dunstan walks away. Suddenly, he turns and bolts back, rushing past the Guard, through the gap in the wall.

He vanishes into the forest beyond. The Guard is torn: wanting to give chase, too scared to cross the gap.

EXT. STORMHOLD FOREST EDGE – NIGHT.

Dunstan scrambles through the trees. He stops, his expression of triumph melting into total confusion and then awe: beyond the forest is an utterly BIZARRE LANDSCAPE. At its centre, an OTHERWORLDLY MARKET TOWN.

Stalls line the main street and alleyways. STREET CALLS and lugubrious HURDY-GURDY music. Lights in every window. Lanterns and FIREFLIES and coloured SMOKE.

Even from here we can tell that in crossing the wall, Dunstan has not just left his village: he's left the human world altogether and entered an enchanted realm.

EXT. STORMHOLD MARKET TOWN – CONTINUOUS.

A magical festival of weirdness. Spellbound, Dunstan wanders from stall to stall, each selling wares more astonishing than the last – EYE-BALLS in jars; CLOTHES that seem to be made of the night sky; CRYSTAL ANIMALS that turn out – when Dunstan inspects them – to be ALIVE.

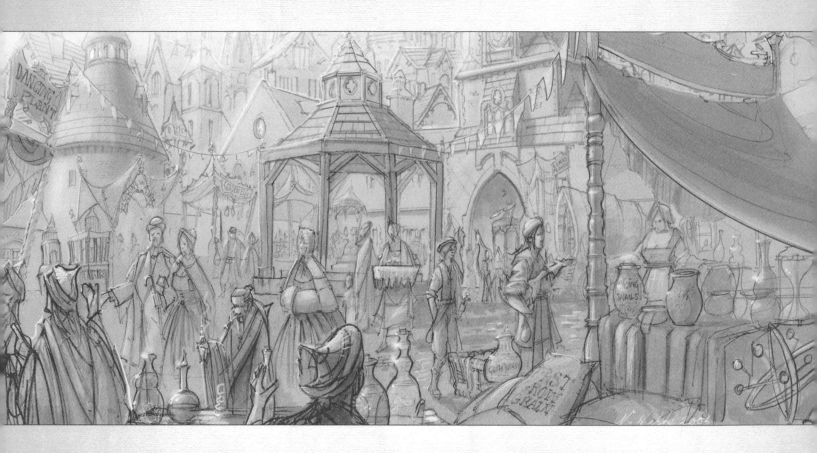

Finally he stops, captivated, by a stall selling an array of amazing GLASS FLOWERS. An ugly old lady, DITCH-WATER SAL, attends the stall. Behind, a stunning SLAVE GIRL lounges on the steps of a YELLOW GYPSY CARAVAN.

Dunstan picks up a glass BLUEBELL. It CHIMES.

> SAL
> I don't deal with time wasters.

Sal sniffs him, a look of distaste clouding her face.

> SAL (CONT'D)
> Especially human ones.
> (to Slave Girl)
> Get over here. Tend the stall. I'm off to the Slaughtered Prince for a pint.

And she's off, making briskly for the inn across the market square. The girl, just a few years older than Dunstan, slips into Sal's place, smiling seductively.

> SLAVE GIRL
> See anything you like?

> DUNSTAN
> (grinning)
> Um... Definitely.

> (then, nervous)
> I mean... I didn't mean... Well, I did, but... What I meant was... That one. The blue one. How much is that?

> SLAVE GIRL
> I can't recall. I think it might be the colour of your hair. Or it might be all of your memories before you were three. I can check, if you like.

Confused, and unable to take his eyes off her, Dunstan rifles in his pocket and brings out three coins.

> DUNSTAN
> This is all I have. Do you have anything I could buy for this?

> SLAVE GIRL
> Hmmm. Let's see...

She strokes her finger round Dunstan's palm, pretending to count the coins, deliberately taking ages. It's a charged moment. She breaks it with comical abruptness.

> SLAVE GIRL (CONT'D)
> No. We don't take money at this stall. Sorry.

She smiles at her little game. Dunstan releases his breath, which he's been holding, and laughs nervously. She picks up a glass SNOWDROP.

> SLAVE GIRL (CONT'D)
> Anyway, you shouldn't buy the blue-bells. Buy this one instead. Snowdrop. It'll bring you luck.

> DUNSTAN
> But... you won't accept money.

> SLAVE GIRL
> This one costs a kiss.

She tucks the snowdrop into Dunstan's pocket and leans over for her payment. He is fearful, but can't resist. It's quite a kiss. He pulls away, dizzy, intoxicated.

Checking that the coast is clear, she takes his hand and leads him to the caravan. He babbles nervously.

> DUNSTAN
> I'm sorry... I don't know your name? Mine's Dunstan. Dunstan Thorne. I come from the village of Wall. On the other side of the... And... God, this is peculiar. You know, I didn't used to believe it was true. About your world. The gap in the wall. I thought it was just a fairy tale. I –

Dunstan stops in his tracks. It's only now that he notices a thin silver CHAIN, attached at the girl's ankle and wrist, snaking away into the caravan.

> SLAVE GIRL
> This? Oh. Yes. I'm a princess tricked into being a witch's slave. Will you liberate me?

She sits on the step as Dunstan studies it. It looks delicate. He yanks it. It turns to iron, unbreakable.

With his POCKET KNIFE, he cuts through the chain like butter. It repairs itself immediately.

Exasperated, he pulls a large loop into his hand, cuts, and jerks it quickly away. He's left with the length of chain in his hand, but the missing section regenerates as we watch, broken ends running together like mercury.

> DUNSTAN
> Wait a minute, is this another one of your jokes?

The girl nods sheepishly.

> DUNSTAN (CONT'D)
> You're not really a princess.

> SLAVE GIRL
> I am!

> DUNSTAN
> That old woman isn't really a witch?

> SLAVE GIRL
> No, no. She is. Horrible.

> DUNSTAN
> So what's the joke?

> SLAVE GIRL
> Just the part about liberating me. You can't. It's an enchanted chain. I'll only be free when she dies. Sorry. It wasn't that funny. I don't get out much. As you can imagine.

> DUNSTAN
> If I can't liberate you, what do you want of me?

She smiles coquettishly. Dazed, Dunstan goes to kiss her. She pulls him into the caravan, closes the door.

EXT. STORMHOLD/WALL – MOVING SHOT – NIGHT.

The camera rises off the door and floats high above the forest. From here, we can clearly see the two worlds on either side of the wall.

> NARRATOR (V.O.)
> If a human boy had ever before been seduced by a Stormhold girl, the story of the event has been long forgotten. But although Dunstan returned home that night to his life in Wall, he would not soon forget.

Autumn leaves blow across our field of vision, and snow begins to fall.

> NARRATOR (V.O.) (CONT'D)
> For nine months later, he received an unexpected souvenir.

We move down through the snow-covered Wall village...

EXT. THORNE HOUSE – CONTINUOUS.

...Until we come to Dunstan's door. A hand knocks. The door opens to reveal Dunstan, and we see that the hand belongs to the old Guard, who is holding a MOSES BASKET. Inside it: a BABY. And a small PACKAGE marked "TRISTAN THORNE, CARE OF DUNSTAN THORNE."

> GUARD
> This was left for you at the wall. Says here his name is Tristan.

The Guard thrusts the basket at Dunstan and they stand staring at one another awkwardly for a time before a shell-shocked Dunstan, basket in hand, closes the door.

Off the door, the camera tilts to the starry night sky...

CREDITS.

...Our iconic shot of the single unique star. Other stars appear, clustering together to form the word "STARDUST".

We tilt back down. And once more, we are at...

EXT. DUNSTAN'S HOUSE – NIGHT.

The door opens to reveal Dunstan's son, TRISTAN, 18. He has his father's awkwardness. Also his mother's good looks, but he hasn't yet figured out how to show them off. He's holding a small bunch of wildflowers.

> NARRATOR
> Eighteen years passed, and the baby Tristan grew up knowing nothing of his unconventional heritage.

EXT. WALL VILLAGE – MOMENTS LATER.

Tristan walks through the village. It's deserted.

> NARRATOR
> But never mind how the infant became a boy. This is the story of how Tristan Thorne becomes a man. A much greater challenge altogether. For to achieve it, he must win the heart of his one true love.

EXT. VICTORIA'S HOUSE – NIGHT.

He arrives at a rather nice cottage. Through an upper window, we see a pretty girl, VICTORIA FORESTER, 20, holding court among a group of girls.

Tristan throws a stone at the window. They twitter.

> GIRLS (O.S.)
> It's him! It's him!

Victoria comes to the window.

> VICTORIA
> Humphrey?

> TRISTAN
> No, it's Tristan.

> VICTORIA
> Oh. Did I leave something at the shop?

> TRISTAN
> No, no, I –

Seemingly out of nowhere, A SILVER CANE flies into view and – THWACK! – all the heads are off Tristan's flowers, leaving him holding just the stems.

He wheels round to see: HUMPHREY, 23 – lantern-jawed, expensively dressed, oozing confidence. Huge bunch of flowers. Every boy's nightmare.

HUMPHREY

Tristan Thorne. Shop boy by day, peep-
ing tom by night. Is there no end to your
charms?

Now Victoria has been joined at the window by all
her girlfriends. Some giggle at Humphrey's remark.

VICTORIA

Humphrey, there's no need to be like
that. Be nice to the poor boy.

HUMPHREY
(to Tristan, faux-sympathetic re: flowers)
Ah. Were those for Victoria?

Goaded into action, Tristan picks up a stick and
tries to behead Humphrey's bouquet in retalia-
tion. Humphrey slips immediately into Errol
Flynn mode, parrying expertly.

A cane/stick fight begins. It doesn't last long.
With a few deft strokes, Humphrey has the stick
out of Tristan's hand. A couple more and
Tristan's on the ground, on his back, the cane at
his neck.

HUMPHREY (CONT'D)
You were always useless at fencing at
school, Tristan. In fact, I'm having trouble remembering if there was anything
you were good at.

TRISTAN
Let me up.

HUMPHREY
What's the magic word?

Up at the window, the girls giggle.

TRISTAN
(mumbling)
Please.

HUMPHREY
Can't hear you.

TRISTAN
Please.

Victoria opens her door and looks disapproving-
ly at Humphrey. He frees Tristan and walks into
the house. Victoria peers past him, at Tristan,
with some concern.

VICTORIA
(calling to Tristan)
Are you alright?

Tristan, still on the ground, beams at her cheerfully.

TRISTAN
Oh yes. Fine.

Victoria mouths "sorry" and shuts the door.
Inside, we hear more girlish LAUGHTER.
Outside, Tristan struggles to his feet, his head-
less flowers scattered around him in the dirt.

INT. THORNE HOUSE – KITCHEN – DAY.

The perfect cosy cottage kitchen. Dunstan is
breakfasting as Tristan dashes down the stairs,
coat on, hurried.

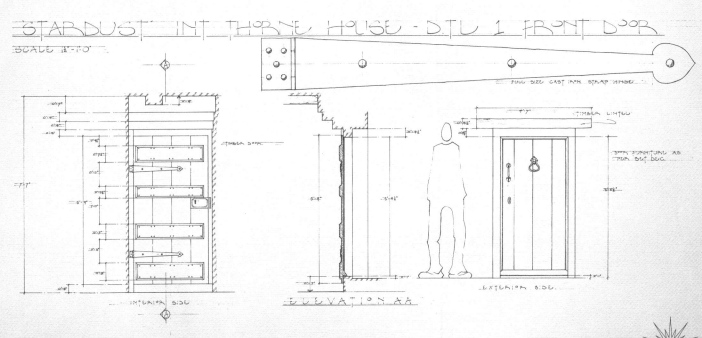

DUNSTAN
Don't you want any breakfast?

TRISTAN
No thanks, father. I'll be late for work.

Tristan opens the door and goes to leave.

DUNSTAN
Are you alright?

TRISTAN
Fine. Why?

DUNSTAN
I don't know... Last night... Did it go... okay?

TRISTAN
(slightly unconvincing)
What? Oh. Yes. Victoria – definitely. Wonderful.

And he's gone. Leaving Dunstan looking concerned.

EXT. WALL VILLAGE STREET – DAY.

The radiant Victoria glides toward a small grocery store. A sign reads: "MONDAY AND SONS GROCERS"

INT. VILLAGE GROCERY SHOP – DAY.

The grocer, MR MONDAY, bustles. Tristan, in an apron, helps a customer, an important-looking middle-aged lady. Victoria enters and, ignoring the long queue, walks to the counter, smiling winsomely.

VICTORIA
Hello Tristan. Pound of sugar, please?

Tristan abandons his customer and runs to fetch the sugar. Mr Monday, not happy, steps in to attend to the increasingly irritated customer. Tristan returns.

TRISTAN
Victoria, I –

VICTORIA
Let's see... Bag of flour. Dozen eggs.
(as he fetches her goods)
Look, I'm sorry about last night. Humphrey was very rude. I also need a sack of potatoes and a pound of butter.

Tristan heaves the sacks of potatoes onto the counter.

TRISTAN
May I see you tonight perhaps?

She looks at the incredibly heavy groceries.

VICTORIA
No. But you may walk me home.

In a love-struck daze, Tristan leaves, proudly hefting the bags. Mr Monday and the queue watch, open-mouthed.

INT. THORNE HOUSE – DUSK.

Tristan uses a large hanging copper pan as a mirror, in which he is practising various poses and demeanours.

TRISTAN
(cheerful)
Father! I lost my job!
(casual)
Oh. Father. Yeah. Hi. Lost my job. Anyway.
(sobbing hysterically)
Father! I l-l-lost my jo-ho-ho-hob! Gaahhh!
(serious)
Father, look –

He is interrupted by Dunstan clearing his throat. It would seem he's been here for some time.

DUNSTAN
You lost your job. Yes. So I heard.

Tristan leans his head against the wall, downcast.

TRISTAN
Well at least that saves me having to choose which way to tell you.

DUNSTAN
Yes, that would have been hard. They were all so good.

TRISTAN
I'm sorry. I'm so sorry. Maybe Mr Monday was right. Maybe I am deluding myself. I'll never be good enough for Victoria. I should just give up.

DUNSTAN
(softening)
He said that? That's poppycock.

TRISTAN

You really want to know how it went last night? Not good. Humphrey turned up.

DUNSTAN

Humphrey?! The man's an ass.

TRISTAN

Victoria seems to think otherwise. I'm wasting my time.

DUNSTAN

Oh Tristan, no...

TRISTAN

What, you're saying I'm not?

DUNSTAN

Do I think it's a waste of time refusing to settle for someone else because the person you love isn't available?
(gesturing around)
I'd say you're asking the wrong person.

TRISTAN

You know it's not the same thing. Victoria's... alive. She just doesn't want me. I'm not like Humphrey. I'm not like any of them. I don't know why I try to be. I'm not.

DUNSTAN

Tristan, with the benefit of my years, I can tell you that all the men I ever envied as a boy have lived unremarkable lives. So you don't fit with the popular crowd? I'd take that as a very good omen.

The camera floats through the window and tilts up to the starry sky – our iconic shot. Over this, we hear the voices of a young woman, YVAINE, and a little girl, CELESTE. We're not sure where they are coming from.

CELESTE (V.O.)

Yvaine! Not again! You're too close! Go back.

YVAINE (V.O.)

Oh, come on Celeste. It's just getting good.

EXT. STARS' POV SEQUENCE – CONTINUOUS.

From space, we see Earth. We then pull focus into...

EXT. A TREE TRUNK – DUSK.

STARDUST

In C.U., we see a MOUSE shinning up a tree, painfully slowly.

> CELESTE (V.O.)
> Where? What? The mouse? You're risking mother's wrath to watch a mouse?

> YVAINE (V.O.)
> He's not really a mouse. He's a goblin lord. Under a curse by a jealous warlock who coveted his bride. The only way he can turn back is by eating a nut grown in the shadow of the Palace of Stormhold.

We pull back to reveal vast, strange royal gardens. Yvaine hams it up softly, bedtime-story style.

> YVAINE (V.O.) (CONT'D)
> For fifty years he's searched. Took him a decade just to scale Mount Huon. And now, at last, he's arrived at the Stormhold Palace and spied a wondrous tree. On it, a single nut. His quest is at an end.

In C.U. we see the mouse continue his arduous climb.

> CELESTE (V.O.)
> Will he get to be a lord again?

> YVAINE (V.O.)
> Uh-huh. He'll eat the nut, and he'll be transformed. Watch. Then he'll go back to his own kingdom, and reclaim his goblin bride and live happily ever after.

We pan up to see a single golden NUT. The mouse's tiny hand reaches out for the nut, fingers wriggling. Suddenly an OWL swoops down and snatches the mouse in its beak. CRUNCH. He flies off, the mouse's tail flapping freely in the wind. Celeste bursts into tears.

> CELESTE (V.O.)
> I hate you! I hate your horrid stories!

> YVAINE (V.O.)
> I'm sorry! I didn't know that would happen! Let's watch something else? The King of all of Stormhold is about to die and all his sons want the throne?

> CELESTE (V.O.)
> Forget it! I'm telling mother!

> YVAINE (V.O.)
> Fine, tell her! I'm sick of being told what

to do. For god's sake. I'm 30 million years old.

EXT. STORMHOLD PALACE GARDENS – DUSK.

By the nut tree, SEPTIMUS, a smug and evil-looking prince, watches a carriage arrive. Absent mindedly, he plucks the nut from the tree and goes to eat it. Noting that the nut looks a bit funny, he shrugs and tosses it away. On his hand is an ornate tattooed "7".

His brother, PRIMUS, climbs from the carriage. He is older, though less self-assured. If we were to glimpse his hand, we'd see a tattoo of the numeral "1".

> PRIMUS
> (anxious)
> What news of our father?

> SEPTIMUS
> (smiling)
> They tell me he is fading fast.

As they walk towards the Palace, we notice the owl, circling above. Suddenly – SQUIT – owl droppings splatter onto Primus' head. Septimus smirks.

> PRIMUS
> A good omen, they say in some parts.

> SEPTIMUS
> But in these parts, my dear brother, merely further proof that of the seven of us, you were always the unluckiest.

The princes arrive at the Palace doors. Two guardsmen bow and go to open them when suddenly they're flung open from inside. Another prince, TERTIUS, dashes out.

> TERTIUS
> Primus! Septimus! Where have you been?! Hurry! Our father is dying!

Septimus pushes past him.

> SEPTIMUS
> And about bloody time, too.

EXT. VICTORIA'S HOUSE – NIGHT.

A stone hits Victoria's window. She opens it.

VICTORIA
Tristan? I clearly said –

TRISTAN
I know. You told me not to come. But I
have something for you. A surprise.

She goes back in, leaving Tristan deflated.
Moments later, however, she appears at the front
door.

VICTORIA
It's not my birthday for another week,
you know.

**EXT. A FIELD NEAR THE WALL – MINUTES
LATER.**

Tristan leads Victoria, her eyes closed. He halts
and she opens them to see: a beautiful PICNIC.
Candles flicker, a cornucopia of food on display. It
takes her breath away. He opens a bottle of champagne and pours.

VICTORIA
I've never had champagne before.

TRISTAN
Me neither.

They drink, smiling at one another. A shared
moment.

VICTORIA
God, this is delicious.

They laugh, delighted. Then her smile fades.

VICTORIA (CONT'D)
Wait, how did you... How could a shop
boy afford all this?

TRISTAN
(stung, trying to hide it)
I'm not a shop boy.

VICTORIA
I know. I heard the news. I'm awfully
sorry for you. What will you do now?

TRISTAN
No, I mean, I'm not a shop boy. I was
just... working in a shop. And now I'm
free to live my life as I truly wish.

VICTORIA
(not really listening)
This... must have been all your savings.

TRISTAN
I can make more! That's the beauty of it!
I never intended to stay in Wall. I'm
going to make my fortune. There's a big
world out there, Victoria.

VICTORIA
You sound just like Humphrey! He's
quite a traveller. I've heard he's going all
the way to Ipswich just to buy me a ring.

TRISTAN
Ipswich? Victoria, I'm talking about
London! Or Paris! Or, or... Wait a minute
– a ring? What kind of ring?

VICTORIA
(happy and conspiratorial)
Word is, he's planning to propose to me
on my birthday.

TRISTAN
He's... And you're going to say "yes"?

VICTORIA
Well I can't very well say no after he's
gone all the way to Ipswich!

TRISTAN
All the...? Ipswich?! Victoria, for your
hand in marriage, I'd cross oceans.
Continents.

VICTORIA
Really?

TRISTAN
For your hand? I'd go to the gold fields of
San Francisco and bring back your
weight in gold.

She laughs and leans in a little closer, her interest piqued. Tristan senses he's onto something.

TRISTAN (CONT'D)
I'd go to Africa and bring you back a
diamond as big as your fist!

Victoria moves closer still.

TRISTAN (CONT'D)
I'd go to the Arctic and I'd, I'd... slaugh-
ter a polar bear! And bring you back its
head!

VICTORIA
(rearing away in alarm)
A polar bear's head??

Tristan curses under his breath. An awkward silence.

TRISTAN
I'm serious you know.

VICTORIA
About the polar bear's head?

TRISTAN
No. About marrying you.

VICTORIA
(affectionately)
You're funny, Tristan. But people like you and people like me, we're just not...
(more awkward silence)
You know, I really should be getting home soon. It's late.

TRISTAN
(brightly, trying to conceal that his dreams are crushed)
Shall we at least finish the champagne?

She shrugs – why not? – and holds out her glass.

We tilt up to the starry sky and move swiftly over the wall and across the strange Stormhold landscape.

NARRATOR
Had Tristan known then how the stars watched Earth, he'd have shuddered at the very thought of an audience to his humiliation. But fortunately for him, nearly every star in the sky was, at that moment, looking in earnest at the land on the other side of the wall, where the King of all Stormhold lay on his deathbed. Which was a coincidence, because it was the King's final act that would change the course of Tristan's destiny forever.

Soaring above the Stormhold Palace, we plunge down towards a domed glass roof and into...

INT. KING'S BEDROOM – NIGHT.

A lavish chamber. The KING OF STORMHOLD lies on his deathbed. Beside him are Primus, Septimus and Tertius. Behind him, three shadowy figures.

The King looks weakly up at his sons.

KING
Where is Secundus?

PRIMUS
He's on his way, father.

KING
Then we shall wait.

A beat. Then a LOUD BANG, and the bedchamber doors fly open to reveal: SECUNDUS. The archetypal Prince Charming.

SECUNDUS
Sorry I'm late, father. I came as swiftly as I was able.
(nodding to his brothers)
Septimus. Tertius. Primus.

KING
(beaming at him)
At last. Now we may begin.
(businesslike, now)
I trust you have prepared the hall of ancestors for the arrival of my remains?
(off their nodding)
Good. So. To the matter of succession. Not so well prepared there, were you? Of my seven sons, there are four of you today still standing. This is quite a break with tradition. I had twelve brothers and –

SEPTIMUS
You had killed all of them for your throne long before your father the king even started to feel poorly. We know. You are strong, father. And courageous.

KING
And cunning. Most importantly, cunning. Secundus. Look out of the window. Tell me what you see.

Secundus does as he is asked.

SECUNDUS
I see the kingdom. All of Stormhold.

KING
And?

SECUNDUS
(hopefully)
My kingdom?

KING
Maybe. Look up.

He does, and we see his POV: the iconic shot of the sky. As he tries to figure out what he's supposed to be looking at, the King grins at Septimus, who calmly walks over and pushes Secundus out of the window.

EXT. STORMHOLD CASTLE - CONTINUOUS.

We are now with Secundus as he plummets to his death. Just as he is about to hit the ground, we cut back to:

INT. KING'S BEDROOM - MOMENTS LATER.

Beside the shadowy figures, Secundus suddenly appears, dishevelled and grey, with a slightly flat face.

We now clearly see that the shadowy figures are actually DECOMPOSING GHOSTS. They are, in fact, the King's other sons: QUINTUS, QUARTUS and SEXTUS. Sextus is horribly charred, Quartus appears frozen and Quintus has a huge hatchet buried in his head. Where we see dry blood, it is a deep royal blue.

Secundus appears, frantically feeling at his squashed face, horrified at the obvious damage.

> QUINTUS
> Can't believe you fell for that!

> QUARTUS
> Sucker!

> SECUNDUS
> (pleased but puzzled)
> Sextus? Quartus? Quintus? You're... alive?

They all shake their heads and raise their eyebrows.

> SECUNDUS (CONT'D)
> You're all...?

They all nod.

> SEXTUS
> Stuck like this 'til a new king is crowned.

> SECUNDUS
> I was that close.

> QUARTUS
> Ah well. At least you still have your looks.

SECUNDUS

Oh please. You're not still annoyed about the whole murder thing, are you? That was ten years ago!

QUARTUS

And a great deal of good it did you killing me, didn't it, Secundus? Now you're king of all Stormhold. Oh no. You're not. My mistake. You're dead.

SEXTUS

Please! Can we all just settle down? I have the worst headache.

QUINTUS

Can I just say, I beg to differ.

From the King's rather hazy POV, the vague figures of Primus, Tertius and Septimus drift in and out of focus. The King reaches out to the figure closest to him.

KING

Una? Is that you?

TERTIUS

Um... no, father. It's me. Tertius.

KING
(disappointed)
Oh. Then where is your sister?

PRIMUS

I'm sorry father. No one has seen Una for years now.

KING
("Who's a naughty boy then?")
Septimus?

SEPTIMUS
(indignant)
What?!

KING

Tradition dictates that the throne must pass to a male heir.

SEPTIMUS

Exactly! Why would I waste my time killing my sister when so many of my cretinous brothers are still alive?!

KING

Indeed. Which is why we shall resolve the situation in a non-traditional manner.

The King removes his ruby pendant. In his hands, the stone turns even redder, glowing. He lets it go: to everyone's amazement, it FLOATS before him, losing its colour and turning moonstone-white as he speaks.

> KING (CONT'D)
> Only he of royal blood can restore the ruby. And the one of you who does so shall be the new king of Stormhold.

The King lies back and closes his eyes. The three living brothers look anxiously at one another, all about to lunge and snatch the pendant from the air. But as they go to move, it JOLTS into motion and HURTLES out of the window, high into the sky.

EXT. SKY – CONTINUOUS.

We follow the pendant as it speeds through the night sky, until, amid the star-peppered blackness, there's a huge EXPLOSION and a burning, meteoric mass begins to hurtle downwards, along with the pendant.

We follow it down towards Earth. As we gain distance and perspective, it becomes apparent that our fireball is a falling star.

EXT. A FIELD NEAR THE WALL – NIGHT.

More awkward silence between Tristan and Victoria. They stare up at the stars as they sip their drinks. Tristan tries to make conversation.

> TRISTAN
> Um... Did you know... An interesting fact, actually... The first champagne glass was actually modelled on the left breast of Marie Antoinette?
> (hideous silence)
> I don't know if there was something wrong with her right one. Probably not, though. Probably just... Anyway.

Suddenly a SHOOTING STAR streaks across the sky and falls way beyond the wall in the distance. An astonishing sight.

> VICTORIA
> A shooting star! Oh Tristan, how beautiful!

> TRISTAN
> More beautiful than a fancy ring from Ipswich?

Victoria giggles.

> TRISTAN (CONT'D)
> (serious – his last chance)
> For your hand in marriage, I'd cross the wall and bring you back that fallen star.

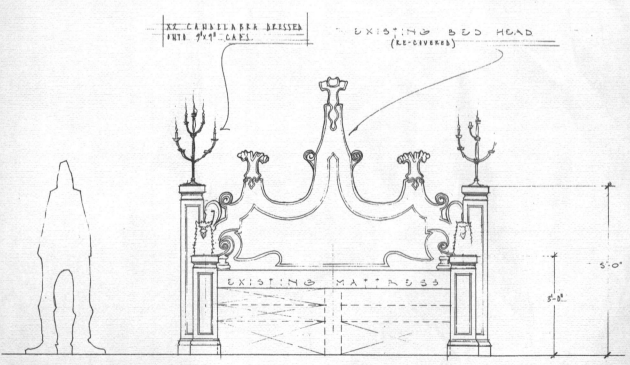

FRONT ELEVATION

VICTORIA
You can't cross the wall! No one crosses the wall. Now you're just being silly.

TRISTAN
I'm not. I'd do it. For you, I'd do anything.

VICTORIA
Tristan, you're drunk.

TRISTAN
Yes I am. And so are you.

VICTORIA
Hmmm. My very own star. It seems that we have ourselves an agreement.

She raises her glass. With barely contained excitement and disbelief, he hurriedly fishes his own empty glass from the picnic basket and clicks it against hers.

EXT. STORMHOLD LANDSCAPE – NIGHT.

In the sky overhead, the shooting star continues its journey, getting ever closer to Earth. As we watch it soar over a curious-looking canyon, we realise we are looking over the shoulder of an old woman. She is LAMIA: the most deeply scary old witch we have ever seen.

Excited, she wheels around and hurries back towards to her lair at the bottom of the canyon.

EXT. STORMHOLD LANDSCAPE – NIGHT.

The star's journey continues over mountains and treetops, getting closer and closer to the ground before finally reaching the moment of impact with a massive EXPLOSION that kicks up a towering cloud of dusty earth.

Tracking low through the forest, we pass through swathes of burned trees towards the smoking crater it has created.

All is quiet as we track toward the epicentre to find: YVAINE. Ethereal, heart-stoppingly beautiful and somewhat startled by her fall. Nearby, the King's pendant lies smouldering.

INT. WITCHES' LAIR – NIGHT.

Lamia bursts into the shabby, cobwebbed entrance hall of her lair, a dimly-lit jumble of once-stately furniture. Here, in an equal state of disarray and disintegration, her sisters MORMO and EMPUSA lie asleep in a mangy four-poster bed.

LAMIA
Mormo! Empusa! Wake up!

They stir; sleepy, confused and irritated.

EMPUSA
What is it?

LAMIA
A star has fallen!

This news snaps them from their stupor. They clamber to their feet and all three hurry into the depths of the lair.

Lamia throws open a cupboard, finds it empty.

LAMIA (CONT'D)
Where are the Babylon candles?!

MORMO
You used the last one, Lamia. Two hundred years ago. Do you not recall?

Lamia cries out in fury.

EMPUSA
Perhaps we can obtain another?

LAMIA
You speak as if such things are freely available, Empusa.

EMPUSA
I know, sister, I merely thought –

LAMIA
You'd have us hunting for a Babylon candle while some other witch finds our star? Fool! There's no time to waste. If we must retrieve it on foot, then we shall.
(turning her back on Empusa)
Mormo! We need information!

From a large bank of CAGES containing various animals, Mormo grabs a STOAT, and hurries away again.

She joins her sisters at a table. As they crowd around, we see the glint of a BLACK BLADE. When finally we get a clear view, they're analyzing the stoat's ENTRAILS.

LAMIA (CONT'D)
If these divinations are correct, the fallen star lies 100 miles away.

EMPUSA
Four centuries, we've waited for this! What hardship a few more days?

MORMO
Which of us shall go, then, to seek it and bring it back?

They all shut their eyes and rummage, as in a lucky dip, before disgustingly holding stoat organs aloft.

MORMO (CONT'D)
I've his kidney.

EMPUSA
I've his liver.

LAMIA
(satisfied)
And I've his heart.

EMPUSA
You'll be needing some years.

They walk to a rusted IRON BOX bound by three cords, each with a distinctive knot. Each witch touches one, and the cords untie themselves and fall away. They open the box. Inside, something golden SHINES brightly.

LAMIA
There's not much left. It is as well that we have found a new one.

MORMO
Soon there will be plenty for us all.

The golden-something seems to avoid Lamia's hand as she reaches in. Finally she grasps it. Then, she eats it.

Lamia rushes over to a large freestanding MIRROR. As Mormo and Empusa look on, she TRANSFORMS into a beautiful woman in her 30s.

All three admire her splendid new body as she tears off her ragged clothes.

EXT. WALL VILLAGE OUTSKIRTS - NIGHT.

Tristan approaches the gap in the wall, just like his father did. The same old man is here, now even older.

GUARD
Dunstan Thorne? Not again?!

TRISTAN
Erm, it's Tristan, actually.

GUARD
Oh. You do look a bit like your father. And I suppose you intend to cross the wall as well, do you? Well you can forget it. Go home.

TRISTAN
Cross the wall as well as who?

GUARD
(flustered)

No one. Nobody. Nobody crosses the wall. You know that. Everybody knows that.

TRISTAN

Oh no, no. Of course. Nobody. I'd better just head for the old homestead, then.

He turns and begins to walk away, just as Dunstan did.

GUARD

Right, then. Night, Tristan. Give my best to your father.

And just as we expect, Tristan turns and bolts back, towards the Guard. But, to his amazement, the feeble old Guard leaps into action, springing improbably over the wall to intercept him before expertly kicking the living daylights out of him.

Once he's certain that Tristan has had enough, the Guard leans over him, smiling sweetly.

GUARD (CONT'D)

Off you go.

And Tristan limps away.

MONTAGE – TRISTAN TRIES TO CLIMB THE WALL.

— At another section of wall, a bruised Tristan begins to climb. He stops, puzzled at his lack of progress. Pull back to see: the wall GROWING higher and higher. Finally, exhausted, he drops to the ground.

— Tristan is back, prepared: a rope round his waist, a heavy iron hook. He slings it over the wall (now back to its normal height) and climbs, pleased with himself until: all the stones RETRACT, leaving a perfectly smooth surface. He claws desperately for purchase, drops to the ground. The rope and hook fall onto him.

— He returns with A WOODEN LADDER, places it against the wall and starts to climb. Soon, he's concerned by a SIZZLING sound and wafts of SMOKE in the air. The wall begins to GLOW red hot and the ladder smokes ominously before – WOOF! – bursting into flames. Tristan leaps off with a shriek. He frantically pats his singed hands and watches his ladder collapse into a pile of ash.

— Back, kitted out with HEAVY BOOTS, SPIKED CRAMPONS, CLIMBING HOOKS and a large CUSHION tied to his back, Tristan gingerly touches the wall. No apparent sign of heat. He touches it again. Huge, lethal metal SPIKES shoot out – WHOOMPH! – missing him by inches. He slopes off, defeated.

INT. THORNE HOUSE – KITCHEN – NIGHT.

Tristan seated, a raw steak on his eye. Dunstan enters.

DUNSTAN

I thought I heard you come in. What happened? Are you hurt?

TRISTAN

No, nothing. I'm fine.

DUNSTAN

In that case I really should teach you how to cook a steak one of these days.
(a beat, then:)
Humphrey again?

TRISTAN

If you must know, it was the Guard. The Guard at the wall.

Dunstan notes his cuts, bruises, shredded clothes.

DUNSTAN

Tristan, he's 97.

TRISTAN

Well, that's given him plenty of time to practise, I suppose. Anyway, it wasn't just him. It was... No, forget it. You wouldn't believe me anyway.

DUNSTAN

Try me.

TRISTAN

It was the wall.

DUNSTAN

And may I ask why you were trying to cross the wall?

Tristan removes the steak, fixes him with a look.

TRISTAN

I might ask you the same thing.

EXT. CRATER – NIGHT.

Still dazed from her fall, Yvaine sits up slowly and takes in her surroundings.

As she gazes around, she notices the King's pendant. Curious, she reaches for it, studying it briefly before deciding – why not? – to put it on.

INT. THORNE HOUSE – ATTIC – NIGHT.

Dunstan and Tristan sit. Before them is the Moses basket.

> TRISTAN
> I... have a mother. I have a mother. I mean... she could still be alive.

> DUNSTAN
> I hope so. I like to think so.
> (a beat)
> You alright?

> TRISTAN
> It's a lot to take in.

> DUNSTAN
> I know. I mean, I can't begin to imagine. I hope you can forgive me for hiding the truth... The people of this village are... I just wanted the best for you.

Dunstan pushes the basket towards Tristan. He reaches in and finds some CHAIN and the GLASS FLOWER.

> TRISTAN
> The chain you cut... Just as you told me. And the flower! The glass flower she sold to you.

> DUNSTAN
> She said it would bring me luck. I know she'd want you to have it.

He tucks it into his buttonhole and touches it tenderly.

> TRISTAN
> She could be... out there. Somewhere. Do you ever... think about that?

> DUNSTAN
> Every day.
> (an awkward silence, then:)
> This was in the basket. I've never opened it. It's addressed to you.

Dunstan hands Tristan the PACKAGE, addressed to him and nods to him to unwrap it. Inside: a CANDLE, and a NOTE.

EXT. SAL'S CARAVAN – 20 YEARS AGO.

The Slave Girl sits scribbling the note, occasionally stopping to wipe away a tear or glance lovingly at the basket by her feet. Ditch-Water Sal potters nearby, now and again casting a cold eye on her.

> SLAVE GIRL (V.O.)
> My dearest Tristan, please know that I only ever wanted the best for you. Had my mistress allowed it, I would have kept you in a heartbeat. I hope you will understand and forgive me. My dearest wish is that we will meet someday, but I urge you to understand that Stormhold is a dangerous place, and more dangerous still for a boy of your bloodline. The safest way to travel is by candlelight.

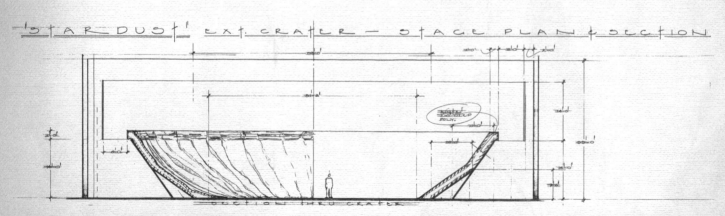

Checking that Sal isn't looking, the girl pops open a secret compartment. Inside are a number of curious looking magical items. She quickly sneaks out the partly used candle and slips it into a package, along with the note, and pops this into the basket.

INT. THORNE HOUSE – ATTIC – NIGHT.

Tristan, reading the letter, clearly moved. Instinctively, he reaches out to touch the candle.

> SLAVE GIRL (V.O.)
> Guard this candle well. To use it, think of me and only me... But believe me darling when I say that even if you choose never to use it, I will think of you every day, for always... Your mother.

> TRISTAN
> Well, do you have a light?

Dunstan passes Tristan a match. Tristan stares into his eyes, clutching the candle. They exchange grins and Tristan lights it. There is a loud rush of air – WHOOSH! – and Tristan vanishes. Dunstan stands alone, grin melting into slack-jawed shock as reality sets in.

EXT. CRATER – NIGHT.

Slowly, painfully, Yvaine struggles to her feet. Gingerly, she straightens up, drained but proud of her efforts. Suddenly, a loud NOISE.

She looks up to see a bright LIGHT. Her smile turns to a scream as it hurtles towards her, finally smashing into her, sending her rolling across the ground. The light fades to reveal an extremely shocked Tristan.

> TRISTAN
> Mother?

Yvaine glares, incredulous, in agony, too angry to speak. Tristan can't believe his reunion with his birth mother has got off to quite such an appalling start.

> TRISTAN (CONT'D)
> Oh no! I'm sorry. I am so, so sorry! I used the candle you gave me, you see, and, oh mother, are you alright?

> YVAINE
> No I'm not. And I'm not your mother. So get off me.

> TRISTAN
> You're not my mother.

> YVAINE
> Do I look like I'm your mother?

Tristan gets up, concerned despite his embarrassment.

> TRISTAN
> Are you... Do you need some help?

> YVAINE
> Yes please. You can help by leaving me alone.

He wanders away, surveying the vast crater. Something hits him and he begins to mutter excitedly.

> TRISTAN
> Oh my god, this must be where... "Light the candle and think of me..." I was thinking of mother... But then, Victoria, the star, just popped... I'm such a –

But he can't berate himself for long – this is where he really wanted to be. He runs back to Yvaine.

> TRISTAN (CONT'D)
> Excuse me, miss, this may seem odd, but: have you seen a fallen star?

> YVAINE
> Oh, you're funny.

> TRISTAN
> No, really. The crater... This must be where it fell.

> YVAINE
> Yeah, this is where it fell. Or if you want to be really specific, up there is where this big weird bloody necklace came out of nowhere and knocked it out of the heavens when it was minding its own business. Over there is where it landed. Very heavily. Breaking its right leg. And right here? This is where it got hit by a magical flying moron.

He's so surprised by the oddness of the revelation, and glad to have found her, he barely notices her fury.

> TRISTAN
> You're a...? Really? I had no idea you'd be a... Well, I apologize for any inconvenience,

but you're coming with me. Back to my village, on the other side of the wall! The
human side! You're going to be a birthday
gift for my true love!

He offers her a hand up. She stares at it.
Impatient, he tries to lift her, but she makes herself as heavy as possible. He gives up, frustrated.

YVAINE
Seems like you'd better start looking for
another birthday present.

Tristan frowns and fishes around in his pocket.

TRISTAN
May I just say in advance, that I'm very
sorry.

YVAINE
Sorry for what?

TRISTAN
For this.

With uncharacteristic deftness, Tristan ties the
silver chain around Yvaine's wrist. She glares at
him, aghast.

TRISTAN (CONT'D)
I think this means you have to come
with me, wherever I want, until I set you
free. Or die.

Yvaine
Don't tempt me.

Tristan ties the other end to his own wrist.
Yvaine struggles away from him. As when we
saw it before, the chain turns from it's fluid-
looking state to iron.

TRISTAN
See? I'm sorry, but you've no choice but
to return with me to my Victoria.

YVAINE
Ah. But of course. Nothing says romance
like the gift of a kidnapped, injured
woman.

TRISTAN
Come on, get up.

YVAINE
I've got a broken leg!

Tristan stares furiously at Yvaine. Finally he

picks her up. She scratches his face. Shocked, he
drops her.

He slumps down beside her and they sit in stony
silence. This is going to be much, much harder
than he thought.

INT. BISHOP'S CHAMBERS – NIGHT.

The King's COFFIN stands in state; his crown, on
a regal cushion, is displayed atop it. Primus is
here, kneeling beside the coffin in reverent
prayer, watched by an agitated BISHOP.

BISHOP
(shooing him)
Hurry on your way now, Primus.

PRIMUS
I'm going, I'm going.

BISHOP
You have a stone to find.
(conspiratorial)
I should like to see you take the throne.
The first benevolent king. I don't doubt
that Stormhold would be a better place
under your rule.

The door bangs open. Septimus and Tertius
stride in.

SEPTIMUS
Really? Fascinating. Don't you think,
Tertius?

TERTIUS
Indeed.

BISHOP
(panicky)
Septimus. Tertius. Well, well. I... Since
you're all here now, won't you join me in
a toast?

SEPTIMUS
A fine idea. Here, let me...

He pours the Bishop's wine into four chalices and
hands them round. The Bishop raises his.

BISHOP
His highness, the new king of
Stormhold. Whichever of you fine fel-
lows it might be. And may the best man
be triumphant.

ALL
(raising their chalices)
The new king of Stormhold!

They drink. Silence. The Bishop clutches his throat in panic. He convulses. And then – bang – he's down. The princes look at one another with anxiety and suspicion. A pregnant pause. Then – huurgh! – Tertius goes down too.

Primus and Septimus stare at one another. Then, to our surprise, Septimus drops to the ground, leaving only a very confused Primus.

Joyously, it dawns on him that he is now king. He reaches a trembling hand toward the crown. Just as he is about to touch it, Septimus leaps up again, laughing.

SEPTIMUS
Your face! You actually thought you would be king! Priceless.

PRIMUS
You killed the Bishop!?!

SEPTIMUS
I think you'll find, Primus, that you killed the Bishop. By drinking out of the wrong cup. And when you've finished wrestling with your conscience, may I suggest that if you'd care to be the first prince of Stormhold fortunate enough to live to see his brother crowned, you'll return to your chambers and leave the quest for the stone to me.

Septimus steps over the bodies and leaves.

INT. WITCHES' LAIR – NIGHT.

Mormo and Empusa help Lamia into a beautiful DRESS. She looks around in disgust at her squalid surroundings.

LAMIA
How have we lived this way all these years?

With a click of her fingers, the entire length of the lair is ILLUMINATED, and we now realise that the witches have been inhabiting only a tiny portion of it.

The rest – a vast, stately hall with a fountain, ornately framed mirrors, huge black glass chandeliers overhead and a sweeping double staircase leading to a mezzanine balcony – is breathtakingly beautiful, yet has clearly been neglected over the centuries.

LAMIA (CONT'D)
In my absence I expect you to make it fit for the queens we are.

A reluctant nod of accord from Mormo and Empusa. Then Mormo hands Lamia a RING and a set of RUNES. Empusa presents her with a black glass HATCHET and FILLETING KNIFE. Lamia chooses the latter.

LAMIA (CONT'D)
When I return with our prize, all of us shall be young again. Never fear, my sisters. I will not fail.

EXT. CRATER – DAWN.

Tristan sleeps while Yvaine hobbles around, stomping on the chain, trying to break free of it. Her efforts wake Tristan, and not, we deduce, for the first time.

TRISTAN
Don't you ever sleep?

YVAINE
Not at night. It may have escaped your notice, genius, but that's when stars have rather better things to do. Coming out. Shining. That kind of thing.

TRISTAN
And it may have escaped yours, but you're not in the sky any more. Coming out is off the agenda. Shining has been suspended until further notice. And sleeping during the day is O-U-T, unless you have some kind of magical ability to sleep while you're walking.

YVAINE
Have you not got it into your thick head yet? I'm not walking anywhere.

He thinks a moment, grabs her wrist, tackles the chain.

TRISTAN
Fine. Sit in a crater. Enjoy.

YVAINE
You're letting me go?

TRISTAN
Yep. I was going to put you back in the

sky after I'd brought you to my Victoria.
But clearly you'd rather stay on your
own in the middle of nowhere.

YVAINE
(yanking her hand away)
And just how were you planning to get
me back to the sky? You can't. You're
lying.

TRISTAN
(smug; she took the bait)
I find the fastest way to travel is by
candlelight.

YVAINE
You've got a Babylon candle?

TRISTAN
(bluffing that he already knew what it
was called)
Yeah, I've got a bubbling candle. Takes
you right where you most want to go.
How do you think I got here?

YVAINE
A Babylon candle.

TRISTAN
That's what I said.

YVAINE
You said "bubbling".

TRISTAN
Did not. Anyway. I was going to give
what's left of it to you.

He produces the candle, his bravado dented
somewhat by the fact that it's now scarcely a
stub.

YVAINE
That barely has one use left.

TRISTAN
So be grateful that I'm not using it up
right now to get the two of us back to
Wall. Unless you can think of another
way to get yourself home, in which case
you can be as ungrateful as you like. In a
crater. On your own.

Yvaine thinks. Then she thrusts her hand out
angrily. Tristan helps her up, trying not to smirk.
Resentfully, she holds him for support. He puts
his arm around her. She smacks it away. Their
journey has begun.

EXT. PALACE STABLES – DAWN.

Primus stands by a magnificent black carriage
and four black horses. A GROOM holding a feed
bag tries to see what he's doing. The camera has
a peek: he's consulting some RUNES. Apparently
satisfied, he puts them away.

PRIMUS
Did you happen to see which way my
brother Septimus went?

GROOM
Indeed your highness. He went north
west.

PRIMUS
Thank you. That information is most
useful.

The Groom nods. Unexpectedly, Primus swipes
the feed bag from his hands. The Groom stares at
him, shocked.

PRIMUS (CONT'D)
I shan't be needing you to accompany
me on my journey. My runes tell me that
Septimus went south. Though by a
funny coincidence, they say the stone is
north west. So you would actually have
done me a favour with your lies. Count
yourself lucky that I am not my brother.
He'd have had you eating those oats.

GROOM
I'm not lying, your highness, truly. Your
brother went north west.

Primus thrusts the feed bag towards him,
sighing.

PRIMUS
Then eat them. Eat the oats you were
about to feed my horses.

The Groom shakes his head fearfully. Primus
grabs a handful and lifts them towards the
Groom's mouth.

GROOM
No! Please! Spare me, I beg you!

Primus drops the oats, mounts the carriage.
Muttering.

PRIMUS
Septimus, Septimus. Always with the
poisoning.

And he's off, leaving the shaken Groom standing alone.

EXT. FARMHOUSE – DAY.

Outside a small farmhouse, BERNARD, 17, sullen and ginger haired, is trying to harness an obstinate GOAT. From inside we hear the fish-wife tones of his MOTHER.

> MOTHER (O.S.)
> And don't take less than a florin for him, Bernard, you understand?

> BERNARD
> Yes Mother.

> MOTHER (O.S.)
> And I want you back with a hen. A good hen and some corn. And some turnips.

Bernard rolls his eyes as only a teenager can, and silently mimics her yakking. Blah blah blah.

> MOTHER (O.S.) (CONT'D)
> And bring back the change. No dilly-dallying. No wenches. And don't even think of stopping at the tavern, Bernard, or you'll be sorry.

> BERNARD
> Yes Mother.

As he turns to begin his journey he's startled to find the beautiful LAMIA, standing right behind him. She holds a coin. Beside her is a small cart.

> LAMIA
> A florin for your goat, boy?

He is thrown by her beauty as well as the coincidence. Even a dim-bulb like Bernard suspects something fishy.

> BERNARD
> I'm supposed to go to market.

Lamia presses the coin into his hand.

> LAMIA
> Give me the goat.

> BERNARD
> He's a bit small to pull your cart.

They both look at the cart. Lamia considers this.

> LAMIA
> Hmmm. You're quite right.

She touches Bernard between the eyes. Confused and frozen in panic, he begins to shrink out of frame.

We cut to Bernard's POV: he is now at eye-level with the goat. The florin coin, dropped, tinkles to a stop. We pull back to reveal: two goats, one white, one ginger, like Bernard's hair. Harnessed to the cart.

> LAMIA (CONT'D)
> That's much better.

Retrieving her coin, Lamia notes with dismay new veins and liver spots on her arm: using magic has aged her.

She mounts the cart, cracks her whip. And they're off.

EXT. STORMHOLD LANDSCAPE – DAY.

Septimus' crew ride their stallions hell for leather.

INT./EXT. PRIMUS' CARRIAGE – DAY.

Primus' carriage speeds onward.

Inside the carriage, the ghostly princes sleep. All except for a worried-looking Tertius, still coming to terms with his newfound ghost-dom.

EXT. STORMHOLD LANDCAPE – DAY.

Tristan and Yvaine walk, as fast as Yvaine's bad leg will allow.

EXT. SAL'S CARAVAN – DAY.

In a field, the yellow caravan where Tristan was conceived. Snaking away from it, the silver chain that held his mother captive. We track along it to reveal: a glorious, exotic BIRD on a perch.

Ditch-Water Sal cooks a hare over a fire. A clatter of HOOVES: Lamia's cart approaches, pulled by her goats.

> SAL
> Who goes there? What do you want with me, a poor old flower seller? A harmless

old biddy. A sweet old –

LAMIA

Oh do shut up. I know what you are. And I swear by the ordinances of the sister- hood to which we both belong that I mean you no harm this day. I wish to share your meal.

SAL

Oh. Well. One can never be too careful. Sit down. I'll get you a seat.

She snaps her fingers at the bird, who TRANS- FORMS back into the Slave Girl. Miserably, the girl retreats into the caravan and returns with a stool.

The girl's task completed, Sal casually turns her back into a bird.

With a stick, Sal spears the crispy hare and holds it aloft.

SAL (CONT'D)

So, stranger. What's it to be? Heads or tails?

Sal chops the hare in two.

SAL (CONT'D)

A woman after my own heart, you are. I always choose heads. Luscious eyes and brains. Nice crispy ears. Don't mind me, though, nothing but dull rump meat to chew on. I'm fine. A little herbal sea- soning livens it up a treat. Care for a sprinkle?

Sal proffers a small glass jar. Lamia takes it and shakes some onto her food. She starts to eat.

SAL (CONT'D)

How is it?

LAMIA

Perfectly palatable.

SAL

So, stranger, where are you headed to on this fine night?

LAMIA

(casually, eating)

I seek a fallen star. She fell not far from here. And when I find her I shall take my great knife and cut out her heart while she still lives. And with my sisters I shall dine upon it... and the glory of our

youth... shall be restored.

Lamia looks increasingly confused by her own words and we can see her trying to work out what the hell possessed her to share her precious information with Sal. Sal claps her hands togeth- er in delight.

SAL

A fallen star? Why that's the finest news I've had in a while. I could do with losing a few years myself. And what I don't eat will fetch a fortune at the market. So, whereabouts do you reckon –

Fury spreads across Lamia's face. She rises to her feet, her plate falling to the ground and shattering.

LAMIA

Limbus grass? You dared to feed me Limbus grass?! You, a lowly harridan? A money-grubbing peddlar? You dare to subject ME to your tuppeny enchantments? To steal truth from my lips by feeding me Limbus grass? Do you have any idea how big a mistake you've made, Ditch-Water Sal?

SAL
How do you know my... Who are you?

LAMIA
Look again.

Lamia's face is calm now. Suddenly, for a terrifying split second, we see a FLASH of her ghastly true form. After recovering from this shock, Sal bows, trembling.

SAL
I shall not seek the star, your dark majesty, I swear. By the rules of the sisterhood. Your rules. Please be –

LAMIA
Seek all you wish. You shall be unable to see the star, to touch it, smell, or hear it. You will not perceive it, even if I were to put its heart in your palm.

Lamia touches her fingertip to Sal's forehead. The clouds darken. The fire goes out, more crockery smashes. And veins, wrinkles and liver spots appear on Lamia's other arm, now aged to match the first.

LAMIA (CONT'D)
You shall forget you ever saw me. Yet the memory will be like an itch on an amputated limb. An itch that will vex and irritate you.

SAL
But that's all, your majesty? You... took an oath. I, I shared my supper with you. You won't harm me?

LAMIA
I swore not to harm you today. Pray you never meet me again, Ditch-Water Sal.

The sky lightens and we focus on the bird, witness to the whole event. We hear GOAT HOOVES as Lamia leaves. A baffled Sal surveys the carnage left behind.

EXT. STORMHOLD FOREST – DAY.

Tristan and Yvaine make slow progress.

YVAINE
So let me get this straight: you think you know we're going the right way because – and I quote – "I just do".

TRISTAN
I do, though. I don't know why. Maybe it's my love for Victoria guiding me back home.

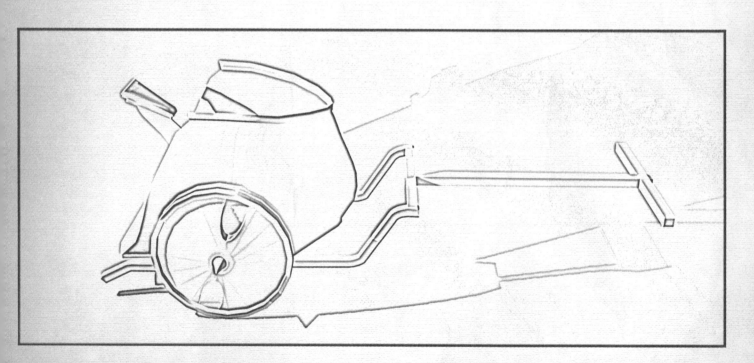

YVAINE

Oh please.

TRISTAN

Look, Yvonne, whether you like it or not –

YVAINE

Yvaine! My name is Yvaine. How many times do I have to –
          (then, re: her leg)
Ow! Will you slow down?!

TRISTAN

What are you doing?

YVAINE

What does it look like I'm doing? I'm sitting down. I'm tired.

TRISTAN

Oh, not this again. I thought we'd agreed we were going to stop for a rest and something to eat in the next village.

YVAINE

We didn't agree anything! I said I don't want anything to eat! I need to rest. So I'm resting. I'm tired.

TRISTAN

And I'm hungry! But I'm not...
          (gestures around, struggling)
eating!

YVAINE

I don't understand why you can't go to the village, eat, and then by the time you come back for me, I'll have –

TRISTAN

What? No, because –

YVAINE

Oh come on Tristan, it's mid-day. I never stay up this late. Please. Let me sleep.

TRISTAN

But you must be hungry, too.

YVAINE

I'm NOT hungry. Okay? I'm a star. I eat darkness. I drink light. I'm not hungry.
          (shouting, getting louder)
I'm lonely, scared, cold, angry, homesick, miserable and tired. Really, really tired. But I'm. Not. Hungry!

Yvaine bursts into tears. Tristan fidgets awkwardly.

TRISTAN

Look, don't... Alright, fine. You sleep here. I'll come back when I've eaten. Just... Just, please don't cry.

Yvaine nods gratefully. Tristan begins to fiddle with the chain at his wrist. To his surprise, it releases easily.

As Yvaine curls up beside a tree, Tristan reaches for her wrist. She offers it willingly, thinking he's going to remove the chain. To her surprise and fury, he instead ties her to the tree. She struggles unsuccessfully.

YVAINE

What are you doing!?

TRISTAN

What does it look like I'm doing? Making sure you don't run away.

YVAINE

Run away?! With a broken leg?

He turns his back, wrestling with his guilt as he walks off. Yvaine glares angrily at him as he goes.

EXT. STORMHOLD BEACH – DAY.

Septimus paces angrily. His large entourage all look anxious. Two lackeys march an especially worried-looking elderly SOOTHSAYER over to him.

LACKEY

Your Highness: the Soothsayer. As you requested.

SEPTIMUS

South you said. And south we went. Still no stone. Do you now propose that we start swimming?

SOOTHSAYER

Sire, I've merely relayed to you what the runes have told me. I can do no more.

SEPTIMUS

Consult them again. Now. Here.

Clearly, refusal is not an option. The Soothsayer takes his runes from their bag and shakes them in his hand.

SEPTIMUS (CONT'D)

Wait. Before we seek the stone, another

question. Am I the seventh son?

The Soothsayer looks uneasy. The runes are thrown. All land with symbols showing. The Soothsayer nods decisively.

> SEPTIMUS (CONT'D)
> Is my favourite colour blue?

Once again, all the runes land symbol-side up.

> SEPTIMUS (CONT'D)
> Has excessive begging and pleading ever persuaded me, on any occasion, to spare the life of a traitor?

The assembled lackeys exchange uneasy looks. This time, all the runes land blank side up.

> SEPTIMUS (CONT'D)
> What does that mean, then?

> SOOTHSAYER
> Um. It means... No.

> SEPTIMUS
> No what?

> SOOTHSAYER
> No, excessive begging and pleading has never persuaded you to –

Septimus nods as he speaks, grudgingly impressed. His 'fair enough' expression comically trivial in light of the rather nasty fact confirmed. Then, he interjects.

> SEPTIMUS
> Throw them again.

They are thrown. As they are about to hit the ground:

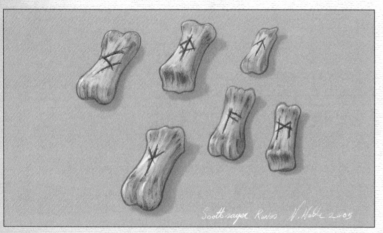

Soothsayer Runes V. Hobbs 2005

> SEPTIMUS (CONT'D)
> Do you work for my brother?

The runes land symbol side up. Septimus touches his finger to his lips – don't even bother. With his other hand, he draws his sword, casually fells the Soothsayer and sheaths it again. He picks up the runes.

> SEPTIMUS (CONT'D)
> Right. Do we continue west?

He throws the runes in the air. He's back on the trail.

EXT. STORMHOLD LANDSCAPE – DAY.

The runes transform in the air: they are now Lamia's runes. She looks at them and whips the goats onwards.

EXT. STORMHOLD FOREST – NIGHT.

Yvaine, still lying beneath the tree where Tristan left her, is awoken by a NOISE. A rustling in the bushes nearby. She sits up hastily, looking around, afraid.

> YVAINE
> Tristan? Is that you?

No reply. From her POV, we see movement. Someone is there, and coming closer. She strains against the chain.

> YVAINE (CONT'D)
> (gripped by panic)
> Who's there?

Suddenly, A UNICORN looms into view. Yvaine reacts in shock and relief. Then, an idea.

> YVAINE (CONT'D)
> Come on... Over here...

And with a few more soft coaxing noises, Yvaine has lured the unicorn over to her. It TOUCHES the chain, which DISSOLVES instantly. She struggles to her feet.

A little more gentle persuasion, and the unicorn dips down before her. She climbs on. And they're off.

EXT. CROSSROADS – NIGHT.

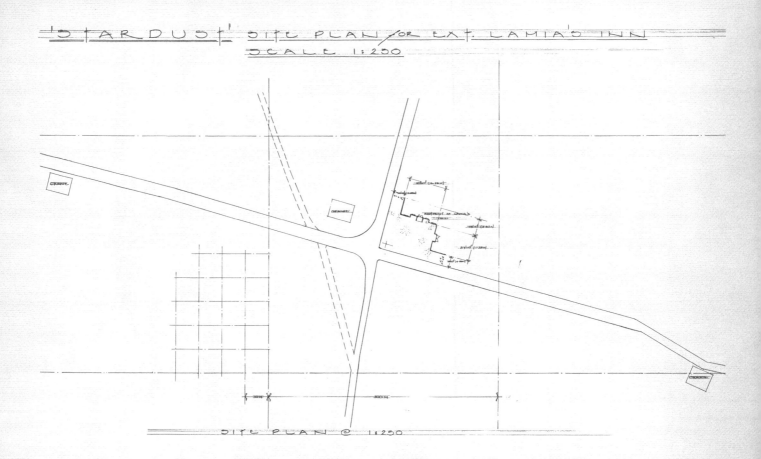

SITE PLAN @ 1:250

A frustrated Lamia, unsure of which way to go, sighs and looks at the ring on her finger. A moment's hesitation, and then she rubs it.

INT. WITCHES' LAIR – NIGHT.

The large free-standing mirror that we saw earlier. Gradually, Lamia now appears in it, looking out at Mormo and Empusa, who stand before it.

> EMPUSA
> Be careful how much magic you use, sister. It's beginning to show.

> LAMIA
> (showing her aged arms)
> One goat and a small enchantment. Hardly extravagant.

> MORMO
> Even using the ring will take its toll. Better to call on us only in dire need, and use your runes to locate the star yourself.

> LAMIA
> I used them. And she should be here. But now they're just telling me gibberish.

Mormo scuttles over to the cages we saw earlier. A stoat looks out nervously. Mormo passes it and opens another cage, dragging out a CROCODILE.

Back at the table, Mormo and Empusa study the entrails.

> EMPUSA
> It is because you must stay where you are, my sister. She is coming to you.

> MORMO
> Oh! Be warned, Lamia – delicacy is needed. Misery has drained her, she's barely shining.

EXT. FOREST – NIGHT.

Tristan returns, carrying bread, wine and a wooden crutch. Yvaine is gone. How could he have been so naive?

> TRISTAN
> (rapping his forehead)
> Idiot.

Defeated, exhausted, he slumps against a tree and closes his eyes.

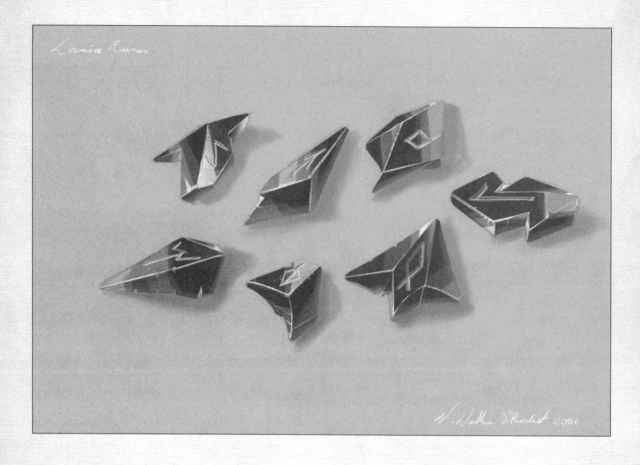

EXT. CROSSROADS – NIGHT.

Lamia gazes at the horizon to see a STORM approaching. Decisively, she walks over to where her goats graze.

She whispers into the ear of the white one and he TRANSFORMS into BILLY, a 40ish man with a white goatee.

She whispers in the ear of the goat-formerly-known-as-Bernard. He becomes Bernard again, a look of relief on his face... swiftly followed by disappointment when, moments later, he changes form again... This time, becoming a boyish, yet sexy, red-haired girl. GIRL-BERNARD reels back, as if dizzy, or drunk.

Girl-Bernard nods, dull-eyed and zombie-like. From her chariot, Lamia fetches her filleting knife. Setting it aside, she raises her hand. FLAMES flicker at her fingers. She touches the chariot and it is engulfed in green FIRE.

The fire grows and takes on substance and form, finally subsiding to reveal: an old INN. Its sign swings in the gathering wind, a picture of the chariot on it.

INT. LAMIA'S INN – NIGHT – CONTINUOUS.

We move through the interior, as the last of the magical flames die. In the main room, we see Lamia, Billy and Girl-Bernard enter from outside. Lamia addresses them.

> LAMIA
> You are Billy the innkeeper. I am your wife. And you're our daughter. Now make everything ready. Our special guest will be here soon.

EXT. A DESERTED ROAD – NIGHT.

Yvaine rides the unicorn, lost, scared and doubtful.

> YVAINE
> I mean, who's to say he'd have even kept his promise about the candle? I refuse to believe he was the only person in Stormhold who could have helped me. And going on and on and on... Victoria this, Victoria that.

A fork in the road. Yvaine slows and rubs her temples.

YVAINE (CONT'D)
Now where the hell are we?
            (rapping her forehead)
Idiot.

She rides on. We pull back. From afar she cuts an even lonelier figure.

EXT. FOREST – NIGHT.

Tristan lies asleep underneath the tree. We tilt up to see the stars.

THE STARS (V.O.)
Tristan. Please protect our sister, Tristan. Yvaine is in grave danger. You must help her. She is heading into a trap. No star is safe in Stormhold...

We track into the sky, closer and closer, and fade to:

INT./EXT. DREAM SEQUENCE – NIGHT.

— A meteoric fireball plunges through space, to Earth.

THE STARS (V.O.)
The last to fall, 400 years ago, was captured by the same witches who seek Yvaine now.

— a beautiful brunette sits, stunned, in a crater.

— Lamia, Mormo and Empusa gently lead her into the lair, appearing for all the world like three kindly old ladies trying to help a lonely, injured girl.

THE STARS (V.O.) (CONT'D)
They tricked her. Cared for her. And when her heart was once more aglow... they cut it from her chest...

— They help the star from a hot bath and into a towel, and lift her onto their table. She closes her eyes. The star's expression turns to terror. The glint of a blade. Then Lamia holds up the star's golden heart.

THE STARS (V.O.) (CONT'D)
And ate it.

— The witches nibble at the heart and stand before the mirror, watching themselves become young and beautiful.

— They seal the glowing remainder of the heart in the box we saw earlier, each witch tying her own knot.

THE STARS (V.O.) (CONT'D)
There's no time to waste. A coach is coming, by any means possible you must get on it. I beg you: wake up.

EXT. FOREST – NIGHT.

A CONKER falls on Tristan's head, waking him abruptly. He looks around, then hearing a VOICE, like rustling leaves.

TREE (V.O.)
Did you not hear them? Wake up.

He looks around, perplexed.

TRISTAN
Oh please, not a talking tree.

TREE (V.O.)
I'm not really a tree. I used to be a wood-sprite. But there was this witch... Long story. And it's true: you really don't have any time to waste.

TRISTAN
I think I preferred the part of this dream where the stars were talking.

TREE (V.O.)
That was no dream. And you must hurry. If you go on foot, you'll never reach her in time. The coach is on the road one mile west of here. Go! Run!

Perplexed, Tristan doesn't move. Suddenly the forest ERUPTS into a mass of movement. Conkers rain down. The woods are ALIVE and the mood has changed completely. This is scary.

TREE (V.O.) (CONT'D)
I said: RUN!

Terrified, Tristan leaps to his feet and begins to run.

INT./EXT. PRIMUS' CARRIAGE – NIGHT.

Primus drives down a road beside the forest. Inside, sit Sextus, Quintus, Quartus, Tertius and Secundus.

TERTIUS

Road.

QUINTUS

Nope. You said that already.

QUARTUS

Reins.

Quintus shakes his head.

SECUNDUS

Rib cage.

QUARTUS

Don't be stupid, it has to be something he can actually see. Otherwise it wouldn't be called I Spy. It'd be called "I can randomly think of something."

SECUNDUS

Excuse me, I can see a rib cage. I can see Sextus' rib cage.

They all look. Indeed, it is showing through Sextus' decomposing skin and mouldy, shredded clothes.

EXT. FOREST – NIGHT.

Tristan runs blindly through the madly rustling forest. It's almost as if the trees are parting to create a path.

INT. PRIMUS' CARRIAGE – NIGHT.

In contrast, the urgently unexciting game continues.

QUINTUS

Good guess. But wrong.

SECUNDUS

It's not rib cage?

QUINTUS

No. Next guess?

QUARTUS

I'm so bored of this. I actually don't even care.

EXT. FOREST – NIGHT.

A breathless Tristan continues his scary sprint.

INT. PRIMUS' CARRIAGE – NIGHT.

And still it goes on...

QUINTUS

Give up?

SECUNDUS

Yes.

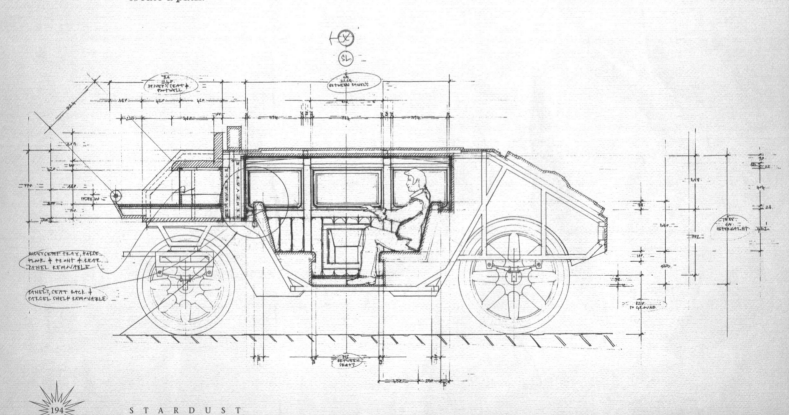

QUINTUS
It was "rample".

TERTIUS
What the hell is rample?

QUINTUS
It's the bit you put between the horse's teeth.

QUARTUS
That's called a "bit".

QUINTUS
Is it?

SEXTUS
Will you all shut up! I don't know how you can sit playing stupid games when the runes say that Septimus is back on track. I thought we were backing Primus to win.

EXT. FOREST – NIGHT.

Tristan keeps running as the forest rages around him. In the distance, he sees the lights of the carriage.

INT. PRIMUS' CARRIAGE – NIGHT.

...And on.

SECUNDUS
Okay, my go. I spy with my little eye...

Sextus sighs deeply.

EXT. PRIMUS' CARRIAGE – NIGHT.

Finally, Tristan bursts out onto the road, just as the carriage approaches. Frantically, he flags Primus down. Primus sees him, but instead of stopping, he whips the horses – SNAP! They speed past, a thunder of HOOVES.

Tristan stands deflated, when suddenly there is an almighty noise – CRACK! – and a huge BRANCH falls from a tree, blocking the road. Primus is forced to stop. Tristan mouths "thank you" to the tree as he runs over.

Primus looks doubtfully at this odd young fellow but accepts his help in moving the branch.

That done, he climbs back onto the carriage and throws Tristan a COIN.

PRIMUS
Thank you.

TRISTAN
I don't need money. I need a lift.

PRIMUS
I'm afraid I can't take passengers. You see, I am on a quest of enormous importance, and –

TRISTAN
Then all the more reason to take me! There may come a time when you need another pair of hands. Maybe providence sent me to you just as it sent you to me.

Primus considers this.

PRIMUS
Get on.

EXT. PRIMUS' CARRIAGE – NIGHT.

Tristan rides alongside Primus. Holding the reins in one hand, Primus briefly consults his runes.

TRISTAN
If it's not too forward of me: what sort of a quest is it that you're on?

PRIMUS
My destiny. My right to rule.
(holding out his hand)
Prince Primus of Stormhold.

Tristan takes it and bows too, unsure of the etiquette.

TRISTAN
Your highness. Tristan Thorne. I'm –

They round a corner and Tristan is silenced by the view: an incredible mountain range. He gasps.

PRIMUS
If this view pleases you, I insist that one day you visit my castle on Mount Huon. Now that's what I call a mountain. Her foothills alone are bigger than this.

TRISTAN
And you're most welcome to visit me in my village. We have an annual cheese-

rolling competition. And our duck-pond was voted the cleanest in all Suffolk.

PRIMUS
You are most kind.

They ride on in silence.

EXT. DESERTED ROAD – NIGHT.

It's raining heavily, now. Thunder and lightning. Yvaine, drenched and forlorn, rides through the storm. In the distance, she spies the welcoming lights of the inn. Joy and relief. She spurs the unicorn in to a gallop towards it.

EXT. LAMIA'S INN – NIGHT.

As Yvaine approaches, the PATTER of rain seems to form words of warning. She dismounts and limps to the door.

Lamia opens it, looking like an average innkeeper.

LAMIA
Goodness me, come in out of this wretched rain, my dear. We have food and drink. A warm bed. Plenty of hot water for a bath.

YVAINE
A bath? I've never had one of those.

LAMIA
Never had a bath!? Why it's a treat you'll enjoy, my love, on a cold night like

this. It'll make your heart glow.

Lamia puts an arm around Yvaine and steers her in. She notices Yvaine's limp and supports her more.

INT. LAMIA'S INN – CONTINUOUS.

Through flames, we see a TIN TUB, beside a blazing fireplace. Lamia sits Yvaine down on a seat beside it.

LAMIA
How do you like your bath? Warm, hot or boil-a-lobster?

YVAINE
I honestly don't know.

LAMIA
Then let me choose for you. Let's get you out of your wet things. And I'll have my husband take your horse to the stables. Billy!

Lamia claps her hands. We see the ex-goat standing behind the bar. He is chewing slowly on a tea towel.

Yvaine looks concerned. Lamia claps again, and glares at Billy as he shuffles out.

Girl-Bernard, still actually a teenage boy, goes with some enthusiasm to help Yvaine undress.

INT./EXT. STABLES – NIGHT.

Billy leads the reluctant unicorn into the stables.

INT. LAMIA'S INN – MINUTES LATER.

Lamia's finger dips into the bath. Underwater, a ribbon of green fire leaves her fingertip to encircle Yvaine's leg.

Yvaine lies happily in the steaming bath. We notice a slight glow around her, a shimmering, twinkling corona.

LAMIA
Feeling better?

YVAINE
Much. Thank you. The warm water has actually done me a world of good.

LAMIA

Ah, you see? The powers of a nice hot
bath! And your leg? Any improvement?

Yvaine stretches her leg out of the water, gingerly at first, and then wiggling her toes with growing wonder.

YVAINE

That. Is. Extraordinary... I don't... You
know, I actually thought it was broken.
But now...

She wiggles her toes, flexes her leg up and down.
Delighted and baffled at the same time.

LAMIA

It's the very least I could do. I'm just
glad you're feeling better. You seem happier in yourself, too.

YVAINE

I do feel happier. Less troubled.

LAMIA

Wonderful! Nothing like a nice soak to
wash your cares away. Warm the cockles
of your heart.

With assistance from a delighted Girl-Bernard,
Yvaine climbs from the bath and slips into a robe.

**INT. LAMIA'S INN – BEDROOM – MOMENTS
LATER.**

A small room containing an inviting-looking bed.
Yvaine glitters even more brightly than before.

LAMIA

Now I'm only a simple innkeeper's wife,
but I've been told I have a healer's
hands. I'd be glad to give you a massage.

YVAINE

What's a massage?

LAMIA

You've never...? Well, bless my soul.
Nothing like a massage to send you off
for the finest and deepest night's sleep.

YVAINE

I do have trouble sleeping at night...

Lamia gestures for her to lie down. She climbs
up, and the camera jibs down under the bed to
reveal the knife.

LAMIA

Lie on your back, dear. And why not
close your eyes? Drift off better that
way.

Yvaine lies down and Lamia begins to open
Yvaine's robe. She is interrupted by shouting
from outside.

PRIMUS (O.S.)

Service! Hello!?

EXT. LAMIA'S INN – NIGHT.

Primus paces angrily, cross at being left in the
rain.

TRISTAN

Maybe we should try the next inn. Carry
on a little longer. If your stone really is

as close as the runes say.

Unheard, the ghosts shout out in protest.

> GHOSTS
> No!

Unseen, Tertius does a pointless jig before Tristan. Secundus, equally frantic, waves his arms at Primus.

> TERTIUS
> No! It's here!

> SECUNDUS
> She's here! It's here! The stone is here!

The door is opened by Billy.

> PRIMUS
> At last! We require accommodation. Help my friend take the horses to your stable.

Primus heads inside as Tristan begins to unhitch a horse. Looking around for Billy, Tristan is surprised to find him nibbling at the hem of his jacket.

INT. LAMIA'S INN – BEDROOM – NIGHT.

Lamia tries to hide her fury at the interruption.

> LAMIA
> Relax here, my love. I'll be back just as soon as I've taken care of this customer.

INT. LAMIA'S INN – MOMENTS LATER.

A frustrated Primus – followed by his ghostly brothers – wanders in to find the inn empty.

> PRIMUS
> Hello? Hello??

Spotting the tempting, steaming bath he decides not to wait. He begins to strip off his wet clothes. The ghosts avert their eyes in revulsion.

INT. LAMIA'S INN – KITCHEN – SIMULTANEOUS.

Lamia pours a glass of WINE, to which she adds the contents of a small, nasty-looking bottle.

INT. LAMIA'S INN – MOMENTS LATER.

Yvaine comes down the stairs and is shocked to see Primus sitting in the bath. She turns away quickly.

> PRIMUS
> I'm accustomed to better service. But you're awake now, and that's what counts. A hot meal would be in order. What can you offer me?

Before Yvaine can reply, Lamia enters with the wine.

> LAMIA
> I'll thank you not to bother my guests, sir. I am the lady of this inn. I've a pot of stew on the stove. A drink while you wait?

> PRIMUS
> Until my brother is dead, I've vowed to drink only my own wine. But my friend in the stables would be glad of a drop, I'm sure. Your best room, perhaps?

Lamia nods and walks out with the wine, irritated. Alone with her now, Primus eyes Yvaine up lasciviously.

> PRIMUS (CONT'D)
> I'm sorry, I just assumed... Travelling alone, are you? I've just stabled my coach and my four black stallions...

Yvaine peers at him suspiciously. The ghosts surround her, shouting and pointing at the pendant around her neck. Primus, oblivious, continues talking to Yvaine (ad lib), though we can't hear him over the ghostly ruckus.

> GHOSTS
> The stone! Primus! LOOK! Here!

After continuing (ad lib) for some time, they eventually give up, exasperated. We now catch the tail end of Primus' attempts at seduction.

> PRIMUS
> ...the largest in all of Stormhold, they say.

Yvaine ignores him but continues peering, trying to work something out.

> YVAINE
> You look very familiar. I've seen you somewhere before.

> PRIMUS
> Well alright. I confess it. I am Prince Primus of Stormhold.

> YVAINE
> That's it! The Stormhold Palace!

> PRIMUS
> (now I'm in)
> Indeed.

> YVAINE
> (excited at having remembered at last)
> You're the one who... A bird did a...

She motions a splatting on her head

> PRIMUS
> (deflated)
> What? How on earth could you possibly...
> (then, suspicious)
> Do you know my brother?

> YVAINE
> Fortunately not. Now if you'll excuse me.

She turns to go back upstairs, her collar falling open a little as she does so, revealing the stone.

> PRIMUS
> That stone! Come here, let me see it.

The ghosts cheer – finally! Yvaine rolls her eyes. Absolutely no way she's getting any closer to a naked guy in a bath.

> PRIMUS (CONT'D)
> Please! I believe it to be mine.

INT. LAMIA'S INN – BEDROOM – NIGHT.

Lamia bursts in and gets the knife from under the bed.

INT. STABLES – NIGHT.

We follow zombie-Girl-Bernard, carrying a glass of wine. She opens one horsebox to find Tristan, drying a horse. She puts the wine on the floor and turns to go.

TRISTAN
Thanks, that is just what I needed. My name's Tristan. Glad to meet you, Miss –

GIRL-BERNARD
Bernard.

Tristan, foxed, watches her shuffle out. He goes for the wine, but stops: an almighty BANG from the horsebox opposite. He looks to see: the door fly off its hinges.

INT. LAMIA'S INN – NIGHT.

Yvaine eyes Primus with thinly veiled hostility as she walks towards him, holding the stone that effectively destroyed her peaceful life in the heavens. We may note her shimmer fading now.

YVAINE
Yours, is it? Did you throw this?

PRIMUS
(taken aback, aggressive)
Excuse me? You don't seem to have understood me, young lady. I am the first-born of Stormhold and I command you to bring it to me. Now!

Before he can finish, he's interrupted by the loud NOISE from the stables. Both look around in concern.

ON THE STAIRCASE

Lamia, armed and halfway down the stairs, HEARS it too.

INT. STABLES – NIGHT.

As we cut back, the door flies off its hinges and the unicorn comes CRASHING though, charging at Tristan.

It knocks the wine from Tristan's hand. Where the wine has splashed, the hay on the ground is smoking and charred, as if burned by acid. Tristan looks to the unicorn, back at the ground, and runs out.

INT. LAMIA'S INN – NIGHT.

All at once, Lamia runs in, the front door flies open and Tristan bursts in, shouting.

TRISTAN

Prince Primus! Don't touch anything they give you! They tried to poison me!

The camera jibs down under the water and we hear a muffled commotion. The water turns deep blue.

A PAN AROUND THE ROOM

On the shocked reactions of Tristan, Yvaine (no longer shimmering), Girl-Bernard, Secundus, Tertius, Quintus, Quartus, Sextus and finally, a ghostly Primus – naked, but politely framed, more shocked than anyone to see:

IN THE BATH

Primus, slumped down, a slash of blue blood at his throat. And standing behind him, Lamia, holding her horrible knife, stained blue.

TRISTAN AND YVAINE

Spot one another. Stunned, they run together, but are stopped by Lamia, who grabs Yvaine from Tristan.

LAMIA

Billy! Get him!

DEAD-EYED BILLY

We've barely noticed him, standing silently behind the bar, but now he runs at Tristan with his head down. Tristan sidesteps him, but he backs up, charges again.

THE UNICORN

Races in through the front entrance of the inn. He cuts in front of Tristan to run at Billy. Heads lowered, Billy and the unicorn rush at one another at full tilt.

HORN VERSUS FOREHEAD.

At speed. Guess which wins.

LAMIA

Lets go of Yvaine, throwing her across the room, and turns on the unicorn as it shakes its head to disengage the impaled Billy – in death, a goat once more. The unicorn rears up at Lamia, knocking her to the ground.

TRISTAN

Runs to Yvaine. She points in horror to the unicorn and swats at Tristan urgently as he pulls her away.

YVAINE

No! We have to help him!

TRISTAN

Forget it, we have to go, these people are insane, they'll kill us!

LAMIA

On the ground, the unicorn poised to attack. With a sweep of her arm, she creates a WALL OF GREEN FIRE, around Tristan, Yvaine and herself, shutting it out. She gets up and strides towards the pair, a witchy Terminator.

Tristan and Yvaine back away until – against the wall of fire – they can go no further. Tristan stands protectively in front of Yvaine. Lamia keeps on coming.

LAMIA

The burning golden heart of a star at peace is so much better than your frightened little heart. But even so, better than no heart at all.

With unthinkable menace, she displays her knife.

TRISTAN AND YVAINE

Cower. Lamia almost upon them. Tristan fumbles in his pocket and pulls out the tiny stub of Babylon candle.

TRISTAN

Hold me tight and think of home.

Lamia raises her knife to strike.

Tristan wraps one arm around Yvaine and plunges the other, holding the stub, into the fire. He screams. Lamia, realizing what he is doing, screams too. There's a WHOOSH, and they disappear, leaving Lamia alone, her knife slicing through the empty space where they stood and shattering as it connects with the wall.

EXT. CANDLE JOURNEY SEQUENCE – NIGHT.

Tristan and Yvaine's POV as they fly at astonishing speed out of the inn and into the dark, stormy sky. The inn, the road and the twinkling lights of

Stormhold get smaller and smaller until we stop in a cloud.

EXT. CLOUD – NIGHT.

Tristan and Yvaine stand on a grey cloud. Thunder rumbles, lightning forks flash, and black rain sheets down violently. They have to scream to be heard.

> TRISTAN
> What the hell did you do?!

> YVAINE
> What did I do? What did you do? "Think of home?" Great plan. You thought of your home and I thought of mine and now we're halfway between the two.

> TRISTAN
> You stupid cow! What did you think of your home for!?

> YVAINE
> You just said "home"! When someone says "home", I think of my home! I don't think of your home! Why would I think of your home? If you wanted me to think of your home, you should have said!

> TRISTAN
> A crazy lady was about to cut your heart out and you wanted me to give more spe-cific instructions? I'll bear that in mind next time. Perhaps you'd like it in writ-ing? A diagram, maybe?

The magnitude of what just happened hits Yvaine, and she starts to cry. Angry tears of fear and frustration.

> YVAINE
> Don't come on like the big selfless hero, Tristan! It's not like I was any use to you dead! I mean, happy birthday Victoria darling, I hope you'll accept this blood-soaked carcass as a token of my –

Suddenly, out of nowhere, a COPPER NET falls onto them and they're dragged through the clouds, out of shot.

EXT. SKY VESSEL – NIGHT.

Lying on a deck, trapped in the copper net, Tristan and Yvaine look up to see a dozen PIRATES staring down.

Behind them, other PIRATES haul in copper nets, full of glowing LIGHTNING. Muscling his way through is CAPTAIN SHAKESPEARE. Mid-40s, slickly dressed, built like a fridge. Definitely the daddy. A SKINNY PIRATE sneers.

> SKINNY PIRATE
> Look, Captain Shakespeare, a little bonus. Caught ourselves a couple of Lightning Marshals.

> CAPTAIN
> Don't look like Lightning Marshals to me.

> SKINNY PIRATE
> But they were right in the middle of the storm, Captain! Why else would anyone be up here during a storm?

> CAPTAIN
> Hmmm. Why would anyone be up here in a storm... Let's think.
> (shouting)
> Maybe for the same god-forsaken reason we are?

The pirates cower. The Captain prods Tristan with his foot.

> CAPTAIN (CONT'D)
> Now, who are you?

Tristan and Yvaine cling together, too scared to speak. The Skinny Pirate, copying, prods Tristan with his foot.

> SKINNY PIRATE
> Cat got yer tongue?

> CAPTAIN
> Fortunately for the birds, I ain't ever seen such a thing as a flying cat. Any of you ever seen a flying cat?

The other pirates shake their heads, clearly afraid of the Captain.

One VERY OLD PIRATE raises his hand. Several others elbow him nervously 'til he puts it down.

> CAPTAIN (CONT'D)
> I'm gonna wager that their tongues are still in place... for the time being! Let's see if a night in our lovely brig will loosen their lips...

The pirates surround Tristan and Yvaine and drag them towards the brig.

We pull back to see the vessel in all her glory: a magnificent FLYING SHIP, gliding through the stormy sky.

INT. THE BRIG – MINUTES LATER.

In C.U., an old iron key. A hand removes it, leaving an open keyhole through which we spy: Tristan and Yvaine, tied together, back to back. We move through the hole.

YVAINE
They're going to kill us aren't they.

TRISTAN
I don't know.

YVAINE
(smiling wanly)
You know, it's funny: I used to watch. Watch people having adventures. I envied them.

TRISTAN
Are you familiar with the saying: be careful what you wish for?

YVAINE
What, so ending up with my heart cut out, that'll serve me right, will it? Thanks.

TRISTAN
No! No. I didn't mean that at all. I admire you for dreaming. I could never have imagined an adventure this big in order to wish for it. I just thought I'd find this lump of celestial rock, take it home, and that would be it.

YVAINE
And you got me. I am sorry, you know.

TRISTAN
Don't be. How else would a shop boy like me ever have had an adventure like this?

YVAINE
If there's one thing I learned in all my years watching Earth, it's that people aren't what they may seem. There are shop boys, and there are boys who just happen to work in shops for the time being. And trust me, Tristan, you're no shop boy. You saved my life. Thank you.

She squeezes his hand. We see it is charred black

from where he thrust it into the fire. Not wanting to spoil his newly heroic image, he silently grimaces in pain.

EXT. CROSSROADS – DAWN.

Septimus arrives where the inn stood, to find Lamia's chariot, a dead goat and the corpse of Primus, still in the bath. He and a Lackey stop beside the bath.

SEPTIMUS
Well, well, well. The last brother dead. It would seem that I am king.

He walks triumphantly back towards the rest of his entourage.

SEPTIMUS (CONT'D)
King!

The ghosts appear behind him.

PRIMUS
Not yet, brother.

SEPTIMUS
All that remains now is to find the stone.

LACKEY
Your brother does not have it?

SEPTIMUS
I suggest you find out.

Septimus walks away as the Lackey begins reluctantly to delve in the cold blue water around the naked corpse. The ghosts exchange looks of distaste. Eeew.

As Septimus passes Lamia's chariot, a HAND shoots out and grabs his ankle. He looks down to see a cowering, traumatised and slightly charred Bernard.

BERNARD
Help me... please?

A flash of shock and revulsion, and then Septimus reaches down and grabs Bernard by the collar.

SEPTIMUS
What happened here? Where's my stone? Do you have it?

BERNARD
No... I... I don't know. The man... Your brother? I heard him speak of a stone. The girl had it.

SEPTIMUS
What girl?

BERNARD
I don't know. A girl. She got away. All of this – it was a trap set for her. Your brother just strayed into it, I swear.

SEPTIMUS
A trap set by who?

BERNARD
A woman you should pray you'll never meet.
(off Septimus' glancing)
She's gone. She took your brother's carriage.

SEPTIMUS
And this woman wanted my stone?

BERNARD
What? No. She wanted the girl's heart. She said the girl was a star. She wanted

to cut out her heart and...

As Bernard trails off in disgust, a look of dawning comprehension spreads over Septimus' face, turning to sheer gleeful greed. He ends the sentence with relish.

SEPTIMUS
...Eat it.

He drops Bernard.

SEPTIMUS (CONT'D)
Oh my god. Do you have any idea what this means?

He grabs Bernard's collar again and begins dragging him towards the horses.

SEPTIMUS (CONT'D)
It's imperative that I find her.
(to Lackey)
This idiot is coming with us.

Lackey, still elbow deep in bathwater, looks doubtful.

LACKEY
But sire... We haven't enough...

Septimus hoists Bernard onto the Lackey's horse, mounts his own and snaps the reins. All the horses thunder away, leaving the Lackey alone amongst the carnage.

LACKEY (CONT'D)
...horses.

INT./EXT. PRIMUS' CARRIAGE - DAY.

Primus' magnificent black carriage sweeps past the camera, apparently out of control, with no one driving.

Inside we find Lamia. Much older, and furious at being thwarted. As she brushes her hair from her face, a clump of it comes out in her hand, making her gasp. She looks at her reflection in the window and away again, disgusted. Reluctantly, she uses her ring.

INT. WITCHES' LAIR - DAY.

We sweep past the animal cages, many empty. Mormo and Empusa stand by the mirror, talking to an angry Lamia.

EMPUSA
We have asked again. And the answer is the same: she is airborne.

LAMIA
Well she can't remain so forever. Inform me as soon as she touches ground. Immediately – do you understand?

MORMO
Watch your tongue, sister. It is you and not we who have lost her.

EMPUSA
Lost her and broken the knife. Even if you apprehend her, how will you complete the deed?

MORMO
Perhaps you should return now, and one of us set out in your place.

LAMIA
Don't be absurd. I'll bring her home and deal with her there. Be sure everything is ready for our arrival.

INT. THE BRIG – DAY.

Tristan and Yvaine are right where we left them.

YVAINE
Do you think someone is trying to tell us something?

TRISTAN
Like what?

YVAINE
I mean one way or another, we always seem to end up stuck together.

TRISTAN
What are you talking about, "someone"? What, destiny or fate or cosmic messages or something? I don't believe in all that.

YVAINE
Really? Most people on Earth do. It used to amuse me, how they look to the stars for answers about the future. Like we have any idea what will happen next! Imagine how boring it'd be for us to watch you if we did.

TRISTAN
People who want to know the future are usually ones who desperately want something they fear they'll never have.

YVAINE
And you claim not to be one of them?!
(off his lack of response)
Tell me about Victoria, then.

TRISTAN
There's not much more to tell you.

YVAINE
Because... the little I know about love is that it's unconditional. Not something you can buy.

TRISTAN
This wasn't about buying her love. It was a way to prove how I felt.

YVAINE
Ah... And what's she doing to prove how she feels about you?

Tristan puzzles this over for a moment.

TRISTAN
Look, Yvaine... you'll understand when you meet her. Providing we don't get murdered by pirates first.

YVAINE
Hmmm. Murdered by pirates. Heart torn out and eaten. Meet Victoria. Can't quite decide which sounds more fun.

INT./EXT. PRIMUS' CARRIAGE – DAY.

Lamia rides anxiously onwards. The camera pulls further and further back until we can see miles of road. And, gaining on her in hot pursuit: Septimus and his crew.

EXT. STORMHOLD LANDSCAPE – CONTINUOUS.

Septimus and company gallop through the countryside. From certain angles, we can see the ghostly princes seated behind the living riders. Septimus is delirious.

SEPTIMUS
(shouting to Bernard)
Don't lose sight of those tracks!
(to himself)
Thank you, dear lady, whoever you may be. Not only have you killed my brother,

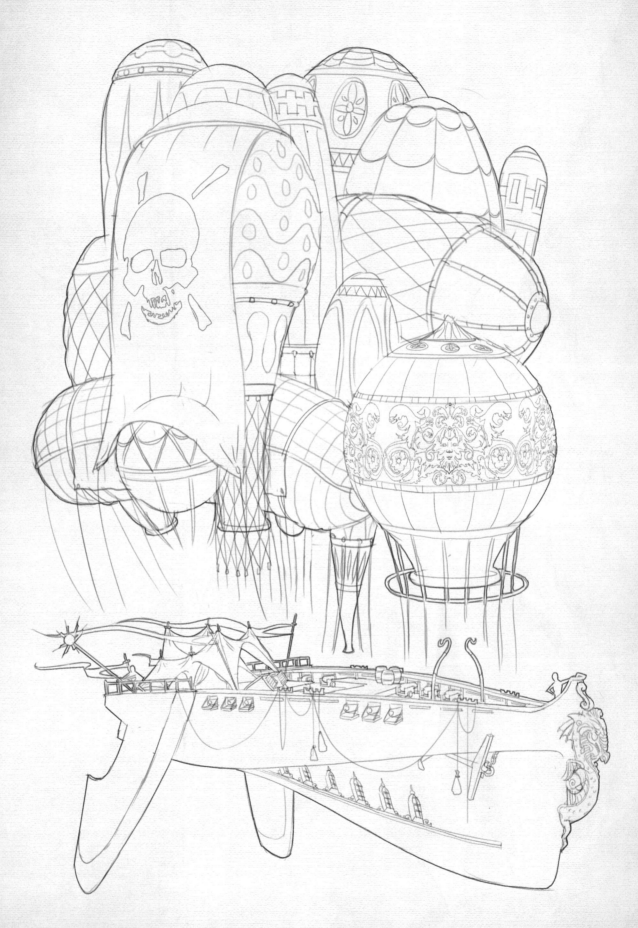

but in pursuing the girl, your coach tracks will lead me right to her!
> (to Bernard)

Can you even begin to comprehend what this means? Everlasting life! King forever! The last king of Stormhold.

The ghosts react in abject disgust.

EXT. SKY VESSEL – DAY.

The Sky Vessel cruises on through the clouds.

INT. BRIG – DAY.

Captain Shakespeare looms over his captives. He really is scary. Tristan and Yvaine try to speak but he won't let them.

> CAPTAIN
> So. This is the part where you tell me who you are and why you're up here. Or...
> (to Yvaine)
> I'll break his spine across my knee!
> (to Tristan)
> And snap her pretty little fingers one by one...
> (clicks fingers)
> Like dry twigs.

> TRISTAN
> My name is Tristan Thorne and this is my wife Yvaine, and –

> CAPTAIN
> Your wife? Far too young and radiant to belong to just one man! It's share and share alike aboard my vessel, sonny boy.

The pirates laugh.

> TRISTAN
> If you dare –

> CAPTAIN
> You may think you're showing a little spirit in front of your lady friend. But if you talk back to me again I'll feed your tongue to the dogs, you impertinent little pup.

The pirates cheer.

> TRISTAN
> Sir, I beg you –

> CAPTAIN
> Better. But still interrupting. Let's see. A hanging's always good for morale. Maybe we'll watch you dance a gallows jig.

The pirates cheer.

> CAPTAIN (CONT'D)
> Or perhaps I'll just tip you over the side and have done with it.

The pirates boo, disappointed.

> CAPTAIN (CONT'D)
> It's a very long way down – plenty of time to reminisce about your pitifully short lives.

> YVAINE
> We were lost!

> CAPTAIN
> Lost!? No one gets lost up here! There's nowhere to get lost from!

> TRISTAN
> I promise you it's true! All we want to do is get back home, to a place called Wall and –

CHING! The Captain draws his CUTLASS.

> CAPTAIN
> Wall? That's one lie too many, my son.

> TRISTAN
> But, but, it's true! I was born there.

> CAPTAIN
> So if you're really from Wall, tell me this: who is Victoria's consort?

> TRISTAN
> (taken aback)
> You... know Victoria?
> (clearly the jig is up)
> Okay. Point made. Me and Yvaine aren't really married. And yes, if I ever get home, I do hope to make Victoria my wife.

> CAPTAIN
> You hope to marry Queen Victoria?

> TRISTAN
> Ah, ah, Queen Victoria? In that case I mean... Prince Albert?

INT. BRIG – MINUTES LATER.

Captain Shakespeare is holding Tristan by the ankles out of a porthole. We can hear Yvaine screaming.

> CAPTAIN
> Thought you could just wander onto my patch, did you? Take my lightning? Or what? Do a little sightseeing? You think I'm here for your amusement? Thought you'd spin me a line about Queen Victoria, be the first to trespass on Captain Shakespeare's territory and live to tell the tale? Like I'd fall for it? Like I'm stupid? Big mistake, Mr Thorne. And the last one you'll ever make.

EXT. DECK – CONTINUOUS.

The crew, ear-wigging at the brig entrance, rush to the side. We take a pirate's POV in this mad dash, arriving just in time to see the Captain let go of Tristan's ankles, dropping him through the clouds to his doom.

Moments later, the Captain bursts onto the deck, dragging a struggling, shouting Yvaine behind him.

> YVAINE
> Brute! Murderer! Pig!

> CAPTAIN
> I'm taking the girl to my cabin. And mark my words: anyone who disturbs me for the next few hours will get the same treatment.

> SKINNY PIRATE
> (aghast)
> What, you'll...?!

> CAPTAIN
> No, you idiot! I'll sling you over the side.

> SKINNY PIRATE
> Oh, I see.

The Captain hauls Yvaine to his cabin, throws her in.

INT. CAPTAIN'S CABIN – CONTINUOUS.

Yvaine is thrown to the ground, still screaming. The door SLAMS behind her. She falls silent and gets up.

Sitting here is Tristan, wearing only his underpants. The Captain fetches WINE and THREE GLASSES as he talks. His voice is now well-spoken and lighter – almost fey.

> CAPTAIN
> So that went well, I thought. There'll be a few pants in the wash tonight, I'll wager! Now, sit down and tell me news of my beloved England. I want to hear absolutely everything.

> YVAINE
> Just a second – I can't believe your crew fell for that. And where in god's name did you get that mannequin from?

> CAPTAIN
> (shrugging)
> Works every time. An ounce of bargaining, a pinch of trickery and a soupçon of intimidation, et voilà – the recipe for a towering reputation without ever having to spill a drop of blood. Ever tried getting bloodstains out of a silk shirt? Nightmare.

> TRISTAN
> What I can't understand is how they're not going to recognize me among their number.

> CAPTAIN
> Tristan, dear boy, when I'm done, your own mother won't recognize you. Now we have no time to waste, we have only two hours before we make port. First and foremost...

He throws open a pair of double doors to reveal a WALK-IN WARDROBE full of piratey FINERY, some displayed on dressmakers' mannequins.

> CAPTAIN (CONT'D)
> It's so good to see you out of those dreary clothes – so very small-town errand-boy. Howlingly parochial.

Captain rifles through a rail, selects an outfit and flings it at Tristan.

> CAPTAIN (CONT'D)
> Here. Très you. I wore it as a younger man. I hate to throw anything away. You know the day you do it'll come back in fashion – be oh-so de la mode.

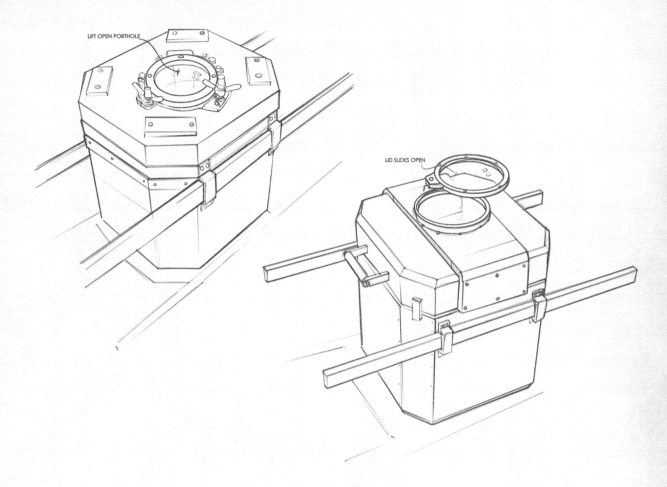

LIFT OPEN PORTHOLE

LID SLIDES OPEN

He gestures to another rail, indeed full of GOWNS.

                    CAPTAIN (CONT'D)
Now you, darling. I have some lovely dresses. Take your pick.

                    YVAINE
Oh no, really, I'm fine.

                    CAPTAIN
Honey, you're wearing a bathrobe. Now, England, England. I want to hear everything.

The Captain helps Tristan with his shirt buttons.

                    TRISTAN
You're not from England, though, are you? Your accent –

                    CAPTAIN
Oh, no! Sadly no. But from my earliest youth, I lapped up the stories. People told me they were nothing more than folklore. But my heart told me they were true. As a boy I'd scurry away from my father at the market while he did his deals. Just to peek over the wall. Dream of perhaps crossing it one day, seeing England for myself.

                    TRISTAN
              (what a weird parallel)
You were here, looking over there...

The Captain scrutinizes Tristan.

                    CAPTAIN
Hair.

INT. CAPTAIN'S CABIN – MOMENTS LATER.

An uneasy-looking Tristan – now in a barber's cape – is seated at the table, the Captain behind him with a pair of SCISSORS. He's midway through giving Tristan a very short – and not terribly nice – haircut.

                    CAPTAIN
Always did my best to fit in, of course. Tried to make my father, Cap'n Ghostmaker, proud. Forged a decent

reputation as a ruthless marauder and cold-blooded killer. But I couldn't help myself. One day I could resist it no longer: I slipped through the gap, into England.

TRISTAN
You slipped through the gap?! Past the Guard?!

CAPTAIN
The old fella? I just waited 'til he fell asleep.
(eager to continue)
And I arrived in England a blank canvas: a heart and soul and body waiting for reinvention. Finally, I could be the man I wanted to be.

YVAINE
That must have been... lovely.

CAPTAIN
Oh I adored every moment. Strolling down Pall Mall. Perusing the latest fashions on Savile Row. Catching the latest Gilbert and Sullivan musical at the Savoy Theatre. Then back to my lodgings to sip tea from a beautiful bone china teapot.

The Captain appraises his handy work, and swaps his scissors for a COMB. Presently we see that this is a special comb: it's making Tristan's hair GROW.

TRISTAN
Why did you come back?

CAPTAIN
My father died. Always promised him I'd take over the family business. Keep the old girl flying.
(sighs)
Ah, you've no idea the lightness it brings to my heart, being able to confide in you charming young people. The pressure of maintaining the whole Captain Shakespeare persona for the sake of the crew... I don't know, sometimes...

YVAINE
Persona?

CAPTAIN
Oh, I'm very much a man of my own creation. Even chose the name specially. Took me ages. See, I'm thinking: legendary British wordsmith. My enemies

and crew are thinking: Shake. Spear.

He makes scary throttling and stabbing motions. Tristan and Yvaine exchange doubtful looks.

CAPTAIN (CONT'D)
It's little things like that make me happy.

Tristan's hair is now extremely long. The Captain starts snipping at it again.

TRISTAN
I don't understand... Surely it would make you happier to actually be yourself? Why fight to be accepted by people you don't actually want to be like?

YVAINE
(sarcastic)
Yeah, why would anyone do that to himself?

TRISTAN
(not getting it)
Exactly.

Yvaine smirks at Tristan, amused: he could so easily be talking about himself. Realising, he looks away.

EXT. CLIFF-TOP PORT TOWN – DAY.

The sky vessel has 'docked'. It floats beside a cliff top, gangplank down. Nearby we see other vessels and hear the bustle of a rowdy port town.

Near the docks, we find an artfully camouflaged HUT. A door opens and Shakespeare, Yvaine and the crew shuffle through, the crew toting several heavy-looking crates.

INT. FERDINAND THE FENCE'S DODGY DEN – DAY.

A wooden crate, blinding light bursting out from within as several of Captain Shakespeare's men struggle to nail the lid on it. The Captain and Yvaine look on, with another shady character, FERDINAND THE FENCE.

Behind them we see myriad stocks of magical objects, some of which we might recognize from the market.

FERDY THE FENCE
This doesn't look very fresh to me,

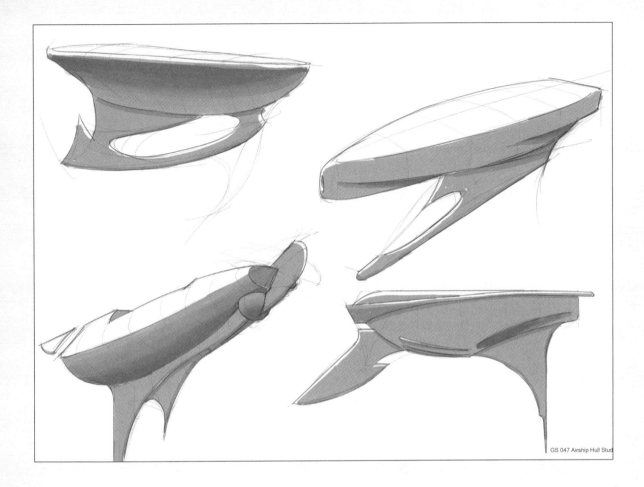

GS 047 Airship Hull Stud

Captain.

The Captain reaches for a leather-covered container – not unlike a hip flask or quiver – unscrews a stopper.

> CAPTAIN
> I'll give you a little taste shall I, young Ferdinand?

> FERDY THE FENCE
> No, no, Captain, I'll take your word for it, I –

As Ferdy raises his hands in protest, the Captain points the container at him and opens it for a split second. A bolt of blue lightning leaps out, hitting Ferdy's hand. He's thrown backward, landing in a heap. The pirates roar with laughter.

> CAPTAIN
> I think it's still crackling, very much alive, Ferdy – still très fresh.

Ferdy gets up, brushes himself down, holding his hand.

> CAPTAIN (CONT'D)
> So. Name your best price.

> FERDY THE FENCE
> For ten thousand bolts?

> CAPTAIN
> Ten thousand bolts of finest quality grade A.

> FERDY THE FENCE
> Yeah... see, here's my problem: It's hard to shift, it's hard to store, if I get the Revenue men in here, sniffing about...
> (shrugs)
> Best price? A hundred and fifty guineas.

The pirates have just finished unloading the boxes.

> CAPTAIN
> (to Skinny Pirate)
> Put the merchandise back on board and prepare to sail!
> (to Ferdy)
> Ferdinand? Always a pleasure.

The pirates reluctantly go to pick up the boxes. Ferdy raises a hand to stop them.

>   FERDY THE FENCE
>   One sixty.

>   CAPTAIN
>   Seeing as I'm feeling particularly gener-
>   ous today – I'll settle for two hundred.

>   FERDY THE FENCE
>   Two hundred! You've had your head in
>   the lightning barrel, Captain! You've
>   been sailing up where the air's too thin.

>   CAPTAIN
>   You're being very rude.
>   (off his nervous look)
>   Take it as a compliment, young Ferdi-
>   nand. In our line of business it doesn't do
>   to be too amicable. Two hundred.

>   FERDY THE FENCE
>   One eighty.

>   CAPTAIN
>   Two hundred.

>   FERDY THE FENCE
>   That's not negotiation! I'm changing my
>   number! One eight five.

>   CAPTAIN
>   Did I hear two hundred?

>   FERDY THE FENCE
>   From you, you did. One nine five. My
>   final offer.

>   CAPTAIN
>   One nine five it is.

Ferdy looks surprised and delighted. They shake hands.

>   CAPTAIN (CONT'D)
>   So with sales tax, that's... Let's see...
>   Two hundred.

>   FERDY THE FENCE
>   (glumly resigned)
>   Put 'em in the back.

The pirates move the boxes to the back of the warehouse, leaving only Yvaine, Ferdy and the Captain. Ferdy starts shifting COINS from one BAG into ANOTHER.

>   FERDY THE FENCE (CONT'D)
>   (changing the subject)
>   Hey, you'd be the man to ask – have you
>   heard these rumours about a fallen
>   star? Everybody's talking about it.
>   Think about it, Captain. Find that and
>   we could shut up shop and retire.

Yvaine freezes.

>   CAPTAIN
>   A fallen star? Really?

>   FERDY THE FENCE
>   You haven't heard anything on your
>   travels?

A long inscrutable look. Then the Captain shakes his head.

>   FERDY THE FENCE (CONT'D)
>   Not anything? Not even a little sniff of a
>   whisper? Everybody's talking about it
>   down the market.

>   CAPTAIN
>   Which market? The market near the
>   wall? Ferdy, you're wasting your time,
>   listening to gossip from the kind of pond
>   scum trading down there.

Before the Captain can continue, who should walk in but Ditch-Water Sal. Here for some shady wares, no doubt.

>   CAPTAIN (CONT'D)
>   Oh, my word, speak of the devil.

>   SAL
>   Oh, yeah? What was you saying then?

>   CAPTAIN
>   What a wonderful woman you are, Sal.
>   How the world wouldn't be the same
>   place without you.

He takes the bag of cash from Ferdy's hand.

>   CAPTAIN (CONT'D)
>   But you two have business to attend to.
>   Sal. Ferdy. Good day.

EXT. SKY VESSEL DECK – MOMENTS LATER.

The crew pour up the gangplank behind the Captain and stop in surprise: A stranger in pirate gear lounges on deck, his feet up. He looks damn fine. He draws on a pipe and tries not to cough. He is, of course, Tristan.

> TRISTAN
> Ah, Captain Shakespeare. I've been expecting you.

A hearty handshake, then the Captain turns to his crew.

> CAPTAIN
> Meet my nephew: the fearsome buccaneer Tristan Thorne. He'll be joining us for the final days of our journey home.
> (to Tristan, grinning)
> I have the perfect gift to keep you amused on the way.

He pushes Yvaine towards Tristan, who laughs.

The crew look at him with concern. Hastily, Tristan seizes Yvaine and gives a triumphant gesture and manly growl more befitting a buccaneer who has just been presented with a wench.

Appeased, the pirates give a lusty cheer of support.

MONTAGE – ABOARD THE SKY VESSEL – DAY/NIGHT.

— Stunning views over Stormhold as the Captain teaches Tristan to sail the ship.

— Tristan and Yvaine exchange contented glances as the wind rushes through their hair on deck.

— Dining in the Captain's cabin, Tristan feeds Yvaine a mouthful of food, the first she's tasted. A joyful revelation. We may notice in the low light of the cabin, that she is beginning to twinkle again.

— The Captain coaches Tristan in sword-fighting.

— The Captain teaches Yvaine to play the piano.

— Tristan and Yvaine help trawl for lightning. In their first net: a fine, glowing haul. The crew applaud.

— Tristan's sword-fighting improves a little.

— Captain Shakespeare teaches Yvaine to Waltz.

— Tristan helps Yvaine climb high into the rigging

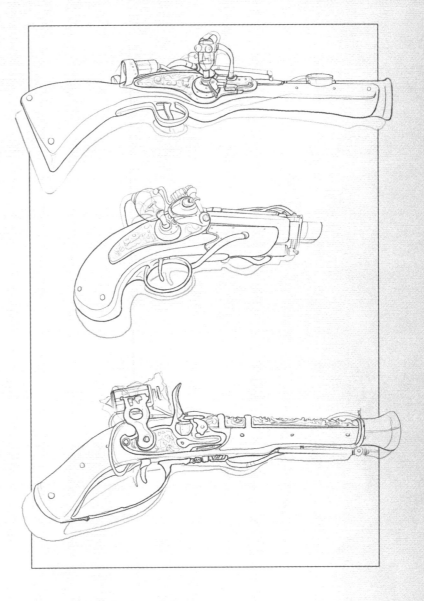

and they enjoy the wind rushing past and the glorious view.

— Yvaine, helping the cook, secretly dips her finger into some stew, having found a liking for food.

EXT. SKY VESSEL DECK – DAY.

The Captain is coaching Tristan in sword-fighting.

> CAPTAIN
> Much better! Almost had me there.

> TRISTAN
> Captain, may I ask you something? This vessel... How high can it go? I mean, could you fly to, I don't know, the stars?

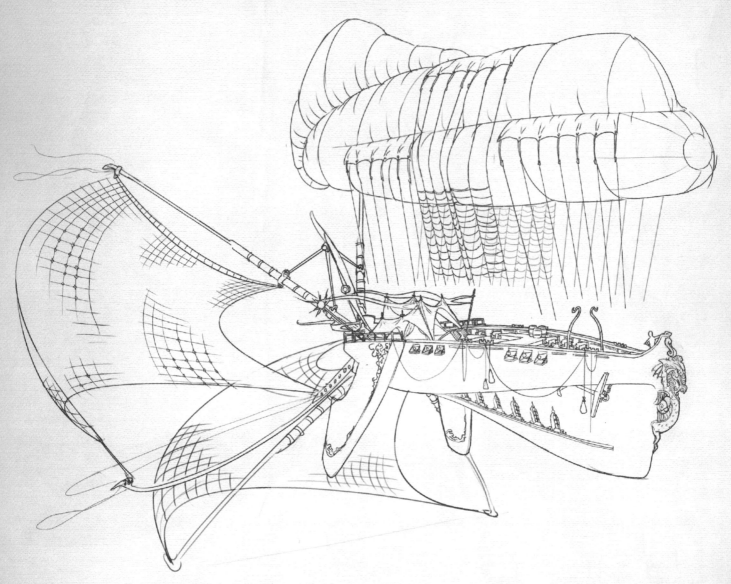

CAPTAIN
Why would anyone want to do that?

TRISTAN
Some people dream of travelling to space, don't they?

CAPTAIN
I do know one way you can get there. Well kept secret. Get a submission out of me now and I'll tell you it.

Eyes blazing with determination, Tristan launches into a sequence of artful attacks and parries, finally getting the better of the Captain.

CAPTAIN (CONT'D)
Touché. I'm impressed. Okay...
(leaning in, whispering)
There's something called... a Babylon candle.

TRISTAN
That was it?! I know THAT! How do you think we got onto a bloody cloud in the first place?!

CAPTAIN
You had a Babylon candle? How on earth...? Do you have any idea how rare they are?

TRISTAN
I, I... No. It was a gift.

CAPTAIN
Really? Gosh. Incredibly hard to find. Very few ever made, you see. Wish we'd had this conversation earlier – the chap I just sold to, Ferdy the Fence? Once in a blue moon, he'll see one. Most of his clients trade at the market near the wall. So you could ask around when you

get there. But don't get your hopes up too high.

EXT. SKY VESSEL – DECK – NIGHT.

A moonlit night on deck. A GRAMOPHONE is playing, and the Captain is teaching Yvaine ballroom dancing.

> YVAINE
> Is this right?

He nods.

> CAPTAIN
> Yvaine... I... know what you are.

She springs away from him, and the glittering corona around her dims a little. He pulls her gently back.

> CAPTAIN (CONT'D)
> Don't fear. No one on this vessel will harm you. But there are plenty who would. Just... When you return to Stormhold... Be careful. Your emotions give you away, Yvaine. You must learn to control them. You've grown a little brighter every day. And I think you know why.

> YVAINE
> Well it's obvious, isn't it?

> CAPTAIN
> To me, yes. But I don't think he's realised yet.

> YVAINE
> Who? Tristan? Don't be absurd! He's known I was a star ever since we met.

> CAPTAIN
> (smiling to himself)
> So you've not realised it either.

> YVAINE
> (irritable)
> What are you talking about? Of course I know why I'm glowing! I'm a star. And what do stars do best?

> CAPTAIN
> (affectionate, teasing)
> Well, it's certainly not the waltz.

Tristan arrives, taps the Captain politely on the shoulder and takes Yvaine in his arms to dance.

As they begin, the shimmer around Yvaine again begins to glow more brightly than ever.

INT. FERDINAND THE FENCE'S DODGY DEN – NIGHT.

Lamia menacingly circles Ferdinand the Fence.

> LAMIA
> Due west you say?

Ferdy nods. Lamia flicks a shiny gold coin into the air in Ferdy's direction. Ferdy opens both hands to catch it. At the top of its arc Lamia HALTS it with a hand motion.

> LAMIA (CONT'D)
> And you're certain he had a girl with him?

Ferdy nods – and continues nodding.

> LAMIA (CONT'D)
> You're sure? Absolutely sure? Sure you're not lying?

Ferdy shakes his head. Lamia clicks her fingers – RELEASING the coin to drop into Ferdy's open hands. He catches it with a crooked smile. Lamia goes to leave.

> LAMIA (CONT'D)
> You better be telling the truth, you two-faced dog.

> FERDY THE FENCE
> I can get you one of those. Anything you want –

> LAMIA
> (struck by a thought)
> What are the chances of getting a Babylon candle?

Lamia – curious – walks back towards Ferdy. Ferdy laughs. Then an intake of breath, and:

> FERDY THE FENCE
> Slim. I'll tell you what though, I knew a girl once who had a friend, whose brother knew this fella, who –

Lamia gently places her index finger on Ferdy's lips.

> LAMIA
> Enough.

Ferdy frantically tries speak but finds that he is now able only to make strange SQUAWKING NOISES.

EXT. SKY VESSEL DECK – DAY.

Tristan watches the sun set, a new man. The vessel makes its descent to land. Yvaine joins him and they share an almost-wistful smile. The moment is interrupted by the Skinny Pirate.

> SKINNY PIRATE
> Um, just to warn you: the Captain has decided to land the ship himself, so you might want to hold on. Tight.

Over on the wheelhouse, Shakespeare gleefully spins the wheel and enjoys the increasingly strong breeze.

Yvaine and Tristan clutch the balustrade and each other. They laugh and shriek as the ship gathers speed.

EXT. A LAKE IN STORMHOLD – DAY.

The airship makes a slightly erratic splashdown. It's a spectacular sight.

EXT. GANGPLANK – CONTINUOUS.

The Captain hugs Yvaine. He hands Tristan a glass CONTAINER brimful of bright, sparking lightning.

> CAPTAIN
> (pointing)
> So there's the road you'll need for Wall. Good luck on your journey home, Yvaine, wherever that may be. And good luck to you, Tristan. With your Victoria.

> TRISTAN
> How can we ever thank you enough for your kindness?

> CAPTAIN
> Don't mention it.
>   (off Tristan's warm smile)
> No, seriously. I mean: don't mention it. Reputations, you know? A lifetime to build –
>   (clicks his fingers)
> Seconds to destroy.

Tristan nods. Now he gets it.

> CAPTAIN (CONT'D)
> Oh, and Tristan...

He whispers something in Tristan's ear.

> CAPTAIN (CONT'D)
> Just think about it.

Tristan joins Yvaine and the pair turn to leave. The Captain waves after them.

> CAPTAIN (CONT'D)
> (slightly camp)
> Well, give my regards to England! It's been a pleasure to meet you both.

The pirates look perplexed at this.

> CAPTAIN (CONT'D)
> (shouting, in tough voice)
> Mind you don't wear that wench out, Captain Tristan!

This is more like it. The pirates give a loud cheer of approval.

The Skinny Pirate, clearly aware all along of the rather flimsy subterfuge, rolls his eyes affectionately.

EXT. DOCKSIDE – CONTINUOUS.

Tristan and Yvaine walk a little way down the dock.

> YVAINE
> What did he say to you?

> TRISTAN
> What did he say when?

> YVAINE
> Just then. When he whispered to you.

> TRISTAN
> Whispered? Oh. Nothing. No... He just – he said I should use the lightning to get you a new Babylon candle. Barter. Y'know.

INT. FERDINAND THE FENCE'S DODGY DEN – DAY.

Septimus is here with his lackeys, interrogating a terrified Ferdy.

SEPTIMUS
For the last time: where is the girl?

Alas, Ferdy can't speak, only squawk.

SEPTIMUS (CONT'D)
(almost out of patience)
The girl with the stone! Where did she
go?

Ferdy squawks with increasing desperation.

SEPTIMUS (CONT'D)
Are you mocking me? Because if you
are, believe me, you have seconds to
live.

Ferdy squawks one more time. And it's one too
many for Septimus. He draws his sword, swiftly
skewers Ferdy and walks away, furious.

He holds his bloodied sword at arm's length
toward one of his lackeys.

SEPTIMUS (CONT'D)
Clean this for me.

He regards the late Ferdy with distaste.

SEPTIMUS (CONT'D)
Thoroughly.

INT. PRIMUS' CARRIAGE – DAY.

Lamia, gazing at her reflection in the window,
prods purposefully at her face, which has aged
even further as a result of casting the spell on
Ferdy.

At her magical touch, her fallen face TIGHTENS a
little. She smiles, admiring her handiwork.

Suddenly, her breasts DROOP dramatically. She
gasps in surprise and annoyance.

LAMIA
Oh bollocks.

From O.S., we hear stifled laughter: Empusa and Mormo, who, unbeknownst to Lamia, have been watching her. Mormo clears her throat loudly, making Lamia jump.

MORMO
If you've quite finished squandering your magic on your rather counterproductive beauty routine, you may be interested to know that the star has returned.

EMPUSA
She's back on land!

LAMIA
I know, damn it! I couldn't reach the lake in time.

MORMO
No matter – we have found her. She's on the road to the village of Wall. If you take the shortcut across the marshes, you should arrive in time to intercept her.

EXT. PRIMUS' CARRIAGE – DAY.

An invisible whip cracks. The horses speed to a gallop.

EXT. STORMHOLD COUNTRYSIDE – DAY.

Tristan and Yvaine walk cautiously between a ditch and a hedgerow. Distantly, we hear VOICES, getting louder. With astounding speed, he pushes her into the ditch, leaps in after her and pulls a bough down over them.

The gloom is lit only by the starry glow around Yvaine. They breathe loudly in the darkness, suddenly awkward at finding themselves pressed so close. An unexpected electricity. Yvaine tries to diffuse it.

YVAINE
(whispering)
Are you trying to break my leg again? It might be nice to have full mobility for a bit longer, if that's okay by you.

TRISTAN
(whispering)
I'm sorry. I just... We can't risk people seeing you. I don't trust anyone.

The voices remain distant but they continue to whisper.

YVAINE
But at this rate, if we keep stopping... I mean, we've only got two more days 'til Victoria's birthday.

TRISTAN
We'll make it. We're making good time.

As Yvaine goes to speak, the voices get louder. Tristan touches a finger to her lips. They lie in silence as the voices pass right above them, then begin to fade.

TRISTAN (CONT'D)
Leave it a minute.

They lie in silence a while longer. Then:

YVAINE
Aren't you tempted?

TRISTAN
Tempted by what?

YVAINE
Immortality. Say it wasn't my heart. Not me. Just a star you didn't know.

TRISTAN
Do you seriously think I could kill anybody? But even then. Everlasting life? I imagine it would be sort of... lonely.

There's a long silence. Yvaine turns her head away, not wanting Tristan to see the tears welling in her eyes. He's right. It is lonely.

TRISTAN (CONT'D)
Unless you had someone to share it with. Someone you loved. I suppose that would be different.

Silence. The voices nowhere to be heard.

TRISTAN (CONT'D)
I think we're safe now. Shall we?

Tristan lets go of the branch and daylight floods in. He climbs out and offers Yvaine his hand. She takes it.

EXT. LAKE – DAY.

Septimus and his entourage study the tracks in the dirt. No doubt about it: Lamia stopped here. Septimus sighs. They're going to have to investigate further.

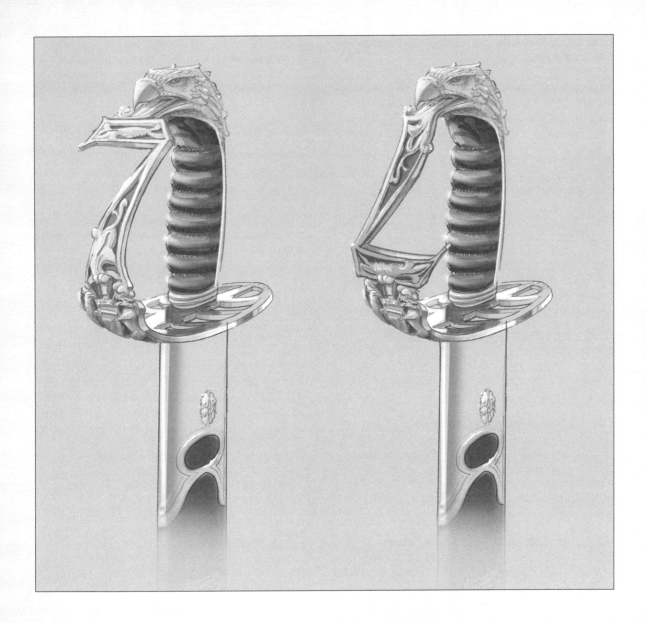

SEPTIMUS

Be ready: Captain Shakespeare has a fearsome reputation.

The lackeys nod anxiously, hesitating briefly before following Septimus down the path towards the lake, where the Sky Vessel is still docked.

INT. CAPTAIN'S CABIN – DRESSINGROOM – DAY.

Oblivious to the imminent siege of his vessel, the Captain stands in his walk-in closet. He begins to play A RECORD on his GRAMOPHONE before admiring his reflection in the mirror. He has changed his clothes and is now wearing a petticoat and camisole.

EXT. SKY VESSEL – DECK – SIMULTANEOUS.

Septimus' men confront the pirates. A huge fight breaks out: the royal entourage versus the pirates.

INT. CAPTAIN'S CABIN – ANTECHAMBERS – SIMULTANEOUS.

Septimus bursts in, sword drawn, and stalks carefully through the room, looking for the Captain.

We INTERCUT rapidly between the mayhem on deck, Septimus' approach, and the Captain in his dressing room, where he tries various poses in the mirror with A FAN and FEATHER BOA whilst cavorting enthusiastically to the music.

INT. CAPTAIN'S CABIN – DRESSINGROOM – CONTINUOUS.

Finally, Septimus finds the Captain. Still frolicking before the mirror, now holding an elaborate pink dress. This is not what he was expecting.

SEPTIMUS
What the hell is this?

The Captain drops the dress in shock.

CAPTAIN
What are you doing here?

SEPTIMUS
My name is Prince Septimus. And you're going to tell me where I can find the girl.

EXT. SKY VESSEL – DECK – MOMENTS LATER.

The battle continues.

INT. CAPTAIN'S CABIN – MOMENTS LATER.

We can see from the Captain's dishevelled state that he has put up a fight. But, unarmed, he hasn't stood a chance, and now Septimus has him pinned to the desk, sword to his throat.

SEPTIMUS
For the last time, twinkletoes, where is the girl? I'm going to count to three. One... Two...

He looks up in alarm as the door flies open and, with a rowdy shout, the entire pirate crew pile in and barrel towards him.

Trapped, Septimus turns and runs towards the window, smashing through it and leaping down into the lake.

EXT. STORMHOLD CLIFF TOP – DAY.

Despite the steep slope, Tristan and Yvaine are keeping a quite a pace. Yvaine turns to check on Tristan, who has fallen behind, and finds him squinting at her.

YVAINE
What? What is it?

She pats her hair, shoulders, behind, craning to see if she has something on her.

TRISTAN
I was just... You... Did you know you sort of... glitter? I only started noticing it these last few days. Is that... normal?

YVAINE
Let's see if you can work it out for yourself... What do stars do?

TRISTAN
Attract trouble?

Yvaine stops until he's caught up, then pushes him in mock crossness. They carry on walking side by side.

TRISTAN (CONT'D)
(playful)
Do I have another guess? Is it... know exactly how to annoy a boy called Tristan Thorne?

Yvaine stops again, and her face falls. It takes a moment for Tristan to realize why: a stone MILE MARKER at the side of the road. It reads: WALL 60 MILES.

YVAINE
How long will that take? Two days?
(off his nod)
But we don't have two days. Victoria's birthday is tomorrow.

TRISTAN
Well remembered.

They start to walk again, subdued.

INT. SKY VESSEL – CAPTAIN'S CABIN – DAY.

The pirates are still in the doorway looking at the Captain, now standing up, though somewhat wobbly.

CAPTAIN
Get out! All of you!

SKINNY PIRATE
Did he hurt you Captain?

The Captain buries his head in his hands and shakes it.

SKINNY PIRATE (CONT'D)
Did you tell him where your nephew and the girl went?

The Captain shakes his head again.

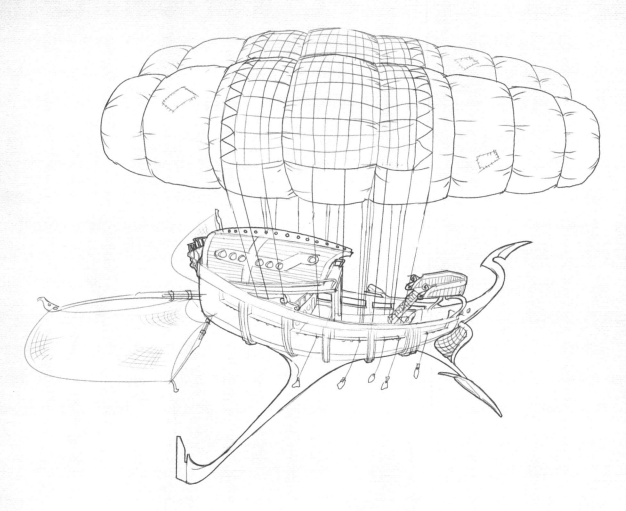

SKINNY PIRATE (CONT'D)
So what's the problem?

CAPTAIN
It's my... reputation.

SKINNY PIRATE
No, no! Nonsense!

The others join in with sympathetic noises of protest.

VERY OLD PIRATE
It's alright Cap'n. We always knew you was a whoopsie.

The other pirates "shhh" him and elbow him sharply out of the way. They all beam at the Captain affectionately.

SKINNY PIRATE
You'll always be our Captain, Captain.

ALL PIRATES
Aye!

The Captain breaks into a smile. Sits up straight, smoothes his rumpled camisole top. And gives his crew a triumphant hand gesture and a proud piratey growl.

They return it with enthusiasm.

EXT. LAKE – DAY.

Septimus emerges from under water, swims to the bank of the lake and climbs out, cold, wet and furious.

Here, a confused Bernard waits on horseback.

BERNARD
Prince Septimus! Your men! They're dead! All of them!

SEPTIMUS
Oh really.

He pushes Bernard off the horse, leaps into the saddle and rides away. Alone and unsure of what to do, Bernard makes his way up the gangplank of the pirate ship.

EXT. UNDER A BRIDGE – DAY.

Tristan and Yvaine are hiding again. We hear hooves approaching. From their POV, we see Ditch-Water Sal's caravan. Yvaine squints curiously. Something clicks.

> YVAINE
> Oh my god, Tristan! I recognize that woman! From when I went with the Captain?

Tristan "shhh"es her.

> YVAINE (CONT'D)
> (whispering urgently)
> When he went to sell lightning to... what was his name? Ferdy the Fence? He said she traded at the market near Wall! We could hitch a lift!

> TRISTAN
> (forgetting to whisper)
> Ferdy the Fence? Ferdy the Fence?!

He throws the branch aside, leaps up and shouts to Sal.

> TRISTAN (CONT'D)
> Stop!!!

Sal stops, curious. Tristan and Yvaine sprint over.

> TRISTAN (CONT'D)
> Excuse me madam, but my name is Tristan Thorne, and –

> SAL
> (pointing at his lapel)
> Thief!

Sal's bird flies from its perch and begins to flap wildly, adding to the chaos as Sal screams.

> SAL (CONT'D)
> That's my flower! Eighteen years, I've been looking for that. Give it to me now!

> TRISTAN
> Give it to you? Never!

> YVAINE
> How dare you? That was a gift from his mother!

Sal blanks Yvaine and makes a grab for the flower. Tristan draws his sword, and she backs away, shocked.

> SAL
> Perhaps I was mistaken.

> TRISTAN
> It's obviously very valuable to you. And you can have it. In exchange for what I need: a Babylon candle.

> YVAINE
> And safe passage to the wall.

> SAL
> A Babylon candle? How dare you!? I don't deal in black magic!

> TRISTAN
> I think Ferdy the Fence might have something different to say about that.

> SAL
> He may do. And he may also be able to recommend someone else at the market who can sell you one.

> TRISTAN
> What about giving us a lift to the wall, then?

> SAL
> Well why didn't you say so in the first place? For that flower I can offer you passage. Food and lodging on the way.

> TRISTAN
> Safe passage.

> SAL
> I swear you shall arrive at the wall in the same condition that you're in now.

Sal holds out her hand for the flower. Tristan takes one last look and hands it over.

> SAL (CONT'D)
> Do you have any idea what manner of thing it was that you had?

> TRISTAN
> Some kind of lucky charm?

> SAL
> A very lucky charm indeed. Protection. In fact, the exact thing that would have prevented me from doing this:

She touches Tristan's forehead and he turns into a MOUSE. Sal scoops him up into her hands.

Yvaine screams and runs at her, but it's as if a

force field prevents them from touching – thanks to Lamia's spell, Sal can't perceive her presence.

> SAL (CONT'D)
> Much better. My little caravan is far too small for regular passengers. But I'll keep my word: you shall not be harmed.

INT. CARAVAN – MOMENTS LATER.

Sal drops Tristan-the-mouse into a little cage. She throws in a handful of nuts after him.

> SAL
> Your food and lodging, just as I vowed.

She chuckles at her little joke and locks the cage with a key. Yvaine stands at the door, watching aghast.

> YVAINE
> Would I be correct in thinking that you can neither see nor hear me?

There is no reply as Sal walks towards her.

> YVAINE (CONT'D)
> Then I'd like to tell you that you smell of pee. You look like the wrong end of a dog. And I swear that if I don't get my Tristan back as he was, you'll regret it forever.

Sal passes her, smiling and oblivious.

EXT. STORMHOLD CLIFF TOP – DAY.

The same 60-miles-to-Wall marker we saw earlier. Septimus, on horseback, pauses briefly to note this before speeding onwards.

EXT. STORMHOLD LANDSCAPE – DAY.

Sal's yellow caravan clatters across the countryside.

INT. CARAVAN – DAY.

Yvaine pokes her finger through the bars of the cage. Tristan-the-mouse sniffs it and walks off.

> YVAINE
> Tristan. Tristan! If you can understand me, look at me now.

He doesn't respond. She puts her head in her hands.

> YVAINE (CONT'D)
> I can't bear seeing you like this. I mean, I know it's probably worse for you. But I... Look, she's a witch, and a witch's promise can't be broken. And if she welches on the deal, I'll become her personal poltergeist until she changes you back.

The mouse returns to the bars and stands. Yvaine smiles until she realizes that he is actually looking past her. Disappointed, she notes the real object of his interest: a large wheel of CHEESE on a shelf. He scuttles off and Yvaine slumps back, depressed.

> YVAINE (CONT'D)
> You really are a mouse now, aren't you.

She breaks off a lump of cheese and begins to feed him.

YVAINE (CONT'D)
You know when I said I knew little about love? That wasn't true. I know a lot about love. I've seen it, centuries and centuries of it, and it was the only thing that made watching your world bearable. All those wars. Pain, lies, hate... It made me want to turn away and never look down again. But when I see the way that mankind loves... You could search to the furthest reaches of the universe and never find anything more beautiful. So yes, I know that love is unconditional. But I also know that it can be unpredictable, unexpected, uncontrollable, unbearable and strangely easy to mistake for loathing, and... What I'm trying to say, Tristan is... I think I love you.

The cheese has run out. The mouse sniffs Yvaine's fingers. He pauses briefly and scuttles off.

YVAINE (CONT'D)
Is this love, Tristan? I never imagined I'd know it for myself. My heart... It feels like my chest can barely contain it. Like it's trying to escape because it doesn't belong to me any more. It belongs to you. And if you wanted it, I'd wish for nothing in exchange - no gifts. No goods. No demonstrations of devotion. Nothing but knowing you loved me too. Just your heart, in exchange for mine.

The mouse scratches around, completely uninterested. Finally he scampers back to the bars to stare at the cheese.

EXT. STORMHOLD MARKET TOWN - CARAVAN - NIGHT.

The caravan has finally arrived. Sal is on the step with the cage. She unlocks it and frees the mouse.

SAL
The wall is one mile away. Though the walk may take you a little longer than normal. Transformation can leave your brain scrambled for a while, so they tell me.

She touches her finger to the mouse's head and Tristan returns to his human form. Dazed, he falls down the steps. Yvaine rushes over, kneels protectively by him.

SAL (CONT'D)
There: safe and sound. Never let it be said that Ditch-Water Sal is anything but true to her word.

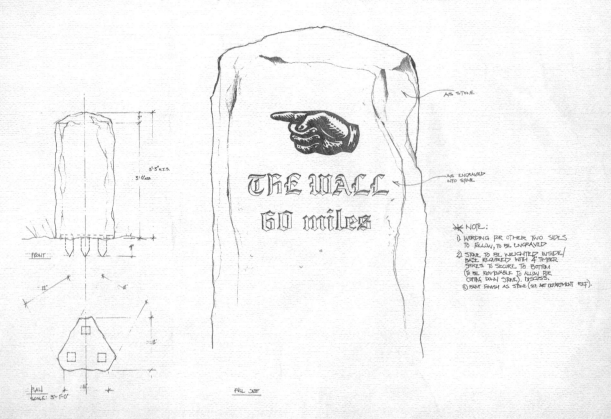

TRISTAN
You wretched old...

Tristan stands unsteadily and goes to draw his sword, but falls over again. Sal chuckles some more.

SAL
I warned you. Save your strength.

Yvaine helps Tristan up.

YVAINE
I've been so worried about you.

She gives him a huge hug. He looks disoriented, weak.

TRISTAN
Victoria?

She lets go of him.

YVAINE
I think I preferred "Mother".

TRISTAN
Sorry. I'm feeling a little bit...

He falls down again. With a sigh of resignation, she places his arm around her shoulder and hoists him up.

YVAINE
Come on. There's an inn over there. Victoria's birthday's not 'til tomorrow. I think you need a bath and a good night's sleep before you present me to her.

They head for the inn, with all the grace of parents competing in the three-legged race at sports day.

INT. SLAUGHTERED PRINCE INN – BEDROOM – NIGHT.

Tristan lies snoring on the bed. Yvaine kneels beside him and whispers softly in his ear.

YVAINE
Tristan. Your bath's ready.

No response. He's comatose. She speaks louder.

YVAINE (CONT'D)
Lovely hot bath. All ready for you.

Still nothing. She shakes him gently. Then harder.

YVAINE (CONT'D)
(shouting)
Tristan!
(off the total silence)
I'm getting used to these one sided conversations. Come on, let's get you in the bath.

Businesslike, she starts to undo his shirt, but stops, suddenly overwhelmed by an unfamiliar feeling. She blushes. Kisses him lightly on the lips. He sleeps on.

Glancing over at the bath she shrugs and begins to disrobe.

INT. SLAUGHTERED PRINCE INN – BEDROOM – MOMENTS LATER.

Yvaine lies dreamily in the steaming bath.

TRISTAN
Excuse me, but I think you're in my bath?

Yvaine wheels around to see Tristan. She screams.

YVAINE
Why, you – avert your eyes!

TRISTAN
I'm not looking! I'm not looking!

He covers his eyes and shuffles over with a towel. She grabs it, climbs out and wraps up.

YVAINE
Okay, you can open them now.

He opens his eyes. She looks beautiful.

TRISTAN
Did you really mean what you said in the caravan?

YVAINE
What I... But, but you were a mouse! You wanted cheese! You didn't... I asked you to give me a sign if you understood me!

TRISTAN
And risk you being too embarrassed to keep saying all those nice things?

Yvaine covers her face, mortified.

TRISTAN (CONT'D)
Do you want to know what the Captain
really whispered to me?

She keeps her face covered but nods vigorously.

TRISTAN (CONT'D)
He told me that my true love was in
front of my eyes... And he was right.

Yvaine lowers her hands. She can hardly believe
what she's hearing. He kisses her. And what a
kiss it is.

As they embrace, the light around Yvaine grows
brighter and brighter.

EXT. SLAUGHTERED PRINCE INN – NIGHT.

All the ghostly princes – except Tertius – perch
morosely on a high ledge. Tertius floats above
them, only his backside visible. Finally, he pops
his head out, flushed and delighted.

TERTIUS
Oh come on, you have to see this.

SEXTUS
No thank you.

TERTIUS
Suit yourself.

With a gleeful expression, he pops his head back
inside.

QUARTUS
Pervert.

Secundus gestures to the inn sign above them.

SECUNDUS
Ironic, isn't it?

The others make noises of resigned agreement.

QUINTUS
(nodding in accord)
Yeah.
(a beat)
What is?

SEXTUS
Septimus will be here by morning. Find
the girl. Get the stone. And be king.
Forever.

SECUNDUS
Unjust. But still. We'll be free.

QUARTUS
Liberated from these wretched bodies.

SEXTUS
Resting in eternal quietude.

PRIMUS
Finally at peace.

QUINTUS
Anyone for a game of rock-paper-
scissors?

INT. WITCHES' LAIR – NIGHT.

Mormo and Empusa talk to Lamia in the mirror.

MORMO
You're very close. She's in the market
town. One mile from the gap in the wall.

LAMIA
(horrified)
You speak as if this is good news! Do I
need to remind you that Wall is not part
of our universe? If she crosses that
threshold into the human realm, our
star will become nothing more than a
pitted lump of metallic rock.

EMPUSA
(sharply)
Then I suggest you hurry up.

**INT. SLAUGHTERED PRINCE INN –
BEDROOM – DAWN.**

Yvaine sleeps in Tristan's arms. He is awake,
staring at her. Decisively, he gets up, dresses.

He looks at Yvaine, asleep. He draws his dagger...
and cuts a lock of her hair. Wrapping it carefully
in his lace handkerchief, he hurries out.

**INT. SLAUGHTERED PRINCE INN –
RECEPTION – DAWN.**

The Receptionist is sprawled on a sofa, asleep
with his dog. Tristan clears his throat. The dog
growls.

RECEPTIONIST
(eyes still shut)
What? What do you want?

TRISTAN
So sorry, but I need a pen and paper.

RECEPTIONIST
Ask me again at a more reasonable hour.

TRISTAN
I can't. I have to go. Look, if my friend wakes before I return please can you give her a message?

Reluctantly, the Receptionist opens his eyes, now grumpily resigned to being awake.

RECEPTIONIST
Go on.

YVAINE
Have you seen my friend?

RECEPTIONIST
He left. Absurdly early.

YVAINE
He left?

RECEPTIONIST
Told me to tell you he's gone to see Victoria because he's sorry but he's found his true love and he wants to spend the rest of his life with her.

YVAINE
What? Are you sure?

RECEPTIONIST
I'm positive.

EXT. STORMHOLD MARKET TOWN – DAWN.

Tristan walks past the deserted stalls, past the yellow caravan – he nods to the bird – and into the forest.

INT. INN – BEDROOM – DAY.

Yvaine stirs from her slumber. She turns over sleepily.

YVAINE
You know, that was the first time I've ever slept at night. I can't believe it.

She stretches happily until she feels that there is no one beside her. She sits up abruptly.

YVAINE (CONT'D)
Tristan?

EXT. THE WALL – DAY.

The old Guard is asleep. Tristan strides through the gap and pauses to take in the enormity of the moment: he's back in England.

INT. SLAUGHTERED PRINCE INN – RECEPTION – DAY.

The Receptionist is drinking coffee. Yvaine runs in.

EXT. WALL VILLAGE – DAY.

Tristan walks through the deserted village.

EXT. STORMHOLD MARKET TOWN – MOMENTS LATER.

Yvaine, no longer glittering, walks slowly through the market on her way to the wall. A hive of activity as stall-holders set up their stalls for the day.

She passes the flower stall by the yellow caravan. The Slave Girl, released from her bird form for a day's work, looks up from arranging the glass flowers.

SLAVE GIRL
Hey... Hey! You! Stop! Wait!

Yvaine, not recognizing her in her human form, just smiles wanly. Tears stream down her face as she marches on to her unintentional suicide.

Concerned, the girl runs from behind the stall in pursuit. The chain stops her before she can catch up.

EXT. VICTORIA'S HOUSE – DAY.

Tristan picks up a pebble to throw at the window, thinks a moment, then drops it.

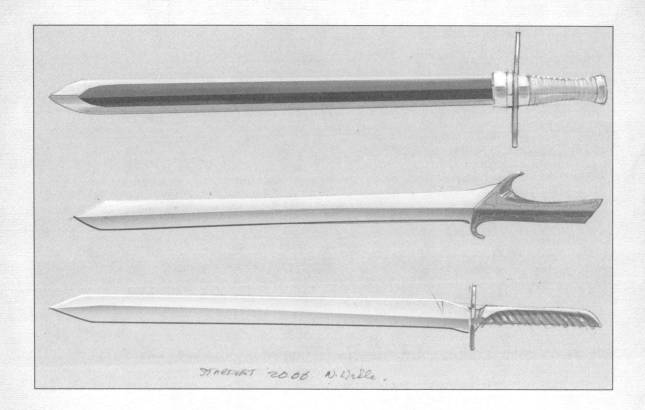

STARDUST 2006 N.Wille.

INT./EXT. CARAVAN – DAY.

As Yvaine disappears from her view, the increasingly frantic Slave Girl opens the caravan door and peeks in. Inside, Sal is sound asleep.

She quietly shuts the door and padlocks it.

EXT. VICTORIA'S HOUSE – DAY.

Tristan walks boldly to Victoria's front door and knocks.

Victoria opens it and reacts in shock. She barely recognizes this handsome and confident young man.

> TRISTAN
> Happy birthday.

> VICTORIA
> Tristan?! What happened to you?

> TRISTAN
> I found the star.

Victoria excitedly grabs Tristan's hand.

> VICTORIA
> Oh Tristan, I can't believe you did it!
> Where's my star? Can I see it? Is it

beautiful?

> TRISTAN
> The most beautiful thing in the world.

He takes the folded lace handkerchief from his pocket and hands it over. She stares at it, disappointed.

> VICTORIA
> It's awfully small.

> TRISTAN
> This is just a little piece. A token. For your birthday. The rest of it I love too much to part with.

> VICTORIA
> You...? But what about our agreement?

> TRISTAN
> Love isn't something you barter for, Victoria. It doesn't have a price tag. It isn't something to be bought or traded.

Victoria is frantic. Tristan looks unbelievably hot, has done the impossible for her and is now unavailable. What girl could resist?

> VICTORIA
> So forget the star. Keep it. It's not the star I want. You know what I want.

She gives him her most seductive look. It's a good one. Getting no response, she drapes her arms around him.

TRISTAN
Yes. I do.

To our horror Tristan puts his arms around her too. He leans her back in true romantic hero style, his lips only inches from hers, seconds away from the moment he'd so dearly wished for. Victoria closes her eyes.

TRISTAN (CONT'D)
You want to grow up and get over yourself.

Her eyes snap open and Tristan drops her.

As he turns to go, we see Humphrey has been here for who knows how long. Open-mouthed, shaking his head in disbelief.

HUMPHREY
Tristan Thorne. You must have some kind of a death wish.

He draws a SWORD, concealed in his silver-topped cane.

Tristan glances at Victoria – looking pleased at the prospect of a duel – and quizzically back to Humphrey, who continues to wave his sword.

Tristan sighs and unsheathes his own. He spins it in a breathtaking display recalling Indiana Jones. Humphrey shrinks away in surprise and alarm.

Tristan holsters his sword. He gestures at Victoria.

TRISTAN
All yours. You really do make a perfect couple. The best of luck to you both.

And again, he turns and starts on his way.

Even in the midst of this humiliating state of affairs, Victoria can't resist the lure of material treasures. Still sitting on the floor, she tears open the handkerchief and looks into it. Annoyed, she screws it up and tosses it after him.

VICTORIA
Why would I want that? Just a measly handful of stardust.

Tristan stops, regards her quizzically and picks up the handkerchief. He opens it slowly and stares inside to see... dust. His good mood turns to panic.

TRISTAN
Oh my god, Yvaine! She can't cross the wall.

And, leaving a confused Humphrey and Victoria behind, he bolts away, running as fast as he possibly can.

EXT. THE WALL – STORMHOLD SIDE – DAY.

Yvaine gets closer and closer to the gap in the wall.

INT./EXT. SAL'S CARAVAN – DAY.

The Slave Girl, sitting in the driving position, spurs the horses to go.

Inside, Ditch-Water Sal falls from the bed to the floor.

The caravan rumbles through the market, creating havoc, and out into the forest, in pursuit of Yvaine.

Inside, a furious Sal, in her nightgown, wrestles with the locked door and is repeatedly flung to the ground.

EXT. FOREST NEAR THE WALL – DAY.

Tristan runs. Faster than he's ever run before.

EXT. STORMHOLD LANDCAPE – DAY.

Septimus gallops onwards.

INT./EXT. PRIMUS' CARRIAGE – DAY.

Lamia spurs the carriage on.

EXT. THE WALL – STORMHOLD SIDE – DAY.

Yvaine pauses by the gap in the wall, then walks into England. While she is still in the gap, hands grab her from behind. She wheels round to find the Slave Girl.

SLAVE GIRL
Stop! If you go through, you'll die.

YVAINE
What?

SLAVE GIRL
If you set foot on human soil, you'll turn
to rock.

YVAINE
Who are you?

Before the girl can respond, a livid Sal smashes
through the locked door of the caravan and tugs
on the chain, pulling her to the ground. She tugs
some more, dragging the girl across the grass
towards her.

SAL
Wretched slattern! Where have you
taken me?

They are interrupted by A CLATTER OF
HOOVES. Primus' carriage arrives. The door
opens and Lamia emerges. Sal drops the chain in
shock.

LAMIA
(to Yvaine)
Planning to enter Wall, were you? If
death is what you wish, my dear, I'd be
more than happy to assist you.

SAL
Are you talking to me?

LAMIA
Ah. You. Small world. You don't recall
our meeting of course. Anyhow, no, I
wasn't. I was talking to the star.

SAL
What star? My slave girl is no star – any
fool can see that. If she was, I'd have had
the heart out of her chest a long time
ago, trust me.

LAMIA
Trust you? Not a mistake I'd be likely to
make again. What's it to be, Ditch-Water
Sal. Heads or tails?

SAL
Pardon?

LAMIA
I think I remember you always liked
"heads".

Lamia points her finger at Sal. Sal points back,
trying to defend herself with magic of her own,
but Lamia's is too strong. Sal struggles with the
effort.

The old Guard peeks over the wall, watching.
Horrified.

Another blast of magical force from Lamia, and
Sal's head VANISHES. No blood – it's just gone.

A pause and then, like the proverbial chicken,
headless Sal starts to run around madly, banging
into the caravan and several trees. Finally, she
stumbles and doesn't get up. Then, a puff of
SMOKE. And she's vanished.

Instantaneously, the chain leading from the
Slave Girl to the caravan turns to a mercury-
like liquid, splashing onto the ground. Free at
last. But not for long. Yvaine and the girl cling
together.

Lamia, now horrifically AGED after this last bout
of magic use, beckons to them.

LAMIA (CONT'D)
(to Yvaine)
Time to go.

SLAVE GIRL
She's not going anywhere!

LAMIA
I think you'll find she is. It's alright, you
can come too. Looks like you're out of a
job, and my sisters could use some
domestic help.

She points her bony fingers at them and two
lengths of the now-familiar mercury CHAIN fly
from her hand, wrapping themselves around the
women's wrists.

They scream as Lamia ties the loose ends to the
carriage and climbs into driving position.

LAMIA (CONT'D)
You can travel in the carriage, or be
dragged behind it. Your choice.

Whimpering, the pair climb in and shut the door.
A crack of Lamia's whip and they're off.

EXT. WALL – WALL SIDE – DAY.

Tristan, panting, arrives at the wall. Coming in
the opposite direction is the old Guard. He

STARDUST

motions for Tristan to enter the gap.

> GUARD
> Be my guest. I quit. Eighty years I stopped you people going out and I didn't even know what was over there. Never crossed my mind that what I should have been worrying about was those people from the other side coming in.

> TRISTAN
> What happened?

EXT. WALL – STORMHOLD SIDE – CONTINUOUS.

The former scene of the drama, deserted. The yellow caravan stands alone. We hear an anguished cry.

> TRISTAN (O.S.)
> NO!

Moments later, Tristan runs through the gap.

INT./EXT. SAL'S CARAVAN – CONTINUOUS.

In the debris inside the caravan, Tristan spots his glass snowdrop. He snatches it up.

A desperate scrabble to unhitch Sal's horse. And, with the greatest urgency of his life, Tristan mounts and gallops away.

INT./EXT. PRIMUS' CARRIAGE – DAY.

The carriage speeds Yvaine towards the witches' lair and her doom.

Inside, Yvaine sobs, comforted by the Slave Girl.

EXT. THE WALL – DAY.

Septimus arrives at a gallop, realising to his frustration that he is too late. He slows, cries out in frustration and protest, and, following Lamia's tracks, charges off in pursuit.

EXT. WITCHES' LAIR – DAY.

The carriage pulls up. Mormo and Empusa hobble out excitedly. Lamia drags her two grim-faced captives from the carriage, still clinging together.

> EMPUSA
> The star!

> MORMO
> And who else?

> LAMIA
> A slave for us. It'll be nice to have someone to help mop up when we've finished with our little guest.

> EMPUSA
> Good work, sister. And just in time too, I see: you look awful!

They all laugh. Soon they'll be young and lovely again.

EXT. STORMHOLD LANDSCAPE – DAY.

Tristan – riding for his life. Or rather, Yvaine's.

INT. WITCHES' LAIR – DAY.

Empusa pushes the fearful Slave Girl towards the filthy animal cages and thrusts an old dishrag into her hand.

Mormo and Lamia lead a stoic Yvaine up the stairway towards the mezzanine, where a large table stands – just as we saw them do with the star in Tristan's nightmare.

EXT. STORMHOLD LANDSCAPE – DAY.

Septimus rides at an intense gallop.

EXT. NEAR THE WITCHES' LAIR – DAY.

Tristan arrives at the vast canyon and begins to make his way down the treacherous path towards the lair.

INT. WITCHES' LAIR – DAY.

Mormo straps Yvaine to the table.

EXT. WITCHES' LAIR – DAY.

Outside the lair, Tristan peers in through a window. He is interrupted by a DAGGER at his neck. He turns to find Septimus.

SEPTIMUS
Who are you? What business do you
have here?

Tristan looks down at the hand holding the
dagger and sees on it an intricate tattoo of the
number "7", similar in style to the one we saw on
Primus' hand.

TRISTAN
(a flash of recognition)
Septimus. I knew your brother, Primus.

SEPTIMUS
And unless you wish to renew your
acquaintance with him in the afterlife, I
suggest you answer my question. What
are you doing here?

TRISTAN
I might ask you the same thing.

The camera jibs down. Tristan's dagger is drawn,
and he's holding it to Septimus' belly.

Septimus gives a nod of grudging resignation and
the two sheath their weapons. Now they're in
this together.

SEPTIMUS
Right. There are four of them. Do as I say
and we may stand a chance.

TRISTAN
Wait. How do I know you can be trusted?

SEPTIMUS
You don't. Why? Do you have a choice?
Now listen...

**INT. WITCHES' LAIR – SEPTIMUS'
FANTASY PLAN.**

As Septimus talks through his plan, we see flash-
es of an idealized reality in which it takes place,
executed to perfection.

SEPTIMUS (V.O.)
We enter, taking them by surprise. First
we go for those two...

Septimus and Tristan burst heroically in, swords
aloft. By the cages, Septimus fells Empusa and
the Slave Girl with two neat swipes of his sword.

SEPTIMUS (V.O.) (CONT'D)
...We keep moving...

By the table, Septimus spears Mormo and
Tristan takes down Lamia.

SEPTIMUS (V.O.) (CONT'D)
...Then you get your little star...

Tristan releases Yvaine. She hugs him happily.

SEPTIMUS (V.O.) (CONT'D)
...and I get my stone.

Yvaine removes her necklace and offers it up to
Septimus. He takes it, and holds the stone nobly
aloft. In his hand it TURNS RED once more, glowing brightly. Tristan and Yvaine bow to him.

SEPTIMUS (V.O.) (CONT'D)
Got it? Good.

INT./EXT. WITCHES' LAIR – DAY.

Tristan and Septimus stand either side of the
entrance, swords drawn. Septimus gives the nod.
With a battle cry, they run in. As planned,
Septimus runs at Empusa and the Slave Girl.

TRISTAN

Still at the entrance, frozen. Overcome by fear.

THE GHOSTLY BROTHERS

Breathlessly watch the proceedings throughout.
Looking not unlike decomposing spectators at a
sporting event.

SEPTIMUS' SWORD

Poised to strike the Slave Girl, whose back is to
him. She turns, arms raised protectively. Their
eyes meet. Septimus lowers his sword, bewildered.

SLAVE GIRL (UNA)
Septimus?!

SEPTIMUS
Una? It can't be...

THE GHOSTLY BROTHERS

Break into smiles of happy recognition as they
too realise: this is their sister.

GHOSTS
Una!

A FLAMETHROWER

REFLECTED CEILING 2.

REFLECTED CEILING 3.

'STARDUST' - WITCHES LAIR INT-
- CEILING PLANS ¼"-1'-0"
#405.

Aimed at Septimus. Or that's what it looks like. Though the fire is, in fact, coming from Empusa's fingertips.

Septimus stumbles back, patting frantically at his shirtsleeves, which are ON FIRE.

He raises his sword to make a counter-strike but the sword becomes RED HOT, forcing him to drop it.

SLAVE GIRL (UNA)

Terrified, makes a break for it, running for the exit.

OVER BY THE TABLE

Yvaine struggles to see what is going on. Mormo and Lamia seem oddly unbothered. Lamia moves calmly to the corner and begins doing something. We can't see what.

AT THE ENTRANCE TO THE LAIR

The Slave Girl/Una sees Tristan and stops running.

> SLAVE GIRL (UNA)
> Tristan?

Afraid that she's a witch, Tristan shields himself. Una grabs his hands and gently lowers them.

> SLAVE GIRL (UNA) (CONT'D)
> Tristan, I'm your mother.

He knows she is telling the truth. They hug fiercely.

A RUSH OF FLAME

From Empusa's fingers. And Septimus is alight again.

Through his panic, he spots a MACHETE on the table. He seizes it and THROWS it with enormous force.

It SKEWERS her through the middle and she hurtles backwards, CRASHING through the free-standing mirror and slamming into the wall, where she remains standing – pinned there by the machete.

A final snarl of defiance, and then she's gone.

Picks up his fallen sword, and walks boldly towards the staircase, oblivious to the few small flames still dancing on his smoking shirt.

AT THE ENTRANCE TO THE LAIR.

One witch down provides a spark of hope for Tristan, but his mother's sense of urgency has not diminished. She shakes him.

> SLAVE GIRL (UNA) (CONT'D)
> I know my brother: he won't save her, Tristan. He cares only for the stone. And believe me, if he had the first inkling of what she is, he'd eat her heart in a

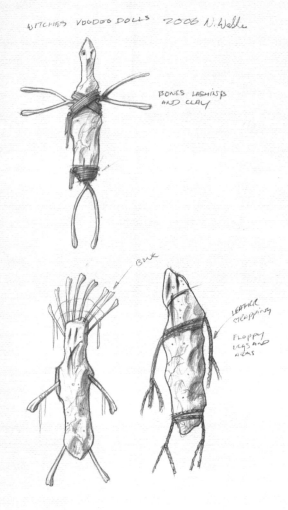

WITCHES VOODOO DOLLS 2006 N. Walle

BONES LASHINGS AND CLAY

BONE

LEATHER STRIPPING

FLOPPY LEGS AND ARMS

moment.

A panic-stricken look on Tristan's face as he recalls:

INT. WITCHES' LAIR – SEPTIMUS' FANTASY PLAN REDUX.

The final, joyful scene from the plan replays, with Yvaine and Tristan hugging as Septimus holds his stone.

SEPTIMUS (V.O.)
Then you get your little star...

Abruptly, the mood changes. An evil grin on Septimus' lips as he turns on them, pushes Yvaine to the ground, raises a dagger high and plunges it towards her chest...

INT./EXT. WITCHES' LAIR – DAY.

Back to reality, as a haunted-looking Tristan turns to his mother. Realizing that he must summon his courage.

SEPTIMUS

Continues to walk towards the staircase leading up to the mezzanine – and Yvaine.

LAMIA

Smiles down calmly. In her hand we now see: A CLAY DOLL. Swiftly, she snaps its right arm.

Septimus' sword CLANGS to the ground. He looks down in dismay at his arm: hanging by his side, useless and limp.

THE GHOSTS

Wince and groan in horror.

THE DOLL

Has its leg twisted by Lamia.

Septimus cries out as his leg flies up, bending at a terrible, improbable angle. He falls to the ground in agony.

THE FOUNTAIN BELOW THE MEZZANINE BALCONY

With a sly look, Lamia holds the doll over the water.

LAMIA
Let's put those flames out, shall we?

The doll drops from Lamia's fingers and into the fountain. It vanishes beneath the surface.

SEPTIMUS

Rising a couple of feet off the floor. Floating, in fact. Panic in his eyes, his mouth silently opening and closing like a fish, clothes dark and wet, hair drifting eerily. He struggles, his limbs moving slowly, heavily, as if underwater. And then no more.

THE GHOSTS

Look at one another. Suddenly, Septimus appears beside them. Coughing and dripping wet.

Quintus guffaws loudly, then looks around to realise that he's the only one laughing. Suddenly grasping the wider implications for his fate, he stops.

QUARTUS
So... what happens now?

SECUNDUS
We have to learn to live with each other.

SEXTUS
Forever?!

Septimus sighs in disgust.

LAMIA

Turns decisively back to Mormo and Yvaine.

LAMIA
Let's get on with it.

AT THE ENTRANCE TO THE LAIR

It's time. Tristan takes what he know might be his last look at his mother. She kisses him on the forehead.

SLAVE GIRL (UNA)
Be the man that I know you are.

LAMIA

Sharpens a horrifying glass hatchet.

AT THE ENTRANCE TO THE LAIR

Tristan shoos his mother to safety.

TRISTAN
Go outside. Go!

And he walks purposefully into the depths of the lair.

ON THE MEZZANINE

Lamia, Mormo spot him approaching.

Yvaine sees him too. Her eyes light up and we see her begin to shimmer again.

YVAINE
Tristan!

LAMIA
(to Mormo)
Get him.

MORMO

Leaps over the mezzanine balcony, landing, menacing and determined, in Tristan's path.

THE ANIMAL CAGES

Ill-fated beasts peer from behind the bars.

Tristan, trapped beside them, doesn't take his eyes off the approaching Mormo as he skilfully uses his sword to break the locks. CHING CHING CHING CHING CHING.

A thunderous stampede: dozens of sharp-toothed STOATS, a vast monitor LIZARD, some nasty-looking WILD BOARS and several fierce WOLVES swarm onto Mormo. She is knocked from her feet and vanishes from view, screaming, beneath a whirl of claws and teeth.

LAMIA

Reacts in horror.

TRISTAN

Has to look away.

OUTSIDE THE LAIR

Una watches in amazement as the animals flee past her, bolting for freedom.

BACK INSIDE

Tristan's hand shakes as he grips his sword and walks towards the staircase up to the mezzanine.

Glancing back briefly at the very dead Mormo and the equally dead Septimus, he walks on, even as Lamia walks down the stairs and continues towards him.

Tristan stops, sword drawn, unsure of her next move.

LAMIA (CONT'D)
So what's it to be, Prince Charming? Frog? Or tadpole?

Lamia points a lethal finger at him. Tristan raises his hands in futile self-protection.

But NOTHING happens.

Both react in surprise. Baffled and angry, Lamia tries again. Still nothing.

The explanation dawns on Tristan. He delves into his buttonhole and produces: THE GLASS FLOWER. Playfully, he sniffs it before grinning at Lamia and placing it back in his pocket.

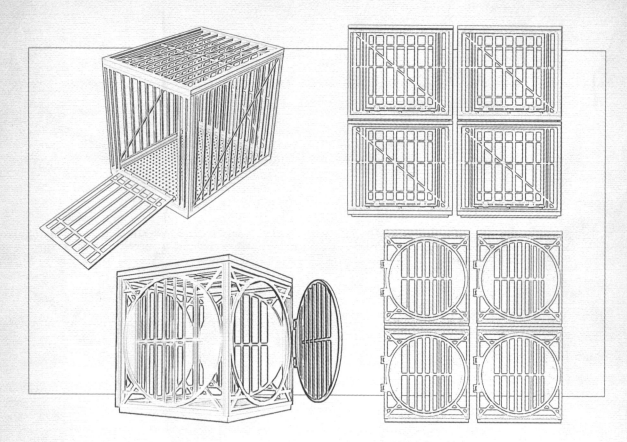

A flicker of frustration, then Lamia shrugs and points instead to A HUGE VASE. It HURTLES across the room at Tristan. He leaps out of the way.

Lamia tries again. This time, the vase hits him in the back, SHATTERING and knocking him to the ground.

Tristan struggles to his feet, clearing the debris off himself and surreptitiously takes his LIGHT-NING CONTAINER in hand.

He opens it and is FLUNG BACK by the recoil as a BOLT narrowly misses Lamia, instead hitting a piece of FURNITURE behind her, which EXPLODES.

He lets out another huge blast. It hits Lamia in the chest, knocking her flying back into the fountain.

LAMIA'S FACE

Reflected in the water. She is stunned and injured, but alive. And she's seen something. She reaches into the fountain.

TRISTAN

Oblivious, moves slowly and cautiously in for the kill while she's down. A NOISE behind him makes

him hesitate.

SEPTIMUS

Rises awkwardly from the ground and lurches unsteadily forward.

Tristan wheels around, shocked and somewhat relieved to see him alive.

TRISTAN
Septimus...

But to his surprise, Septimus' head LOLLS backwards and he lurches forward, raising his sword to attack.

THE CLAY DOLL

Is in Lamia's hand once more. She moves its arm again and Septimus' sword comes crashing down, almost catching Tristan before he can dodge the blow.

AN UNBELIEVABLY COOL SWORD-FIGHT

Commences between Tristan and the zombie-puppet Septimus, controlled by Lamia.

Lamia walks confidently back up the stairs as she continues to manipulate the doll.

Yvaine looks on in hope and horror.

The ghosts cheer Tristan on, with only the spectral Septimus comically conflicted about who to cheer for.

IN A CORNER

Things are not looking good for Tristan. Septimus is bearing down on him, and it has become apparent that no matter how many times Tristan skewers him, the already-dead Septimus is not going to go down. He's unstoppable.

A SWATHE OF ROPES

Lead up to the lair's many huge CHANDELIERS, keeping them suspended. This gives Tristan an idea.

He slices at one.

ABOVE THE MEZZANINE

The BIGGEST CHANDELIER in the room CRASHES down, narrowly missing Yvaine, and SMASHING in the fountain.

Tristan panics and cuts another rope.

ON THE STAIRCASE

Another chandelier smashes down, just missing Lamia.

ZOMBIE SEPTIMUS

Lurches at Tristan, sword flailing lethally. Panicking, Tristan takes a final swipe at the ropes.

Septimus' sword bears down and is just about to make impact when he is CRUSHED by a chandelier that plummets down from overhead.

TRISTAN

Holding the cut end of the rope, is hoisted into the air towards the ceiling.

AT THE MEZZANINE

Tristan SWINGS himself over the balcony and artfully collides with Lamia, knocking her flying.

Tristan and Yvaine's emotional reunion is halted before it has even begun, however, as Lamia scrambles back to her feet and grabs two knives from the sacrificial table.

She comes at Tristan, a blade in each hand, blazing.

Tristan is no match for her: in no time she has his sword out of his hand, out of reach, and him backed up against the table where Yvaine lies. The two cower, terrified and helpless.

Lamia raises her knife and brings it down hard. There's a hideous slicing noise, Tristan and Yvaine both scream, and we're not sure who has been struck.

Both look down to see...

The STRAP that bound Yvaine to the table. Sliced clean through. It falls away.

Lamia throws her knife to the ground and begins to sob.

> LAMIA
> Youth, beauty... it all seems meaningless now. My sisters are dead. Everything I cared about, gone.

Tristan and Yvaine remain frozen in disbelief.

> LAMIA (CONT'D)
> Go.

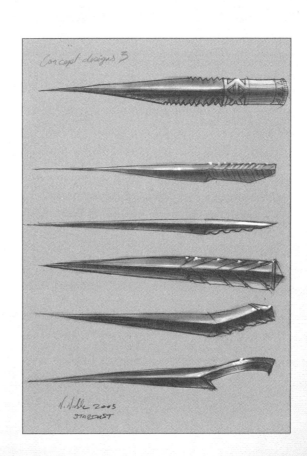

Tristan scrabbles to undo the remaining straps.

> LAMIA (CONT'D)
> (screaming now)
> Go!

Yvaine finally struggles free and is helped up by Tristan. The two flee down the stairs. Yvaine's shimmering growing stronger and stronger.

With a final glance back at the weeping, defeated Lamia, the pair race towards their freedom.

Lamia's sobs echo through the vast room as Tristan and Yvaine dash it's length. Just as they near the exit, the sobs turn to menacing laughter.

THE DOORS

Slam shut in their faces.

OUTSIDE

Una pounds at the doors, her hope turned to despair.

BACK INSIDE

Lamia outstretches her arms and points at the windows.

BLACK GLASS SHUTTERS

Crash down over the windows.

TRISTAN AND YVAINE

Turn to face Lamia.

LAMIA

Smirks back at them. Beckons. Then, one by one, she makes every MIRROR in the lair IMPLODE towards them, forcing them to run back towards her.

She walks down to meet them, hatchet in hand.

> LAMIA (CONT'D)
> I owe you thanks, boy... What use was her heart to me when it was broken?

> YVAINE
> (to Tristan)
> Hold me tight and close your eyes.

> TRISTAN
> What? Why?

> YVAINE
> What do stars do?

Yvaine takes Tristan's hand and places it over his eyes. She smiles. Closes her eyes. And whispers in his ear.

> YVAINE (CONT'D)
> Shine.

And then, she SHINES. Glowing at first, then burning white, until the corona radiating from her fills the room.

Lamia shrieks, frozen in the blinding light. She is INCINERATED. One moment there, the next, vaporized.

Tristan and Yvaine blink as the light fades.

> TRISTAN
> Why didn't you do that before!?

> YVAINE
> (laughing and crying at the same time)
> I couldn't have done it without you. No star can shine with a broken heart. I thought I'd lost you. But you came back.

> TRISTAN
> Of course I did. I love you.

They kiss.

As they part, Tristan notices, lying by their feet, the STONE, its chain melted in the heat.

> TRISTAN (CONT'D)
> Don't forget this.

As he dips to pick it up, they see Una approaching them, and they move quickly to greet her.

THE STONE

Is TURNING RED in Tristan's hand. A ruby once more.

Tristan and Yvaine — and the ghosts, who have assembled behind them — stare at it in wonderment. Una is the only one present not looking surprised.

> SLAVE GIRL (UNA)
> The last surviving male heir of the Stormhold bloodline. It's you, Tristan.

The ghosts exchange looks of utter puzzlement.

SEPTIMUS
But if he's the new king of Stormhold,
then surely...

WHOOMPH – the ghosts are lifted from their feet
and begin to RISE UP. They exchange looks of
happy surprise before CONDENSING into tiny
GLOBES OF WHITE LIGHT which fly skywards
like fairies. All except for Septimus, that is, who
becomes a little RED LIGHT that swoops downwards and into the nearby fireplace.

The ruby sparkles in Tristan's hand as we track
in...

EXT. STORMHOLD PALACE – NIGHT.

...And out again. The ruby is on a new chain,
around Tristan's neck. Tristan and Yvaine sit on
thrones. A NEW BISHOP holds the Stormhold
crown.

Nearby, Una and Dunstan look on proudly, holding hands.

IN THE CROWD

Victoria and Humphrey crane to see, jostled by
the unicorn and crowds of odd Faerie folk, including the pirates, Bernard – also in pirate gear, having joined their crew – and a proudly beaming
Captain.

The Captain shoots Humphrey a saucy little look.
To Victoria's surprise and dismay, Humphrey
returns it.

THE MOST AMAZING NIGHT SKY WE'VE EVER
SEEN

Twinkles above them. It's as if all the stars have
come out to watch the coronation.

YVAINE
That'll give the astronomers something
to worry about.

**INT. ROYAL ACADEMY OF SCIENCE –
NIGHT.**

The distinguished scholar we saw at the beginning – now 20 years older – stares through the
huge telescope. In shock, he staggers backwards,
tripping over.

His fall goes unfortunately unnoticed by his
fellow scientists, who are all crowded at the

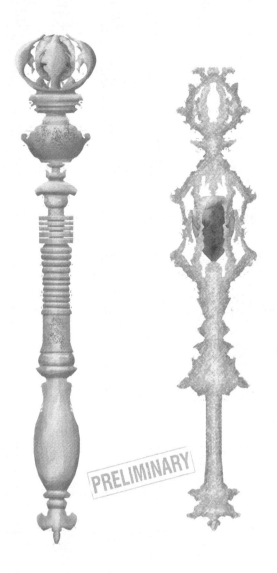

window, pointing and staring in awe at the night
sky above Big Ben.

EXT. STORMHOLD PALACE – NIGHT.

The Bishop steps closer to Tristan: it's time.

BISHOP
I crown thee, King Tristan of Stormhold!

He places the crown on Tristan's head. Tristan
stands. The crowd go wild. He sits back down and
kisses Yvaine.

Una leans in to hand Yvaine a beautiful
LACQUERED BOX.

SLAVE GIRL (UNA)
My gift to you. To you both.

Yvaine opens the box and peeks in. She grins, and

shows Tristan. Now we, too, see the gift: a Babylon candle. Tristan and Yvaine share a smile.

And we pull back, over the cheering crowds, and move slowly up to the dizzying heights of the towering Stormhold Palace turrets.

> NARRATOR (V.O.)
> They ruled for 80 years. But no man can live forever. Except he who possesses the heart of a star. And Yvaine had given hers to Tristan completely.

Leaving the sights and sounds of the coronation behind, we continue our rise. In a warmly lit turret window, we see Tristan and Yvaine in silhouette, 80 years on.

> NARRATOR (V.O.) (CONT'D)
> When their children and grandchildren were grown, it was time to light the

Babylon candle.

The silhouetted Tristan and Yvaine hold one another close, the candle between them. A FLASH of light, the now familiar WHOOSH sound, and the window is left empty.

We continue to move ever upwards, until there's only the night sky.

Our iconic shot. But where there used to be one unique star, now there are two.

> TRISTAN (V.O.)
> And they really did live happily ever after.

FADE TO BLACK.

THE END